Principles of Research in Communication

Thomas D. Stewart

Slippery Rock University of Pennsylvania

Allyn and Bacon

Boston • London • Toronto • Sydney • Tokyo • Singapore

To my loving wife, Victoria, and my children, Tristan and Triona,
without whom none of this would have been possible

Editor in Chief, Humanities: *Karen Hanson*
Series Editor: *Molly Taylor*
Editorial Assistant: *Michael Kish*
Marketing Manager: *Mandee Eckersley*
Editorial Production Administrator: *Bryan Woodhouse*
Editorial Production Service: *Chestnut Hill Enterprises*
Composition and Prepress Buyer: *Linda Cox*
Manufacturing Buyer: *Julie McNeill*
Cover Administrator: *Kristina Mose-Libon*
Electronic Composition: *Galley Graphics, Ltd.*

Copyright © 2002 by Allyn & Bacon
A Pearson Education Company
75 Arlington Street
Boston, MA 02116

Internet: www.ablongman.com

Between the time Website information is gathered and then published, it is not unusual for some sites to have closed. Also, the transcription of URLs can result in unintended typographical errors. The publisher would appreciate notification where these occur so that they may be corrected in subsequent editions.

Library of Congress Cataloging-in-Publication Data
Stewart, Thomas D.
   Principles of research in communication / Thomas D. Stewart.— 1st ed.
     p. cm.
   Includes bibliographical references and index.
   ISBN 0-321-07893-4
   1. Communication—Research—Methodology. I. Title.
P91.3 .S73 2002
302.2'07'2—dc21   2001046130

Printed in the United States of America

10 9 8 7 6 5 4   06

Contents

Preface

Over twenty years ago, as an undergraduate student at Slippery Rock State College, later to become Slippery Rock University of Pennsylvania, I first encountered an introductory course in the methods and analysis of communication research. From that experience, and other courses that followed in my undergraduate and graduate studies, I developed a respect and affinity for the scientific method and its application to the communication discipline.

For the past fifteen years, I have been attempting to inspire that passion in a new generation of communication scholars. However, in that time I have become acutely aware of the anxiety and trepidation with which the majority of students approach the research methods course. Because many students in communication have limited exposure to the sciences and mathematics, they often enter the course with concerns about their success. The very terminology of the scientist frightens many, and mathematical anxiety inspires fear at the mention of statistics. This textbook is the result of my experience with this student population, and is an effort to develop an introductory research methods textbook for second- or third-year undergraduate students with limited scientific and/or mathematical experience.

Although a number of competing textbooks are on the market, many focus either on a specific field within the communication discipline, such as mass media, public relations, or organizational communication, or are written primarily for upper-level undergraduates or graduate students. This textbook was written in a style that should be comprehensible to even entry-level undergraduate students. Although many competing texts provide an abundance of examples of research applications, my experience has shown that students often become confused by the complexity of the examples and have difficulty separating the grain from the chaff. As a solution, this text provides a few continuing examples of hypothetical research that are addressed throughout the entire text, thereby reinforcing important concepts without overwhelming the reader.

It is also important to recognize that the terminology of the communication researcher is difficult for many introductory students to grasp. To assist in their learning the lexicon of science, key terms are included in an extensive glossary, as well as printed in bold throughout the text, with contextual definitions and examples included. To further assist students' comprehension of the various terms encountered in each chapter, the accompanying student workbook contains chapter-end concept reviews, which provide definitions and which students can use to evaluate their ability to recognize and identify key terms, a process especially useful as they prepare for course projects and examinations.

Also included in the accompanying workbook are chapter-end worksheets that require students to put newly acquired concepts into application. The worksheets review introduced concepts and permit the personal application of newly acquired knowledge. As students progress through the workbook, a number of the worksheets encountered are designed to build on the content of previously completed worksheets, permitting the student to better conceptualize the process of research. At the conclusion of the methodology-specific chapters, worksheets are provided to permit small groups of students to do simple, unobtrusive ministudies that will hone their research skills and provide a first-person introduction to the research craft.

Because of the necessary integration of all the various introduced topics, the workbook also includes three optional, more extensive course assignments, each designed to assist in the student's development of an independent research proposal or project. The first of these assignments, at the end of Chapter 3, requires that students define a problem within the discipline that is interesting and develop from that a comprehensive annotated bibliography and search strategy, using the APA citation style. At the end of Chapter 5, the second assignment requires that they begin to develop the information from the annotated bibliography into a literature review. The final assignment, presented at the end of Chapter 7, requires that they begin to formulate from the literature review a research problem that inspires their interest and propose a methodology for its resolution. Each of these assignments is adaptable to specific classroom needs and may be done by independent students or by small groups of students.

Principles of Research in Communication consists of twelve chapters introducing the scientific process. Chapter 1, Epistemology and Science, explores the various ways in which humans acquire knowledge of their world and how the scientific method differs from other epistemological methods.

With that understanding, Chapters 2 through 7 look at the pragmatic steps required as one completes a research study. In these chapters, students are introduced to the process of selecting and developing research problems that guide an investigation, as well as to the process of conceptually and operationally defining the key components of those problems. They are also introduced to techniques for discovering and acquiring the existing knowledge on a topic within their discipline through the use of overview materials, indexes, abstracts, electronic resources, and on-line databases. Chapter 4 explores the development of a conceptual definition into a measured operational definition, with an emphasis on various measurement levels, applications, and assessment of measurement reliability and validity. Chapter 5 addresses methods of probability and nonprobability sampling and the influence of those methods on sampling error. Chapter 6 discusses the multitude of ethical dilemmas facing the communication researcher and the ethical treatment of human subjects. Finally, Chapter 7 introduces students to various factors that influence the selection of a specific research methodology and the internal and external validity of an investigation.

The next section of the book consists of four chapters introducing students to some of the most commonly applied methodologies in the study of communication. Chapter 8 explores the experimental methodology, both in the field and in the laboratory, and introduces some of the more popular single-factor and factorial designs. The use of cross-sectional and longitudinal survey and interview methodology, its advantages and liabilities, and the development of valid questionnaires and interview schedules is the focus of Chapter 9. Chapter 10 introduces students to the nonreactive methodologies of content analysis and interaction analysis, and how these methodologies permit the study of verbal or visual content. The selection of appropriate textual/visual sampling methods, unitizing, and coding and analysis techniques are examined. The final methodology-specific chapter, Chapter 11, explores the variety of inductive research techniques commonly referred to as "qualitative methods," including naturalistic observation, interviewing, and examination of artifacts, as well as the techniques commonly used for their analysis.

The final chapter in the book provides a brief introduction to the use of statistics in the analysis of communication research. Students will encounter the distinctions between descriptive statistics and inferential statistics and learn how to compute such indexes as the measures of central tendency, measures of dispersion, analyses of differences, and analyses of relationship. Although not intended to be a comprehensive treatise on statistical methods, it is intended to provide the necessary foundation for students interested in further study in statistical manipulation of data.

A work such as this is only possible because of the contribution of many talented individuals. It was the introduction to research methods provided by Professor Roy Stewart and Professor Emeritus Timothy Walters of Slippery Rock University that first encouraged my passion for the topic. The graduate instruction of Professor Emeritus Samuel Becker and Professor Donald Smith of the University of Iowa provided the depth of knowledge necessary to further my pursuits. The encouraging support of President G. Warren Smith and Provost Robert Smith of Slippery Rock University in awarding me a sabbatical to develop this work and the encouragement and editorial support of Dean Frank Mastrianna in its development are humbly acknowledged. My colleagues in the Department of Communication have contributed many ideas for the editorial content, and our chairperson, Professor Bruce Russell, has been understanding and supportive throughout the process. Michael Greer, Acquisition and Development Editor at Addison-Wesley Longman, and Molly Taylor, Managing Editor for Mass Communication at Allyn and Bacon, have provided much patient encouragement and direction as the manuscript developed. I appreciate the helpful comments provided by the following reviewers: Alice Crume, SUNY, Brockport; Carol Reese Dykers, Salem College; Thomas Hugh Feeley, SUNY, Geneseo; Mary Gill, Buena Vista University; Rebecca Lind, University of Illinois, Chicago; Richard A. Rogers, Northern Arizona University; Philip Salem, Southwest Texas State University; and George E. Whitehouse, University of South

Dakota. It is, however, the many years of students in my communication research methods classes that deserve most of the credit for the ideas in this text. Without them, it would have been impossible to develop a package such as this. Finally, I must acknowledge the incredible and loving support provided by my immediate and extended family. My wife, Vicki, and children, Tristan and Triona, graciously endured my many long hours at the computer keyboard, and, at times, my overbearing anxiety about producing a quality product. To all of these individuals and to others who have contributed to this effort, I extend my heartfelt thanks. This work is as much theirs as it is mine.

1

Epistemology and Science

Chapter Outline

The quest for knowledge is a seemingly innate human trait. From early childhood, individuals search for predictable patterns and explanations of common events. At an early age, infants recognize that certain patterns of behavior (crying of a specific pattern and duration) will result in a particular response (feeding, changing, or cuddling, among others). It is interesting to note that, like most knowledge, this pattern scheme is shared across a learning community, including in this case the infant, parent or parents, and other key caregivers. This search for predictable patterns and explanations, or for knowledge, continues throughout the individual's life.

Epistemological Methods

Epistemology is "the division of philosophy that investigates the nature and origin of knowledge" (The *American Heritage Dictionary*, 1985), or the study of human knowledge acquisition. Over the years, several epistemologists have developed schemes for understanding the most common varieties of knowledge acquisition. G. C. Helmstadter (1970) developed a hierarchical scheme of six common forms of human knowledge acquisition and development (Figure 1.1). It is possible to arrange the hierarchy of this scheme based on the amount of rigor used in the collection of information and analysis of its quality into a pyramid with three low rigor methods at the base, two intermediate methods in the middle, and the highest rigor method at the apex.

The three low rigor epistemological methods are tenacity, intuition, and authority.

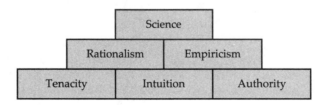

FIGURE 1.1 *Helmstadter's Epistemological Methods*

Tenacity is the acquisition and acceptance of knowledge as a result of its survival over time. Within this category are many of the customs and traditions that we accept, including such things as foods eaten on particular holidays and behaviors expected within particular contexts. Knowledge acquired by tenacity requires little analysis of information quality, but is accepted simply because "it has always been true."

Intuition is the acquisition and acceptance of knowledge because it "feels right," or because it was provided by some extrasensory source. Included in this category are most faith-based beliefs, knowledge based on "gut feelings," and messages from beyond the normal perceptual realm (e.g., "God revealed to me that . . ."). Like tenacity, intuition requires little rigor in the analysis of information quality.

Authority is the acquisition and acceptance of knowledge as a result of its presentation by a respected source. Included in this category is that knowledge that we accept to be true because it is presented to us by the President of the United States, the Pope, our favorite news reporter, or our professor. In each case, the only requirement that we make of the knowledge is that we trust its source.

The two moderate rigor epistemological methods are rationalism and empiricism.

Rationalism is the *development* of knowledge through the application of the rules of logic. The key distinction of this moderate level is the ability to *develop* new knowledge, not simply to *accept* knowledge. Several common forms of logic can be used in the development of this knowledge.

Deductive logic begins with one or more general rules (assumed to be accurate) that are applied to a specific case in order to develop a conclusion. The simplest form of deductive logic is the *syllogism,* which begins with a major premise (general rule), adds a minor premise (additional assumption), and reaches a conclusion:

> All Communication majors must take this class (Major premise).
> You are a communication major (Minor premise).
> Therefore, you must take this class (Conclusion).

It is important to recognize that the rules of logic must be followed to assure an accurate conclusion, and that the major and minor premises are assumed to be true. If either of the premises is inaccurate, the conclusion may likewise be inaccurate.

Inductive logic begins with the collection of several specific cases from which are developed some general rule. This is the form of logic often used as university students select faculty members from whom to take classes. As most students make this selection they talk with friends and acquaintances about their faculty experiences. From those assembled cases they develop conclusions (general rules) about individual faculty members (e.g., "Don't take Stewart for Research Methods"). The most significant concerns of this form of logic are the assurance that there is an adequate number of specific cases to warrant the conclusion and that the specific cases are representative of the context about which the conclusion is drawn. It would, therefore, be inaccurate to draw a conclusion about a faculty member in a particular course if all the assembled information came from experiencing that individual in a different course.

Analogical logic begins with a specific case and then applies it to another specific case based on the similarities between the two. This form of logic is exemplified by the student/mentor relationship. The student often assumes that the mentor's success may be emulated by following in his or her footsteps and so decides to take the same courses in the same sequence as the mentor. The greatest limitation to this form of logic is the need to determine that the cases are truly similar because any deviation may result in inaccurate conclusions.

Causal logic attempts to establish a cause–effect link between events. Several requirements are necessary to draw a causal conclusion: a temporal relationship (the cause must precede the effect), a theoretical connection between events (there must be some reason for believing the cause will yield the effect), and the ability to rule out other potential causes, or alternative causality arguments. These requirements will be explored in greater detail in Chapter 8.

Empiricism is the *development* of knowledge through the observation of real events using the human senses. A simple, though clear, example of such knowledge development is an individual looking out a window to determine the day's weather. The creed of the empiricist is *"seeing, hearing, smelling, tasting, and/or touching is believing."*

The high rigor epistemological method at the apex of Helmstadter's hierarchy is science.

Science is the *development* of knowledge through a combination of rationalism and empiricism. The principle tools of the scientist are the mind, permitting the development of logical relationships, and the human senses, permitting the observation of the expected relationships in the real world. It is the combination of the moderate rigor methods that enhances the overall rigor of this approach, and, as a result of this combination, science is often referred to as a *rational–empirical method*. It is this form of knowledge development that we will concern ourselves with through the remainder of this text, though we should be aware that all humans do, at varying times, use all of the above-mentioned epistemological methods. It would be overwhelming, and quite tiring, if we were to depend on scientific methods for the development of all of our acquired information.

Characteristics of Science

There are several characteristics that differentiate science from the other forms of knowledge acquisition. While none of these characteristics can alone guarantee that the scientific method is being used, the absence of any one guarantees that scientific reasoning is *not* being applied. In other words, these characteristics are *necessary, but not sufficient,* to defining the scientific method. The first two characteristics may seem redundant because they are a part of our definition of science as a rational–empirical method.

Science Is Logical

Because it is a combination of rationalism and empiricism, science requires adherence to the rules of logic.

Science Is Empirical

Science demands that the objects being investigated be observable, either directly or indirectly, using the human senses.

Science Is Problem-Oriented

All scientific inquiry *begins* with a problem of some degree of abstraction, and then develops a procedure or method for the resolution of that problem. Moreover, the investigation concludes with the development of other problems in need of resolution in order to permit the future growth of knowledge.

Science Is Procedure-Driven

Scientific investigation involves the careful advance planning of procedures to be used to gather the data necessary to resolve the motivating problem.

Science Is Community-Based

Scientists operate as part of a *community of scholars* who freely exchange data, procedures, and information in order to allow the growth of knowledge. This community may vary in size and constitution depending on whether the research is *public* or *proprietary.* Public research is that done for the primary purpose of enhancing and improving knowledge, while proprietary research has the purpose of developing knowledge that has an economic benefit to the researcher or his or her employer. Public research is commonly associated with that done at colleges and universities, and the community of scholars is usually quite large and disparate, including all scientists with an interest in the growth of that discipline. Proprietary research is exemplified by corporate investigations (i.e., Microsoft) conducted to enhance corporate offerings (i.e., the practical testing of an improved Web browser). The community in a proprietary study is usually considerably smaller, often including only those within the corporation or institution. However, most notable is that a community exists in both contexts.

Science Is Replicable

Because it is procedure-driven and community-based, the results of scientific investigation can be reproduced, or replicated. Scientists are usually quite careful to completely document their procedures so that a future investigator can follow their "recipe" and reproduce the study. This is quite important in that it permits scientists to rule out potentially *spurious results* or the inaccurate results of investigations that occur as a result of chance.

Science Is Reflexive, or Self-Critiquing

Scientists are constantly evaluating and critiquing their own and other scientists' work. The goal of reflexivity is to search for potential errors in logic or observation made by investigators so that those errors can be corrected. The self-critiquing nature of science is especially evident in the discussion section near the end of most published research. An examination of this section will often reveal numerous mentions of potential concerns with the just-completed investigation and possible errors made by the investigator. The goal of this revelation is the resolution of those concerns/errors in future investigations.

Science Is Evolutionary

Because of its community foundation, and its reflexive nature, scientific findings grow and change over time. With the accumulation of information, and the gradual resolution of errors in logic or procedures, scientists constantly move ever closer to an *approximation of truth* but are seldom satisfied that they have achieved complete, unadulterated TRUTH. As Nunnally (1978) has suggested:

> Each scientist builds on what has been learned in the past; day by day his or her findings must be compared with those of other scientists working on the same types of problems (p. 8).

Science Is Creative

This is perhaps the most surprising characteristic of science for most students. However, the most revolutionary scientific findings are generally the result of the creative scientific mind. In astrophysics, it was the creativity of a scientist that allowed the prediction of the existence of black holes based on an understanding of gravitational theory. It was not until much later that their existence was proven by observation. The creative scientist is one who takes logical reasoning beyond its present application.

Assumptions of the Scientific Method

Knowing how science differs from other methods of knowledge acquisition is one step toward applying the scientific method. However, if we are to adopt the role of the scientist, we must first accept three critical assumptions adopted by all involved in scientific knowledge development (Smith, 1988):

1. *The objects of interest to the scientist are observable.* Remembering that science is a rational–*empirical* method, it is clear that those things that the scientist studies must be perceivable by the human senses. It is not always possible for the researcher to directly perceive these events (*direct observation*), but in those cases some procedure for inferring their presence based on observable data must be developed (*indirect observation*). An example of a directly observable event would be the recording of the number of hours a child spends playing a video game in a given period of time because it can be directly sensed and a time recorded. The evaluation of the child's level of intelligence is, on the other hand, not directly observable (it is impossible to look at a child and determine the level of his or her intelligence). This situation demands a form of indirect observation, perhaps including the use of some cognitive tasks of varying degrees of difficulty, such as an IQ test, to infer its presence.

2. *The objects of interest to the scientist are orderly.* Because science depends heavily on the rules of logic, it must be assumed that the world operates in a systematic and regular pattern. If we were to assume the world to be chaotic and random in its operation, application of the scientific method would be impossible.

3. *The objects of interest to the scientist are explainable.* When "doing science," the scientist must believe that the presence or operation of an object of interest can be explained to result from some *natural antecedent phenomenon* or from some natural occurrence that preceded the object of interest. The first phrase is of particular importance here, as we must remember that we all use a variety of epistemological methods throughout our lives. However, when we are adopting the role of scientist, we must truly believe that those objects we study can be explained. The scientific approach detests the argument that *some things are beyond the realm of human understanding,* an argument sometimes referred to as the "mystification of residuals" (Babbie, 1983).

Schools of Communication Inquiry

When we explore the scientific investigations conducted in the communication discipline, it becomes evident that the various investigators adopt different goals and philosophies. These differing philosophies can be categorized as *schools,* in much the same way that a college or university is composed of different schools (at our university there is a college of arts and sciences, a college of information science and business administration, a graduate college, and others). Each of these schools has a different mission, philosophy, and set of goals. Two schools or philosophies of investigation dominate in the communication discipline, positivism and phenomenology.

Positivism is the oldest of these schools, dating back to the 1920s, when a group of philosophers and mathematicians, known as the Vienna Circle, attempted to unify science with empirical methods. This is a philosophy that we, in the communication discipline, borrowed from the natural sciences (biology, chemistry, and physics) that suggests that everything can be explained, including behavior, using a finite set of rules. In other words, when applied to communication, it is suggested that *a finite set of rules governs all communicative behavior.* (At its most extreme level are the *unification theorists,* who believe that all phenomena, natural or behavioral, may be explained by a single unifying theory, though that theory remains elusive). It is, therefore, the goal of the positivist to discover and understand the operation of those rules. Because these rules are expected to apply to all human behavior, it is expected that the rules will be *generalizable,* capable of being applied to all phenomena.

In order to discover the generalizable rules governing all behavior, the positivist believes in collecting a large amount of observational data from a substantial number of subjects or elements in an effort to search for common trends among those subjects or elements. As a result, the research methods of the positivist often include experiments and surveys, which are then frequently analyzed using statistical methods that permit the generalization of results.

Phenomenology is a more recent school of inquiry, with its roots in the disciplines of sociology, anthropology, and philosophy. The phenomenologist is interested in *understanding of human behavior from the actor's perspective.* The goal of the phenomenologist is much more individualized in scope, with the primary interest being an understanding of why a particular person or group behaves the way it does. There is little interest in the development of broadly generalizable rules.

In order to develop this individualized understanding, phenomenologists generally use qualitative methods that provide *detailed* or *deep description* of the behavior of an individual. These descriptions may result from extensive observation of the individual actor, from extensive interviews, or from detailed analysis of artifacts left by that actor.

Fundamental Scientific Activities

Regardless of the school of inquiry to which an individual affiliates, two interrelated activities constitute the onus of the scientist's efforts, theory development and observation.

Theory Development

The development of theory to explain or predict the operation of the communication phenomena of interest is one of the key activities performed by the communication scientist. F. N. Kerlinger (1979), a highly respected psychologist, defines **theory** as:

> A set of interrelated constructs, definitions, and propositions that presents a systematic view of phenomena by specifying relations among variables, with the purpose of explaining natural phenomena (p. 64).

In short, a theory is *a simplified generalization about how or why something occurs.*

Generally, when we think of theories, we think of complex and rather abstract theories such as Einstein's Theory of Relativity, Darwin's Theory of Natural Selection, or Bandura's Social Learning Theory. While these are accurate examples, we each use theory in everyday applications as well. If we recognize the above definition of a theory, then we can construct a variety of everyday theories that are regularly used. For example, we might create a brief theory of the relationship between student involvement and academic success:

> If you study hard and regularly attend classes, you will succeed in the university.

Notice that this minitheory meets all the requirements of our definition in that it specifies a set of constructs and explains or predicts the relationships among them.

The minitheory is useful in that it allows us to easily see the various components found in all theoretical statements (Smith, 1988):

The **generative force** refers to *those parts of the statement that motivate a change in other components included in the statement.* In the minitheory above, the generative forces are "study" and "attendance," because these are the parts that are expected to motivate a change in a student's academic success.

The second element found in all theoretical statements are the **effects,** *those components that are expected to be influenced by the generative forces.* So, in our minitheory, the effects are changes in student academic success.

The final components to be found in all theories are the **boundary conditions,** *all other factors that must be true for the theory to remain valid.* In some theories these boundary conditions are explicitly presented, while in others, like our minitheory, they are more implicit. For example, as well as studying hard and attending class, it is assumed that the successful student will remain alert while attending and will diligently study the correct material.

As you may begin to recognize then, the common phrasing for all theoretical statements, no matter how simple or complex, could be reduced to:

If X (the generative force), then Y (the effect), under the conditions Z (the boundary conditions).

A great deal of debate exists among scientists regarding the best approach to the creation of a new theory. Some propose an *inductive approach to theory development,* which suggests that the scientist observes phenomena in the natural world with as few preconceptions as possible. From these observations, the scientist looks for common themes from which to develop a theoretical statement.

Other scientists argue that a **deductive approach to theory development** is superior. In this approach, the scientist begins by producing a tentative theory, based on speculation, not observation, and then tests and refines that theory by comparing it to real-world phenomena. The principle advantage of this approach is its ability to speculate about things that are yet unobservable, and it is therefore more likely to result in the development of *revolutionary theory,* which T. Kuhn (1962) defines as theory that challenges the fundamental assumptions of the existing scientific community.

This debate about theory creation is, however, more academic than practical, because it is likely that most scientists use a combination of these approaches.

Observation

The other principle activity in which the scientist is involved is observation of phenomena in the natural world. Observation allows the refinement or development of theory, so the two activities are truly interconnected. In science (remembering its characteristics), these observations generally follow prescribed strategies, or *research methods,* for the collection of evidence that will assist in the creation or verification of theory. These research methods vary from experiment, to survey, to content/interaction analysis, to naturalistic observation, each with its own assets and liabilities. As we will discover in future chapters, the laboratory experiment has a high degree of control associated with it, but is, as a consequence, rather artificial.

Naturalistic observation, on the other hand, is highly realistic, but fails to have much control. As a result, in recent years the scientific community has recognized the need for observational **triangulation,** a term borrowed from the sport of orienteering. In orienteering, one locates a particular geographic point by taking two or more compass bearings and, from those, develops a triangle that precisely locates the point in question. In science, triangulation refers to *looking at any phenomenon using a variety of different research methods,* each with its own advantages and disadvantages, *in order to develop a closer approximation to truth.*

Evaluation of Theory

Every theory that is created or verified by scientific activities undergoes a great deal of scrutiny by the community of scholars as they attempt to determine its value. Among the criteria used in making this determination, the scientific community often considers several characteristics of useful theories.

Clarity. A valuable theory is generally one in which the terms used by the theoretician are clearly and precisely defined and the logic is consistent. Littlejohn (1978) describes this trait as "descriptive simplicity" (p. 18).

Parsimony. A valuable theory generally uses the simplest logical presentation, one in which the relationship of phenomena is presented logically and concisely.

Testability. The third factor influencing a theory's value is the ability to test its validity through observation. If a theory refers to components that cannot be empirically verified, it is of little use to the scientific community.

Validity. The primary concern of this factor is whether the theory is consistent with observations made in the real world. In short, does the theory consistently work in the world around us? Does it have *empirical validity*?

Scope. A fifth factor influencing a theory's value is its ability to be used in a variety of different contexts. If a theory was developed that explained the operation of a single class, during a single semester, at a specific school, it would have limited scope and be of little use to the scientific community. If a similar theory were developed that could be used to understand any class, in any discipline, during any time frame, and at any school, it would have considerably greater scope, and, if all else was equal, more value to the scientific community.

Flexibility. Flexibility refers to the ability of a theory to change as new observation dictates. Because science is evolutionary, it is necessary that theory be capable of adaptation. Littlejohn (1978) refers to this as the theory's "dynamic openness" (p. 21).

Predictability. A seventh factor influencing a theory's value is its ability to make predictions about the world around us. While not all theories are designed to be predictive, a theory's ultimate value is enhanced if the generative force regularly yields a predictable effect.

Utility. A final factor influencing a theory's value, and perhaps one of the most obvious, is its usefulness in explaining, predicting, or permitting control of some phenomenon. In short, the question is whether the theory assists us in understanding communication. Also, as part of this analysis, the scientist takes into consideration the **heuristic value** of the theory, *the theory's ability to generate new areas for future study.*

A Model of the Scientific Method

The typical communication investigation proceeds through an orderly sequence of stages, beginning with the development of a research problem and proceeding to the integration of findings with existing knowledge. While individual studies may vary somewhat from the sequence described here, the model (Figure 1.2) provides us with a conceptual structure to assist in our understanding and application of science.

Problem Development

Because science is problem-oriented, the first task confronting the communication scientist is the identification of a problem. In some situations, this problem may

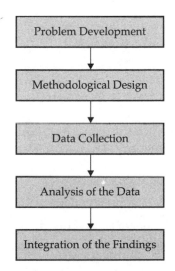

FIGURE 1.2 *Model of the Scientific Process*

emerge as a well-developed statement or inquiry, as is often the case when an investigation builds on a previous study. On the other hand, the problem may, and often does, begin as only an abstract interest in some particular subject. For example, the investigator may recognize an interest in children's use of advertising. Once the idea is recognized, the scientist must begin to assess the current state of knowledge held by the community of scholars. This requires a concerted effort to strategically locate the wealth of information regarding the topic of interest. In our example, it might involve research into children's consumer behavior, children's learning, advertising strategies, and theories of perception. This access to the community of scholars then permits the nurturing of the idea into a well-developed research problem, capable of being scientifically resolved. I cannot overstate the importance of researchers using care and logic during this portion of the investigation. Everything that we do during the remainder of the investigation hinges on the clarity with which we have developed and defined our research problem and its elements.

Methodological Design

Having determined a problem worthy of scientific attention, the next stage in the process is planning a procedure for the resolution of the problem. This stage is particularly important in that science is procedure-driven and replicable. Much thought must go into what observations will be made, what elements will be observed or measured, how the observations will be recorded, and what techniques will be used to interpret the observations. Also, a part of this stage is consideration and resolution of potential ethical issues relating to the research. Because of the significance of this stage in the research process, the majority of the content in a research methods course such as this focuses specifically on it. *As a general rule, no data collection begins until all research procedures or methods are explicitly planned and designed.*

Data Collection

Once the researcher develops procedures that will drive the investigation, he or she adheres to those procedures to make and record empirical observations. The record of the observations constitutes the research data. It is this stage in the scientific process that most students would identify as "actually doing the research." However, it is important to note that, without careful problem development and methodological design, the collection of data would, at best, be suspect.

Analysis of the Data

Once again, the methodological design stage plays an important role in determining how to analyze and interpret the observational data. The goal of this stage is to use logical, and sometimes mathematical, rules to make sense of the empirical data, *to convert the data into information.* In some studies, statistics (mathematical manipulations) are used to reduce data complexity (known as *descriptive statistics*) or to generalize data to a larger group than that observed (*inferential statistics*). In other investigations, data are organized into themes based on interpretive schemes developed by the researcher and supported by the observations. In both situations, however, the strategic plan for analysis is determined during the methodological design stage, *preceding* the collection of data.

Integration of the Findings

The final stage of the research process is the integration of findings into the existing body of knowledge. During this stage, the investigator determines how the newly developed information fits into existing theory, and whether it is consistent or inconsistent with knowledge previously developed by the community of scholars. It is also during this stage that the researcher exercises his or her *reflexivity* by analyzing and reporting any potential errors that may have occurred in the planning or conduct of the investigation. Finally, due to the evolutionary nature of science, the researcher recognizes and records new questions that result from the investigation, questions that may form the basis for a future study.

This model of the scientific process is somewhat idealized. There are numerous examples of investigations that deviate from this ideal. Some investigators, having collected empirical data, recognize additional questions in need of study and begin another study before analyzing the results of the first. It is also common for some stages, particularly data collection and data analysis, to overlap, with the scientist simultaneously satisfying the goals of both. Lest we be tempted to take this, or any, scientific model too seriously, W. L. Wallace (1971) describes the practical process as occurring

> (1) sometimes quickly, sometimes slowly; (2) sometimes with a very high degree of formalization and vigor, sometimes quite informally, unself-consciously, and intuitively; (3) sometimes through the interaction of several scientists in distinct roles, sometimes through the efforts of a single scientist; and (4) sometimes only in the scientist's imagination, sometimes in actual fact (p. 19).

The remainder of this text will, however, be organized around the five basic stages of the scientific process, beginning with the development of a research problem in the next chapter.

2

Problem Development

As we discovered in the last chapter, one important characteristic of science is that it is problem-oriented, originating with a problem of some degree of abstraction. Many novice investigators find the development of this problem the most difficult aspect of the entire research process. However, the clarity and conciseness with which one states the research problem is critical to all of the remaining steps in the investigation process.

Sources of Research Problems

Research problems generally evolve from some combination of three common sources: existing theory or research, practical problems, and observation.

Existing Theory or Research

Often, researchers examine existing theories for missing pieces or for novel applications as the basis for their research problems. For example, many communication investigators have examined psychologist Albert Bandura's (1969) Observational Learning Theory, which suggests that individuals learn those behaviors that they observe others model. Because of the broad scope of this theory, many have recognized fertile ground for new problem development. Some, including Bandura himself, began to speculate that, with the abundance of mass-mediated models in our culture, children might learn a variety of observed behaviors. Among the many questions raised as a result were:

> What is the relationship between children's learning of modeled behavior and whether the model is live or mass mediated?
>
> What is the relationship between children's learning of modeled behavior and whether the model is animated or real?
>
> What is the relationship between children's learning of modeled behavior, and the frequency with which they witness the behavior?

Other investigators locate a theory in a different discipline such as psychology, sociology, or education, and test its application in the communication discipline. Or, they locate a theory in a different field of communication, perhaps interpersonal, organizational, or small-group, and apply it to their field of interest, such as mass communication, in a novel way.

Also, because science is reflexive, previously completed studies comprise a valuable source of research problems. When investigations are published in research journals or presented at professional conferences, researchers often spend considerable time reflecting on the questions that were raised as a result of their research or on potential problems that may have plagued their findings. Other researchers may then use these problems or questions as the foundation for a future investigation.

Practical Problems

A second source of research problems is the practical situations encountered in everyday life that demand some resolution. For example, a communication researcher interested in health care may be interested in how improving physician–patient interaction might improve patient satisfaction. Or, a teacher may be interested in how changing classroom teaching style will influence student perceptions of the classroom climate. In both cases, the goal of the research is some practical application of the results. Therefore, this form of research is often called **applied research,** in contrast to the research whose primary goal is the development of better theory, often called **basic research.** It is important to be aware, however, that it is often difficult to distinguish between the two varieties. Quite often an "applied investigation" will prove helpful in the development of theory, while a "basic investigation" will result in some important new practical applications. The only way to be sure of the form of investigation is by determining the intention of the investigator, and that is not always an easy task.

Observation

A third common source of research problems is casual observation. Many studies are motivated by the investigator observing a trend, or noticing a pattern of behavior in the everyday world, and then deciding to investigate that pattern in a systematic way. For example, in casual observation we might notice that young married couples appear to talk about a different group of topics than do couples that have been married longer. As a result, we might choose to systematically investigate the conversational topics of newlyweds, those married for less than one year compared to those married for ten or more years.

　　As with the previous sources of research problems, this variety will result in basic research if the intent is to promote the development of better theory. If the intent is, instead, to solve a pragmatic problem, it will be applied research.

Research Problem Statements

Regardless of the source of the research problem, investigators generally frame their problem statement in one of two ways: by framing a research question or formulating a hypothesis.

Research Question

A research question, often abbreviated in journal articles as RQ, is an *interrogative statement exploring the relationship between two or more communication concepts.* In other words, it is a question about how the communication process works or how different components of the process are related. Two characteristics of the research question are most important in determining its value. First, the question should explore the relationship between *two or more* communication concepts. For example, how is A related to B, or how are A, B, and C related? Secondly, the question must permit the possibility of empirical observational testing. This criterion omits moral or value questions because there is no way to clearly define and scientifically measure the concepts involved. To help understand the distinction, let's look at some examples.

　　RQ: Are public broadcasting shows better than commercially broadcast shows?

The above is a value-based question that must be answered using human judgment, not scientific procedure. While I may answer the question affirmatively, another person might just as legitimately answer negatively. Only people can make value judgments. Science, as a rational–empirical process, seeks to remain more neutral.

However, with some adaptation the previous research question could become more scientifically valuable.

> RQ: How do public and commercial television programs compare with regard to degree of production complexity?

This question is now rooted in empirical verification. Once we decide what the characteristics of production complexity are, we can empirically observe their relative presence in each variety of television production.

Research questions generally are written in one of two forms: open-ended or closed-ended.

Open-Ended Research Question. The open-ended research question is one that *leaves the direction or form of a relationship between concepts open, simply inquiring into whether* any *relationship exists between/among them*. This is the variety of research question most frequently used when the researcher has little previous research or a limited theoretical foundation on which to build. As a result, it is frequently used in preliminary investigations. An open-ended research question is:

> RQ: How is instructor teaching style related to student perceptions of classroom climate?

In this example there are two communication concepts of interest: (1) instructor teaching style and (2) student perceptions of classroom climate. The relationship between these concepts is not specified. An increase in one could result in an increase, decrease, or other fluctuation in the other concept. The researcher's interest is in finding *any* kind of relationship.

Closed-Ended Research Question. Closed-ended research questions *specify the form or direction of the relationship between concepts, permitting the exploration of a particular variety of relationship*. This form of research question is usually used when there is a great abundance of previous research or existing theory that implies a particular relationship between concepts. In many cases, though not all, the closed-ended question can be answered as either "yes" or "no." For example, based on my knowledge of educational research, I might deduce that more personalized teaching will yield greater student satisfaction, and, therefore, reword my former research problem as a closed-ended research question.

> RQ: Is more personalized teaching positively related to increased student perceptions of classroom climate?

In this question the particular variety of relationship is specified and that the final answer to the research question will simply be "yes" or "no."

Hypothesis

An alternative to the research question, the hypothesis, often abbreviated in research journals as H_n, is *a declarative statement suggesting a predicted relationship between two or more communication concepts.* Wimmer and Dominick (1994) suggest four criteria for good hypotheses: (1) They should be compatible with the current knowledge in the discipline, (2) they should clearly abide by the rules of logic, (3) they should be worded clearly and concisely, and (4) they, like research questions, should be empirically testable. Once again, science cannot make value judgments.

Like research questions, hypotheses also come in two varieties: one-tailed and two-tailed.

Two-Tailed Hypothesis. The two-tailed hypothesis is a *declarative statement that suggests a relationship between/among two or more concepts, but does not specify the form or direction of that relationship.* It is the alternative generally selected when previous research or theory suggests a relationship, but there is some question about the kind of relationship, for example:

> H_1: There is a relationship between instructor teaching style and student perception of classroom climate.

It is clear from this statement that some relationship is expected though that relationship may take any of a number of forms.

One-Tailed Hypothesis. This alternative to the two-tailed hypothesis provides more specificity, as it is a *declarative statement suggesting a particular form or direction to the relationship between/among two or more communication concepts.* This variety of hypothesis is generally favored when previous research or the theoretical foundation permits, for example:

> H_2: As personalization of teaching increases, student perceptions of classroom climate increase.

In this case, the relationship is not only expected but also the specific form of the relationship is explicitly stated.

Any time that researchers propose a hypothesis as a research problem, they simultaneously create a **null hypothesis,** *a hypothesis of no relationship.* The null hypothesis is generally symbolized by H_0. For both of our hypothetical examples, the null hypothesis would be:

> H_0: There is no relationship between instructor teaching style and student perception of classroom climate.

It is important to recognize that the null hypothesis specifies *no* relationship. If we were to create a hypothesis that contrasts with our one-tailed example, which suggested that as personalization of classroom teaching increases student perceptions of classroom climate decreases, it would not be a null hypothesis. Rather, that variety would be labeled an **alternative hypothesis,** or one that *specifies a different form of relationship than that proposed by our original hypothesis.*

Elements of a Research Problem

Regardless of whether a research problem is framed as a question or hypothesis, it is composed of two essential elements: constructs and linkages.

Constructs

The most obvious elements in any research problem are the **constructs.** These are *the terms that represent the things, or concepts, in which the researcher has an interest.* In our previous examples of problem statements, the constructs would be (1) instructor teaching style and (2) student perception of classroom climate. These are the things that the researcher is interested in examining for a potential relationship.

Once we have identified the constructs in the research problem our primary task becomes that of *clearly defining those constructs by relating them to other constructs, or terms,* a process known as **conceptual definition.** The goal of the conceptual definition process is to reduce the ambiguity of the terms used in the problem statement so that the community of scholars has some agreed-on meaning for those terms. Frankfort-Nachmias and Nachmias (1992) suggest that we reduce the **derived terms** from our research problem (those terms with vague or ambiguous meaning) to **primitive terms.** Primitive terms are "those on which there is a consensus on their meaning" (p. 30). In most situations primitive terms are sensory in nature and include colors, smells, tastes, and so on. It is important to be aware that primitive terms may be at different levels of consensus, depending on one's discipline. For example, in communication we would define the color of grass as green, and believe there to be enough agreement. However, a physicist might define the color of grass as that with a reflected light wavelength of 510 to 550 nanometers. Therefore, it is important to be aware of the requirements of the community of scholars in which you carry out research.

An investigator may reference a variety of sources for a conceptual definition. Sometimes the definitions can be borrowed from other scholars in the discipline. If, for example, we were interested in studying "communication apprehension," we might turn to James McCroskey (1977) who, in his research, has provided a clear and often used definition of this phenomenon. Likewise, if we were interested in a conceptual definition for *media violence,* we might access the work of George Gerbner (Gerbner, Gross, Signorielli, Morgan, & Jackson-Beeck, 1979). The advantage to this approach is that it avoids the need to "reinvent the wheel" when trying to develop an agreed-on definition.

However, there are times when existing definitions are either not available or are inadequate for the proposed problem. In such situations, researchers must create definitions by modifying existing constructs. In this case, the researcher must use dictionaries, encyclopedias, annual reviews of research, journal articles, and other sources in an effort to clearly define the intended meaning of the terms used in the research problem. While this technique is more difficult and time-consuming, we should recognize that the breadth of the communication discipline demands that we often look to related disciplines for assistance in developing a conceptual definition based in primitive terms. For example, the constructs in the previous problem examples might be best defined by terms from the discipline of education. Time spent creating clear, well-focused conceptual definitions may be considerable. However, cutting corners at this point will result in considerable difficulty later in the research process.

As the conceptual definition evolves into increasingly primitive, agreed-on, terms, the process begins to blend with the process of creating an **operational definition.** An operational definition is *a statement describing the observable indicators of a construct's relative presence or absence,* in other words, what procedures the investigator will follow in order to observe, measure, or manipulate the construct. We might, for example, be interested in the construct "intelligence." It is possible to conceptually define *intelligence* as 'an individual's ability to solve complex cognitive tasks.' However, in order to empirically measure this ability one must perform some standard procedures. Therefore, we might operationally define *intelligence* as 'one's score on the Stanford-Binet Battery of Intelligence.' This definition provides the "recipe" for empirically observing the construct of interest.

At the point where we begin to operationally define the constructs, those constructs begin to become **variables.** A variable is *a construct capable of taking on two or more values,* or, more simply, a construct that can vary. In a problem statement, it is generally possible to identify up to three different kinds of variables. If we envision a typical hypothesis as "If X, then Y, when Z," the kinds of variables become obvious.

> **Independent variable (X).** The independent variable is *the variable that is expected to influence a change in another variable.* In our earlier sample problem statements, "instructor teaching style" would be the independent variable because it is expected to cause a change in the "student perception of classroom climate."
>
> **Dependent variable (Y).** This is the variable that is expected to change as a result of the actions of the independent variable. In our previous example it would be the "student perception of classroom climate."
>
> **Intervening variable (Z).** The intervening variables are any other variables that might somehow influence the relationship between the independent and dependent variables. These are equivalent to the boundary conditions that we found in our theoretical statements. In our sample problem statements, we have specified no intervening variables, though some, such as the temperature of the classroom, the color of the walls, and the length of the class, may have an influence on the relationship.

A researcher should consider two characteristics when developing effective operational definitions: conceptual fit and reality isomorphism.

Conceptual Fit. The first consideration should be how well the operational definition retains the majority of the characteristics described by the conceptual definition (Frey, Botan, Friedman, & Kreps, 1991). We might conceptually define *media violence* as 'acts that harm another person physically, mentally, or emotionally that is presented to a large, heterogeneous, and anonymous audience using electronic or mechanical reproduction systems.' If we then define it operationally as 'the number of times a gun is fired during a television program,' we clearly have poor conceptual fit. There are many of the characteristics of the conceptual definition that have been omitted in the operational definition. The conceptual fit of our definitions for *intelligence,* used previously, have significantly greater conceptual fit because the Stanford-Binet Intelligence Battery uses a series of progressively more difficult cognitive tasks, the key component of our conceptual definition.

Reality Isomorphism. The second consideration should be *how consistent the operational definition is with the way the constructs exist in the real world* (Smith, 1988). All real-world constructs may be categorized along several dimensions: manifest versus latent, discrete versus continuous, and nominal versus ordered.

1. Manifest versus Latent. *Manifest constructs in the real world are those that can be observed directly, while latent constructs are those that cannot be directly observed, but must be inferred from other observable constructs.* Age, sex, time, and income are all examples of manifest variables, clearly deduced by direct observation. Intelligence, aggression, anxiety, and arousal are, on the other hand, latent, because they cannot be directly observed but must be inferred from other observable factors.
2. Discrete versus Continuous. *Discrete constructs are those that take on a limited number of values and change in distinct steps, while continuous constructs can take on any value within a range from some low to some high.* As a result, sex (M, F), party affiliation (D, R, I), and personal income (capable of change in steps no smaller than $.01) are all discrete constructs, while height, age, and intelligence are all continuous.
3. Nominal versus Ordered. *Nominal constructs are those that are classified without any inherent level of quantification; none is better or worse, greater or lesser than another. Ordered constructs, on the other hand, tend to suggest some level of quantification.* Therefore, sex, and party affiliation are examples of nominal constructs, while class standing (F, So, J, Sr), height, and income are ordered constructs.

The importance of these dimensions is that researchers should, when creating operational definitions, be careful to retain as many of the real-world characteristics as possible. However, in many cases, some sacrifice of true reality isomorphism is necessary. For example, age is a naturally continuous construct. However, when we measure age, it usually becomes discrete, often measured in yearly steps. As researchers, we need to carefully analyze and consider the impact of these sacrifices.

Kerlinger (1979) suggests that all operational definitions fall into one of two categories. The most common form is the **measured operational definition,** which describes the steps an investigator must take to determine the existence or quantity of a construct. Measured operational definitions are encountered in all research studies. The other type is the **experimental operational definition,** which defines the steps the researcher must take in order to manipulate levels of a construct. This variety of operational definition is most often encountered in experimental studies in which the researcher plans to actively manipulate the independent variable in order to identify its influence on the dependent variable.

Linkages

The other essential elements found in research problem statements are the linkages, or *terms that specify the form or direction of the relationship expected between or among constructs.* In open-ended research questions and two-tailed hypotheses, these terms are usually quite general, often suggesting only some form of relationship. In our sample open-ended research question (How is instructor teaching style related to student perception of classroom climate?), the linkage term is *related,* suggests that any form or direction of relationship will be considered.

In closed-ended research questions and one-tailed hypotheses, the linkage terms are generally much more specific, specifying the particular form or direction of the expected relationship. Two general varieties of linkages are most often suggested: linear and curvilinear relationships.

Linear Relationship. This variety of linkage suggests that, *as one construct varies, the other will change in a consistent manner.* For example, if the construct X increases in value, the construct Y will either increase in value or decrease in value at the same time. There are two common forms of linear relationship that may be found in problem statements: positive or negative.

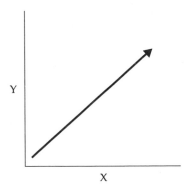

FIGURE 2.1   *Positive Linear Relationship*

Positive Linear Relationship. The positive linear relationship (Figure 2.1) suggests that, *as one construct changes in value, the other construct will change in the same direction.* Therefore, if construct X increases, it would suggest that construct Y increase.

Likewise, if construct X decreases in value, it would suggest that construct Y decrease. This is the variety of linkage specified in our sample one-tailed hypothesis (As personalization of teaching style increases, student perceptions of classroom climate increase.).

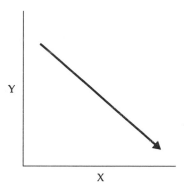

FIGURE 2.2 *Negative Linear Relationship*

Negative Linear Relationship. The negative linear relationship (Figure 2.2) suggests that, *as one construct changes in value, the other construct changes in the opposite direction.* Therefore, if construct X increases in value, construct Y would be expected to decrease. Or, if construct X decreased in value, we would expect an increase in construct Y. An example of such a linkage in a one-tailed hypothesis would be: As a child's hours of television exposure increase, academic performance will decrease.

Curvilinear Relationship. A curvilinear relationship suggests *any relationship that is less direct than the linear form.* It suggests that, as one construct varies, the other also does, but in a less consistent manner. Two common varieties of curvilinear relationships are often encountered: the U-relationship or the inverted-U-relationship.

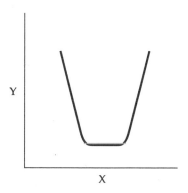

FIGURE 2.3 *U-Relationship*

U-Relationship.   The U-relationship (Figure 2.3) suggests that *a positive or negative change in the value of one construct will result in an initial decline in the second construct, followed by an eventual increase.* This relationship gets its name from the shape of the curve created when the two constructs are graphed on an X–Y axis.

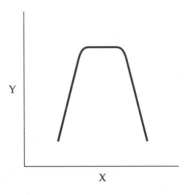

FIGURE 2.4   *Inverted-U Relationship*

Inverted-U-Relationship.   The inverted-U-relationship (Figure 2.4) suggests that, *as one construct changes in value, either positively or negatively, the other construct will initially increase in value to some point where it will plateau, and then begin to decrease.* An example of such a relationship is that discovered between aging and newspaper readership. As one gets progressively older (X-axis), initially the hours of newspaper readership (Y-axis) will increase, then, between 55–65 years they tend to plateau, and at older ages a decline in readership becomes evident.

Careful development of a research problem statement and the evaluation of its components is often tedious, but truly critical to success at later stages in the research process.

3

Access to the Community

Meeting the Community

Science is a community-based endeavor. The next step for the communication researcher is to gain access to the work of the community of scholars. Often, at this point, the problem statement guiding the research is rather abstract and open-ended. The knowledge of the community of scholars will assist the researcher in developing the statement into a more empirically testable and, often, more closed-ended form. The outcome of this step in the research process will be a summary of existing knowledge on the research topic, called a **literature review,** as well as a more refined research question or hypothesis.

Once the general research problem has been formulated, the researcher needs to locate all the relevant knowledge related to that topic. A clear conceptual definition will assist in this process because it provides related concepts that can be used as keywords in the search for knowledge. However, many times the researcher will have an unrefined conceptual definition and will require some assistance in developing a collection of more primitive terms. To assist in this process, one can turn to a number of excellent **overview materials,** *sources that provide a general introduction to the various fields within the communication discipline.* Among the several useful forms of overview material, some of the most useful to the communication student are textbooks. College and university libraries often maintain extensive collections of contemporary texts in the discipline, and students may have a collection from courses previously taken. These texts usually provide a brief summary of the existing knowledge within particular fields and are, therefore, particularly helpful in providing focus to a previously unrefined research problem. Because they are introductions to the field, they also generally provide clear definitions for terms that may prove helpful in developing a list of primitive terms for use in the later, more detailed search. But, perhaps their greatest utility is that they provide some introduction to the key players within the community. Through the use of the citations and bibliographies in these texts the student has a starting point for further investigation.

There are also numerous independent summaries of the communication discipline that may be useful as overview materials. The *International Encyclopedia of Communications,* by Eric Barnouw (1989), provides over 500 articles summarizing the state of the discipline's knowledge, all within four volumes. The detail provided in these articles is generally greater than that found in a student text, and, because they have extensive bibliographies, they are a great resource for community membership. Another extremely useful source is the *Sage Annual Reviews of Communication Research* (1972–), an edited resource that focuses on a different theme each year and provides a comprehensive overview of that research area, often including some original research not found in other sources. That, plus its excellent bibliography, makes it an excellent overview resource. Following a similar, though less theme-oriented approach, is the *Communication Yearbook* (1977–), published by the International Communication Association, a collection of the most important studies and commentaries (with bibliographies) solicited from the membership of this respected international organization.

A final overview source worth consideration is *The Communication Handbook: A Dictionary,* by J. A. DeVito (1986). As well as providing an excellent source of conceptual definitions for many of the terms in the communication discipline, it also provides the reader with over 100 essays surveying the major fields within the discipline, introducing the major players within the community, and providing connections to the most significant works.

One cautionary note regarding all of the aforementioned overview materials: They provide a summary of knowledge prior to their publication dates. Therefore, the most current works within any given field are not going to be included. This means that the researcher's task cannot be completed using only these resources. A more involved search is required. Also, the above list of overview materials is far from comprehensive, as there are many specialized resources available. For a more extensive listing of resources relating to the communication discipline, I would recommend Rubin, Rubin, and Piele's (2000) *Communication Research: Strategies and Sources,* an exceptional handbook for locating the appropriate community of scholars.

Access to the Community

Once the researcher has developed some knowledge of his or her field of interest, the next step is to become more completely integrated into the community. This requires a more detailed search of the available knowledge in books, periodicals, and on-line resources.

The book collection in a college or university library is best suited to the researcher for an overview of the field of interest, as well as for detailed descriptions of communication theory. If, for example, you were interested in Bandura's theory of social learning, the best review of it would be found in his *Principles of Behavior Modification* (1969). Finding books in the library collection usually involves learning the cataloging system of the library being used. In the traditional library, cataloging is done using a series of cards, at least three for each book in the collection. Each volume has a card for the author of the work, one for the title of the work, and one for the subject covered by the book. If the book crosses over several different subjects, multiple subject cards may be present. For most researchers, finding a book using this traditional approach means deciding on the most relevant subject area and searching the catalog for useful sources. If, for example, you were interested in Internet communication and its relationship to personality traits, you might search the traditional catalog under "communication," "Internet," or "personality." Within each subject collection you would need to browse for those books with greatest potential relevance. This is also where a well-developed conceptual definition assists in the search. From the conceptualizing process, you may have discovered that other key terms are related to your initial constructs, allowing you to search under such subjects as "computers," "media," "psychology," and "technology." One important reminder about completing such a search: Be certain to record in a research notebook the important details about discovered books, including their call numbers, authors, and titles, as well as key terms used in conducting the search.

Today the majority of college and university libraries, as well as many community libraries, have moved away from the traditional cataloging approach and have converted to computer searchable systems. The greatest advantage to such systems is the ability to customize the search in highly specific ways. While computer-based systems continue to permit searching by author, title, or subject, the majority of the researcher's search will use **keywords,** *significant words appearing in the title or description of a cataloged work.* Keyword searches work much like the subject search of a traditional card catalog, and entering a single word into the search field of the computer catalog will produce similar results. However, because the system searches titles and descriptions, you may get a greater number of results, or **hits,** than you would by following the traditional method. One important note: If you are searching for a keyword phrase, such as "mass communication" or "personality traits," and you want the search to look for words in those particular orders and combinations, most cataloging systems require that the words be enclosed in some specific boundary markers, usually either parentheses or quotation marks. You will need to check with your local library for the specific phrase maintainers used by your system.

The real advantage to the computer search is the ability to combine terms in varied and unique ways during the search process. This combination is made possible through the use of **Boolean logical operators,** which are simply *logical rules used by the computer to complete a customized search for keywords.* The three most commonly used Boolean logical operators are **and, or,** and **not.**

And. When combined with two or more keywords, this operator searches for *all sources that contain both/all keywords in the statement* (Figure 3.1). If, for example we conducted a search using the keywords "Internet AND personality," the computer would find all sources that contain both of these keywords in either the title or description.

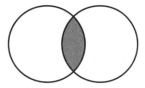

FIGURE 3.1   *Venn Diagram of AND Operation*

Or. When combined with two or more keywords, this operator searches for *all sources that contain any of the keywords included in the statement* (Figure 3.2). If we were to search with the statement "Internet OR personality," the computer would find all sources that mention either of the terms in the title or description. This approach will generally produce more hits than the previous, more focused statement.

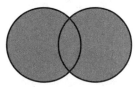

FIGURE 3.2   *Venn Diagram of OR Operation*

Not. When combined with another keyword, this logical operator first *searches for sources with the initial keyword, then omits those that contain the keyword following the NOT instruction* (Figure 3.3). If we were to search for "Internet

NOT E-mail," the computer would first find those sources relating to the Internet, then exclude all those that contain a reference to E-mail in their titles or descriptions.

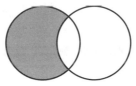

FIGURE 3.3   *Venn Diagram of NOT Operation*

As with keyword phrases, individual cataloging systems have specific rules for the inclusion of Boolean logical operators, such as the need to have them in all upper case or enclosed in parentheses. You will need to ask your local librarian about the rules for your system. Boolean logical operators may be used in combination to form very precise, customized searches (i.e., (television OR video) AND children AND (violence OR aggression). Most systems also permit you to **truncate,** or *shorten,* keywords to enhance the search, usually using either a question mark or an asterisk. Searching for the truncated term "chil*" or "chil?" (depending on the catalog requirements) will find sources with "chil" followed by any other set of letters in the title or description, including such words as *chill, chilled, chilling, child, children, childish,* and so on.

While books provide some important detail regarding the communication discipline, researchers must recognize that they are, by their very nature, not the most timely sources. Therefore, the most significant sources for scholars are **periodicals,** particularly **scholarly journals.** The principal advantages of these journals are their timeliness, because they usually publish the most current research, as well as their nature as **primary sources.** A primary source is a *manuscript written by the original source or person who completed the investigation.* When that source is summarized by another person, as is often done in textbooks, book reviews, newspapers, or other media, it becomes a **secondary source.** Researchers prefer the primary source because it is believed to be a more accurate reflection of the actual situation. Finally, most scholarly journals follow a **blind review policy;** *Articles are reviewed and selected for publication without the reviewers knowing the identity of the contributing author, thereby assuring selection based on quality of scholarship rather than the reputation of the author.*

Searching for periodicals involves the use of **indexes, abstracts,** and **databases.** An index is *a print collection of current article locations arranged topically.* Finding periodical articles within an index is similar to locating a book in the traditional card catalog. Keywords are identified and then searched for in the index listings. A successful search will find a listing of articles, authors, publication names, dates, and pages relating to the keyword searched. The researcher need only record the location information for later access to the articles. Several of the most popular indexes used in the communication discipline are:

Select Scholarly Journals in Communication

Academy of Management Review
Administrative Science Quarterly
American Behavioral Scientist
American Journal of Political Science
American Journal of Sociology
American Journalism
American Political Science Review
American Politics Quarterly
American Sociological Review
American Speech
Applied Psycholinguistics
Argumentation and Advocacy
Broadcasting
Business Communication Quarterly
Child Development
Cinema Journal
Cognitive Psychology
Communication and Cognition
Communication and the Law
Communication Education
Communication Law and Policy
Communication Quarterly
Communication Monographs
Communication Reports
Communication Research Reports
Communication Studies
Communication Theory
Comparative Political Studies
Comparative Politics
Conflict Studies
Critical Studies in Media Communication
Developmental Psychology
Discourse & Society
Educational Technology Research and
    Development
Federal Communications Law Journal
Feedback
Film History
Film Journal
Film Quarterly
Group & Organization Management
Hastings Communications and Entertainment
    Law Journal
Health Communication
Howard Journal of Communications

Human Communication Research
Human Development
Human Organization
Industrial and Labor Relations Review
Information and Behavior
International Journal of Advertising
International Journal of American Linguistics
International Journal of Oral History
Journal of Abnormal Psychology
Journal of Advertising
Journal of Advertising History
Journal of Advertising Research
Journal of Applied Communication Research
Journal of Applied Psychology
Journal of Applied Social Psychology
Journal of Business
Journal of Broadcasting & Electronic Media
Journal of Communication
Journal of Communication and Religion
Journal of Communication Inquiry
Journal of Conflict Research
Journal of Consumer Research
Journal of Current Issues and Research in
    Advertising
Journal of Educational Psychology
Journal of Experimental Social Psychology
Journal of Film and Video
Journal of Gerontology
Journal of Human Relations
Journal of Language and Social Psychology
Journal of Linguistics
Journal of Marketing
Journal of Marketing Research
Journal of Marriage and the Family
Journal of Mass Media Ethics
Journal of Memory and Language
Journal of Nonverbal Behavior
Journal of Personality
Journal of Personality and Social Psychology
Journal of Personality Assessment
Journal of Politics
Journal of Popular Culture
Journal of Popular Film and Television
Journal of Psycholinguistic Research
Journal of Public Relations Research

Journal of Radio Studies
Journal of Research in Personality
Journal of Sex Research
Journal of Social and Behavioral Sciences
Journal of Social and Personal Relationships
Journal of the International Listening Association
Journal of Youth and Adolescence
Journalism & Mass Communication Educator
Journalism & Mass Communication Monographs
Journalism & Mass Communication Quarterly
Language
Language & Communication
Management Communication Quarterly
Mass Comm Review
Media & Values
Media Culture & Society
National Forensic Journal
Newspaper Research Journal
Organizational Behavior and Human Decision Processes
Philosophy and Rhetoric

Political Behavior
Political Communication
Political Science Quarterly
Public Opinion Quarterly
Public Relations Quarterly
Public Relations Review
Qualitative Sociology
Quarterly Journal of Speech
Quarterly Review of Film and Video
Research on Language and Social Interaction
Rhetoric Society Quarterly
Science Communication
Small Group Research
Social Science Quarterly
Sociological Methods and Research
Southern Communication Journal
Symbolic Interaction
Telecommunications Policy
Telecommunications Policy and Regulation
Western Journal of Speech Communication
Women's Studies in Communication
World Communication

Education Index (1929–)

Humanities Index (1974–)

Social Science Index (1974–)

Applied Science and Technology Index (1958–)

Business and Periodical Index (1958–)

Topicator (1965–)

Social Science Citation Index (1972–)

Bibliographic Index (1937–). (This is a specialized index of topical bibliographies, including a minimum of 50 citations, published in books and journals.)

An abstract is similar to an index in that it is a topical listing of article locations, but differs in that it also *contains a brief summary of each listed article*. The advantage to the summary is that it permits the researcher to eliminate articles that seem irrelevant. One should be cautious, however, in dealing with these summaries. Because they are generally secondary sources, errors in the reporting can occur, and there are cases in which the abstract barely resembles the article. As a general rule, *do not trust the abstract to be an accurate summary*. Among the most commonly used abstracts in the communication discipline are:

Communication Abstracts (1978–)

Journalism Abstracts (1963–)

Psychological Abstracts (1952–)

Sociological Abstracts (1952–)

Dissertation Abstracts (This is a specialized abstract of graduate-level research, mostly at the doctoral level. This resource provides information about the investigations conducted, the institution at which they occurred, and the author of the publication. While these studies are not usually printed in scholarly journals, copies can often be obtained from authors or degree-awarding institutions. The greatest advantage of these resources are their extensive bibliographies and lengthy literature reviews.)

Both indexes and abstracts can be found as part of databases, *electronically searchable or machine-readable indexes and abstracts.* The advantage of these collections is the ability to customize the search, much as you customize a search in a computer-based card catalog. Like the catalog, you can search for individual keywords or keywords combined with Boolean logical operators. Some databases permit you to electronically access the complete article as well as providing information about that article. Among some of the more common periodical databases are:

InfoTrac. A collection of three academically oriented databases, including the Health Reference Center, the Expanded Academic ASAP, and the Business and Company ASAP.

WebSPIRS. A collection of a variety of indexes permitting customizable searches.

ProQuest. A collection of several databases, including one of multidisciplinary peer-reviewed journals that may be custom searched.

ERIC. A database of educational resources including papers presented at professional conferences that cannot be found in other sources.

UNCOVER. A commercial database of over 17,000 journal titles published since 1978. Searching for references on this database is free, and reference listings are complete enough for the researcher to locate published articles in the local library. The commercial aspect of the business involves the sale and distribution of copies of hard-to-locate articles.

Lexis/Nexis Universe. A collection of eighteen separate databases containing current events, legal resources, and business information, and a useful resource because the requested documents are delivered electronically to the researcher's computer.

Dissertation Abstracts. An electronic version of the print abstract described in the previous section.

Availability of databases differs from library to library, with several other specialized databases available on a local or regional level. Therefore, researchers should ask their local librarian about databases available for their use, and about special rules for their application.

On-line resources, such as the Internet and E-mail, are a third, and increasingly popular, source of information for the communication researcher. Most Web sites, however, are of dubious usefulness, due to the absence of confirmed source credibility and a lack of evaluation by the community of scholars. Internet sites that are electronic versions of the popular research journals are obvious exceptions to this statement, as are a few other sites that serve as information repositories, including:

http://www.ipfw.edu/comm/resources/default.html
http://www.uiowa.edu/~commstud/resources/index.html
http://www.aber.ac.uk/%7edgc/media.html

Each of the above academic sites provides a broad range of current information regarding the communication discipline, with the last site, situated at the University of Wales, being the most international and comprehensive. Other scholarly sites do exist, but the researcher needs to exercise caution in determining the credibility of the site author and the accuracy of the information presented.

E-mail is another useful on-line tool for the communication researcher because it allows rapid interaction with other members of the research community. It is particularly useful when trying to obtain unpublished details regarding a published work or when trying to gain access to an unpublished paper, thesis, or presentation. Most communication scholars have E-mail access, and their addresses can be found in professional directories published by academic organizations (such as the National Communication Association [NCA], or Broadcast Education Association [BEA]) or by accessing their institution's Web site. It is important to remember, however, that not everyone with an E-mail address actively checks their E-mail accounts, so follow-up letters by traditional postal delivery may be necessary.

Integrating into the Community

Having searched for resources available on a particular topic, the next, rather obvious, step in the process is to collect and read those resources. Hopefully, the researcher has been diligent to this point about recording all source information in a research notebook, thereby making this next step much simpler. When searching for books in the library collection, the researcher will most likely use either the Library of Congress or Dewey Decimal cataloging system. If you are uncertain which system your library is using, or how it is arranged, you should consult your librarian. Finding periodicals in the library is also generally quite simple, though the periodicals may be in a current issues, bound (past issues), or microform (microfilm and microfiche) section, and you will need to consult your library's electronic catalog or librarian for assistance in locating the appropriate section.

If a book or periodical you have discovered is unavailable in your local research library, it is likely that the library can obtain a copy through **interlibrary**

loan. Cooperating libraries make their collections available for loan to other institutions on request. Interlibrary loan is usually achieved by completing a request form available from the reference librarian or electronically through the library catalog. Be aware that requests may take several weeks to process, and that there is sometimes a nominal fee associated with their procurement. At Slippery Rock University, for example, books are obtained for free, but periodicals are photocopied with the cost charged to the person placing the request. If you are uncertain about the interlibrary loan process at your library, once again, ask the librarian.

Papers presented at professional conferences, master's theses, and doctoral dissertations are often among the most difficult resources for the researcher to acquire. While copies of dissertations may often be purchased from University Microforms, the cost is usually prohibitive. With all of the above resources, vigilance is often the most important tool to the researcher. In many cases, copies of the works can be requested by E-mail or conventional mail sent to the author, whose address may be available from a professional or institutional directory. If the search is for a master's thesis or doctoral dissertation, information about its procurement may be available from the degree-awarding institution, particularly the involved department or faculty advisor. It is also possible to find many convention papers through the ERIC database mentioned previously, or through collections of such papers published as **proceedings** by many professional organizations.

Reading articles presented in professional journals is often a particular challenge to the beginning researcher, who feels overwhelmed by the style and jargon of the presentation. The task becomes somewhat simpler if you recognize that the typical journal article consists of five basic parts:

Introduction/Review of Literature. In this section the author provides a brief rationale for his or her interest in the topic of the article, and then provides a rather extensive review of the state of knowledge regarding that topic prior to his or her investigation. It is in this section that beginning researchers may discover important new resources to add to their reference list.

Development of the Research Problem. Near the end of the introduction section, the author will generally reveal the specific research problem(s) that he or she intends to resolve. This problem will serve as the foundation for the remainder of the article.

Methodology. Having developed a problem to guide the research, in this third section the author reveals in some detail the techniques that he or she will use in finding an answer. Included will be details about how the elements were selected for study, what procedures were used, and the analysis techniques used.

Results. This section is usually the most difficult, and sometimes overwhelming, part to the beginning researcher. Within this section the author reveals the specific findings of his or her research, often using sophisticated tables, graphs, and statistics. Even if they seem daunting, beginning researchers should persevere and struggle through this section, as it will help in the future as they acquire understanding of analytic procedures and appropriate research language. The specific implications of the results will become more evident in the final section of the article.

Discussion. In this final section, the author takes the newly discovered information and attempts to integrate it into the prior knowledge base. Generally, as this is accomplished the results are presented in a more understandable, less jargon-laden manner. It is also in this section that the author reflects on the state of knowledge and suggests problems that need to be resolved by future researchers, providing heuristic utility to the study, and suggesting excellent potential problem statements to the reader.

As the researcher acquires and reads each of the resources related to his or her topic, detailed notes about the works should be included in the research notebook. Included in these notes should be some orientation to the work and its purpose, including the research problems being explored, some detail about the methods used to resolve the problems, a brief summary of the general findings in the researcher's own words, and the researcher's own personal reaction to the work including its readability, clarity, conciseness, completeness, and apparent usefulness. The best technique for developing this *summary of the work,* or **annotation,** is to read the article, then attempt to summarize in your own words what you have read. After writing the summary, accuracy can be assured by comparing it to the original article. By using this "read, then write" method a researcher is likely to avoid the temptation to **plagiarize.** *Plagiarism* is "the unauthorized use of the language and thoughts of an author and the representation of them as one's own" (Hult, 1996, p. 43). A well-written annotation is a **paraphrase,** *a rewording of the original work using the researcher's own words and style.*

Credit to the Community

Having found and read the works of the community of scholars within your interest area, generally the next step is the creation of a roster of those community members, usually called a bibliography or list of **references.** The primary goal of this list is to permit other interested researchers ease of access to the same community of scholars you have accessed. One commonly used style for the reference list is found in the *Publication Manual of the American Psychological Association* (1994). Creating a list of references using this style involves awareness of several important rules:

1. The listing of sources compiled on the given topic is entitled "References," with that title centered at the top of the page.
2. Sources are listed alphabetically based on the first significant word in the entry after omitting articles (i.e., *a, an, the*).
3. Authors' names are presented with the last name, followed by the first and, when available, middle initials (e.g., Stewart, T. D.), **not** entire first or middle names.

4. When creating a manuscript, the first line in each source entry is indented five to seven spaces. When a publisher later typesets the entry, it will appear as a hanging indent with the first line projecting to the left of subsequent lines by three spaces.
5. When creating a manuscript, the entries are double-spaced to provide for ease of editing. Once again, when that entry is later professionally typeset, it will be converted to single spacing.

Below are a few of the most commonly encountered APA reference styles in manuscript form:

Books:

The general format for a book entry in your reference list begins with the name of the author(s), followed by a period. Next is the date of publication, enclosed in parentheses and followed by a period. The book title (underlined or italicized, with only the first word and proper nouns capitalized) appears next and is followed by a period. Finally, the city of publication and the publisher are included, separated by a colon and followed by a period. The format for book entries varies, depending on the information that has to be provided.

Book with a single author:
Hult, C. A. (1996). *Researching and writing in the social sciences.* Boston: Allyn & Bacon.

Book with multiple authors:
Frey, L. R., Botan, C. H., Friedman, P. G., & Kreps, G. L. (1991). *Investigating communication: An introduction to research methods.* Englewood Cliffs, NJ: Prentice-Hall.

Edited book:
Emmert, P., & Barker, L. L. (Eds.). (1989). *Measurement of communication behavior.* New York: Longman.

(Note: If the book has a single editor, the correct abbreviation would be [Ed.].)

Essay within an edited book:
Anderson, P. A. (1989). Philosophy of science. In P. Emmert & L. L. Barker (Eds.), *Measurement of communication behavior* (pp. 3–17). New York: Longman.

Second and subsequent editions of a book:
Hoover, K., & Donovan, T. (1995). *The elements of social scientific thinking* (6th ed.). New York: St. Martin's Press.

Periodicals:

Like books, the periodical entry begins with the name of the author(s), followed by a period. The date of publication is enclosed in parentheses and followed by a period. The third element in the entry is the title of the article, with only the first and proper nouns capitalized, with *no* quotation marks enclosing the article title, followed by a period. The fourth element in the entry is the name of the periodical (underlined or italicized, with all significant words capitalized), followed by the volume number (underlined), the issue number when each issue begins with page one (in parentheses), and the page numbers. Like book entries, the format for periodical entries varies. (There is a partial list of important journals in communication on pages 30–31.)

Article with a single author:
Petronio, S. (1991). Communication boundary management: A theoretical model of managing disclosure of private information between marital couples. *Communication Theory, 1*, 311–335.

Article with multiple authors:
Miller, G., Boster, F., Roloff, M., & Seibold, D. (1977). Compliance-gaining message strategies: A typology and some findings concerning effects of situational differences. *Communication Monographs, 44*, 37–51.

Article from a separately paginated issue (when each issue begins with page one):
Planalp, S. (1993). Communication, cognition, and emotion. *Communication Monographs, 60*(1), 3–9.

Magazine article:
Bosak, J., & Bray, T. (1999, May). XML and the second-generation Web. *Scientific American, 280*(5), 89–93.

(Note: If a magazine is published more than once a month, the date of publication is presented following the month [e.g., 1999, May 12].)

Magazine article with no author provided:
Stars on the beach. (1999, July). *Biography*, pp. 50–56.

(Note: When volume and issue numbers are unavailable, the page numbers follow the periodical title, but are preceded by a *p*. [for a single page], or *pp*. [for multiple pages].)

Newspaper article:
Moylan, M. J. (1988, August 28). Proposal to use data from Nazi death tests ignites new debate. *Chicago Tribune*, p. A6.

(Note: When no author is provided, the article title begins the entry, followed by the date, publication, and page[s].)

Other resources:

Unpublished paper or presentation:
Cline, R. (1982, May). *Revealing and relating: A review of self-disclosure theory and research.* Paper presented at the meeting of the International Communication Association, Boston.

ERIC report or paper:
 Feeser, T., & Thompson, T. L. (1990). *A test of a method of increasing patient question asking in physician–patient interactions.* Paper presented at the annual meeting of the Speech Communication Association, Chicago. (ERIC Document Reproduction Service No. ED 325 887).

Doctoral dissertation:
 Stewart, T. D. (1990). Television as a tutorial device: Impact on the mentally retarded citizen. (Doctoral dissertation: The University of Iowa, 1989). *Dissertation Abstracts International, 51*(2), 333.

(Note: The date following the institution name corresponds to the year the dissertation was written, while the name following the author corresponds to the date of publication by *Dissertation Abstracts International.*)

Unpublished thesis or dissertation:
 Stewart, T. D. (1989). *Television as a tutorial device: Impact on the mentally retarded citizen.* Unpublished doctoral dissertation, The University of Iowa: Iowa City, IA.

(Note: If the source was a master's thesis, that information would appear in the place of "doctoral dissertation.")

Internet resource:
 NCA Publications. Retrieved July 13, 1999 from the World Wide Web: http://www.natcom.org/publications.htm

(Note: If you have an author's name, it should precede the title. Likewise, if you have a creation date, it should be included in parentheses (e.g., (1999, July 4).) following the author's name or following the title if the name is unavailable.

On-line journal article:
 Kraut, R., Lundmark, V., Patterson, M., Kiesler, S., Mukopadhyay, T., & Scherlis, W. (1998, September). Internet paradox: A social technology that reduces social involvement and psychological well-being? *American Psychologist, 53*(9), 1017–1031. Retrieved July 13, 1999 from the World Wide Web: http://www.apa.org/journal/amp/amp5391017.html

(Note: Always include retrieval dates in the citation because Web sites change, move, or are removed with great regularity.)

For additional examples and further information regarding the citation of communication resources, consult the APA manual or the APA Web site (http://www.apa.org).

As the researcher collects the current information regarding his or her topic, an adaptation of the reference list often becomes helpful. The **annotated bibliography** is, like the reference list, *a collection of sources related to the researcher's topic of interest,* but *each citation is followed by a short summary of the content of each source with evaluative comments regarding the source supplied by the researcher.* Well-written annotations should generally be two to four paragraphs in length, and should be in the researcher's own words, not the words of the source's author. You will recall that the best strategy for assuring that you are not plagiarizing is the "read, then write" technique, discussed previously. Annotations should include enough detail to permit the eventual development of an *essay summarizing the state of current knowledge on the topic of interest* to be included as part of the **literature review.** It is appropriate to include in the annotation the researcher's own analysis of the source's readability, clarity, conciseness, completeness, and apparent utility. As you may be aware, these are the same elements that you would have included in your research notebook as you collected and read resources. The advantage to the annotated bibliography lies in its alphabetized organization and detailed analysis, permitting easy integration of ideas into the literature review.

The culmination of all this effort is the development of the literature review. This is an essay, written in a formal style, that discusses what scholars have discovered or theorized about regarding a particular topic. Generally, it introduces the reader to the topic of interest as well as the significant scholars who have explored that topic. The literature review should begin with a brief introduction to the topic of interest and the significance of that topic. Within this section, the researcher may suggest why he or she has a personal interest in the topic or why it is an important topic to the communication discipline, perhaps clarifying some theory or providing a solution to a practical problem.

The second section of the literature review is generally the longest. It is in this section that the researcher summarizes the previous knowledge, theory, and research regarding the topic. While developing this review, often aided by the annotated bibliography, the researcher also makes note of gaps, inconsistencies, and possible errors in the knowledge base. Like any research essay or term paper, the literature review may be organized in numerous ways. Related topics may be grouped together into a topical pattern of organization. Research may be summarized along a time line in a chronological pattern. Or, the researcher may provide a generalized look at the topic, and then develop a more specific, detailed understanding. The pattern that the researcher chooses is usually dependent on the information that has been collected.

The final section of the literature review is a critical evaluation of the state of current knowledge. This is a synthesis of the previous section, indicating questions and gaps that have yet to be resolved. The outcome of this section will be the formulation of a specific research problem (question or hypothesis) that the researcher will attempt to resolve in a future investigation.

As the literature review develops, it is important to provide credit within the essay to the various scholars whose work is being discussed. The *Publication Manual of the American Psychological Association* (1994) provides guidelines for including these **internal citations,** *references to the works in the reference list.* If you make reference to a work within the literature review, but have not mentioned the author's name, then you include, in parentheses, each author's last name, and the year of the publication (e.g., (Stewart, 2001)). A reader can then find the specific reference in the listing of references at the end of the literature review. If, on the other hand, you mention the author's name in the sentence, you need only include, enclosed in parentheses, the date (e.g., Stewart (2001) suggested . . .). The above citations are appropriate for all your paraphrases. However, if you directly quote an author, you must also include the page on which the quotation was found, with that page enclosed in parentheses following the quotation, but before the final punctuation (e.g., Stewart (2001) argued that "research methods is important to all communication students" (p. 25).). If you had developed the above sentence without integrating the author's name, you would simply include it, with the date and page number, at the end of the quotation (e.g., "Research methods is important for all communication students" (Stewart, 2001, p. 25).). You will find this style in various sources that you encounter, and, once you are familiar with it, you will find it a natural, easy-to-use alternative to other citation styles with which you may be familiar.

At this point in the research process, you have developed a synthesis of the current state of knowledge regarding your topic of interest and a well-focused research problem to guide your further study. With the first stage of the research process complete, your next step is the development of an appropriate methodological design for resolving the problem.

4

Developing Valid Measurements

Chapter Outline

The focus of the last two chapters has been the development and refinement of a research problem statement, either a research question or hypothesis. Once the general problem statement was formulated, some time was spent identifying the constructs and linkages within the statement, and conceptually defining each of the significant constructs. You discovered that the goal of an effective conceptual definition was to reduce the ambiguous derived terms to a set of primitive terms with agreed-on meaning within the community of scholars. In order to develop such clarity, significant effort was spent assessing the accumulated knowledge of the scholars within our epistemological community. In Chapter 2, you learned that, as the conceptual definition process evolves, the researcher begins to focus on the development of an operational definition that suggests the procedures that the researcher will follow in order to observe, measure, or manipulate a construct. It is at this point that the constructs begin to develop into variables. Care in the development of operational definitions is crucial to assure that the definitions have good conceptual fit and high levels of reality isomorphism. You were also told that Kerlinger (1979) suggested that there are two varieties of operational definitions, measured and experimental. Because measured operational definitions are found in all research studies, they will be the subject of this chapter. If a researcher is to be successful, a great deal of time and effort must go into the development of effective measured operational definitions, or measurement procedures, and the evaluation of those procedures to assess their accuracy.

Measurement

Defining Measurement

To understand measured operational definitions, it is first necessary to understand what we mean by **measurement.** According to S. S. Stevens (1951), *"Measurement is the assignment of numerals to objects according to rules."* We might simplify this slightly by suggesting that it is the classification of observations according to some specified rules. However, to thoroughly understand Stevens's definition, we need to determine the meaning of the word *numerals.* Numerals are *symbols with no inherent quantitative meaning.* In short, a numeral is a label or category that, in itself, suggests nothing about quantity. Some examples of numerals are sex labels (male or female), political party affiliation (Democrat, Republican, Independent), Social Security numbers, and telephone numbers. While the last two appear in numeric form, the "numbers" themselves are meaningless quantities; if we were to perform mathematical manipulations of the "numbers," we would get meaningless results. Nothing about the above numerals suggests quantity; one label is not inherently better or worse, greater or lesser, than another. *When numerals have quantitative meaning associated with them,* they become **numbers.** Some examples of numbers are age in years, annual income, and numeric scores on examinations. Numbers can be mathematically manipulated; we can add, subtract, multiply, and divide these symbols and get meaningful results. It is important for the researcher to remember that *all numbers are numerals, but not all numerals are numbers.*

Levels of Measurement

The goal of the operational definition is the development of *procedures, or rules, for the assignment of numerals to observations,* or the development of a **mapping scheme.** In 1946, S. S. Stevens developed a scheme for classifying variables into four **levels of measurement.** These levels have proven useful to subsequent researchers in determining the appropriateness of research analysis techniques, and are important concepts of which all researchers should be aware. The levels are arranged hierarchically, with the least quantitative level the lowest, building to the highest level of quantification at the apex. As you progress through the hierarchy, each new level has all of the attributes of the previous level, but adds some important component.

Nominal. The lowest level of the Stevens's hierarchy consists of *assignment of a name, label, or category to a variable, but with no quantification of the symbol intended*. One example of a nominal measurement would be the assignment of individuals to the male or female category. Neither category is suggestive of quantity. One is not better or worse, or more or less, than the other category. Other examples of nominal classification would be assignment according to political party affiliation, or selection of a subject's favorite fruit, medium, or ad campaign. The *American Heritage Dictionary* (1985) defines *nominal* as "of, like, pertaining to, or consisting of a name or names." Nominal level measurements are, likewise, simply names attached to observed events. Because of the exclusive use of numerals rather than numbers at this level, mathematical manipulation of the symbols is impossible. For nominal measurements to be effective, they need to meet three critical requirements:

Mutually Exclusive. When the categories of a nominal measurement are developed, there must be some assurance that *every observation will fit into one and only one of the categories*. If I were to assess your favorite pastime, and attempt to map that into the categories of radio, television, or listening to music, you might recognize that the music listening overlaps significantly with the other two activities. Therefore, my mapping scheme would not be mutually exclusive.

Exhaustive. A second requirement of effective nominal categories is that they be exhaustive, or that *every observation have one category in which it may be mapped*. If I were to assess your idea of an ideal pet, and gave you the options of a dog, cat, or fish, I would not be exhaustive in my nominal mapping scheme, especially if your choice was a hamster, gerbil, snake, or parakeet. Often researchers overcome concerns about the exhaustive nature of their nominal categories by adding a category labeled "other." While this does ensure that the categories are exhaustive, it may result in significant problems when it comes to data analysis. Therefore, some care in identifying all possible categories at the time of operationalization is certainly worth the effort.

Equivalent. Finally, all the categories created in a nominal mapping scheme need to be *evaluating and comparing the same attribute of the variable being mapped*. If I were to code television shows according to the categories news, drama, situation comedy, ½-hour, and 1-hour, it is evident that I would be looking at two different attributes of the program. First, I am evaluating the program content, and, secondly, the program length. While each of these attributes might be measured separately, the combination of attributes would result in a less-than-useful mapping scheme.

Ordinal. At the second level of Stevens's hierarchy is ordinal measurement. Ordinal measurement *retains all the characteristics of the nominal level, but with the addition that the numerals are rank-ordered from some low to some high, though with no assumption of equal spacing between the ranked categories*. One example of an ordinal scale would be the assignment of college students according to their class standing (freshman, sophomore, junior, or senior). It is evident that these categories are ranked according to some criteria from a low to a high. However, you will notice that there is no assurance of an equal spacing between levels. It is possible that one student is a freshman, though perhaps only one credit shy of being a sophomore, while another is just beginning course work and is still within the same category. This lack of an equality assumption is perhaps even more evident if you were asked to rank-order three substances based on your preference of a beverage. If the selected substances were iced tea, water, and vinegar, it is assumed that the majority of individuals would select the first two in the number one and two spots, with vinegar being assigned the number three position. However, for most people, the preferential distance between water and iced tea would be significantly smaller than the distance between the second preference and the vinegar. In short, there is no guarantee of equal distances between the levels of the ordinal mapping scheme. A very common measurement item using the ordinal level is, in fact, the rank-order question like that used in the above example.

Interval.   The third level of Stevens's hierarchy is interval measurement. This level *retains all of the characteristics of the previous two levels, but includes for the first time an equality assumption, and the assignment of an arbitrary zero point.* At this level, we not only rank-order observations from low to high, but we assure that the distances between each of the categories is equal to the distance between all other categories, or that the categories progress in equal steps. The other added requirement is the assignment of an arbitrary zero point, or a zero point that is determined and set by the researcher, having no existence beyond the mapping scheme. Perhaps the most commonly used examples of an interval measurement are the temperature scales used by meteorologists. When we examine the Fahrenheit scale, we first notice equal intervals between the temperature markings (e.g., the change between 60 and 61 degrees is the same as the change between 85 and 86 degrees). It is also evident that the 0-degree marking is somewhat arbitrary, because it is possible for the temperature to fall below that level. The arbitrary zero point becomes even more evident when we compare the Fahrenheit scale with the Celsius scale. The 0-degree point differs on each of these scales, and both have observations that can negatively exceed the zero point.

Because of the equality assumption and the addition of an anchoring point, the zero, this is the first level at which we have numbers as opposed to numerals. For the first time it is possible to perform mathematical manipulations that yield meaningful results. As a result of these traits, the interval level of measurement is quite popular among communication researchers, particularly those interested in using statistical data analysis techniques. There are a variety of common interval level measurement scales used by communication investigators. Among the most popular are: the Likert Summated Rating Scale and the Demantic Differential Scale.

The Likert Summated Rating Scale.   The Likert Scale consists of *a series of positively and negatively worded declarative statements, each accompanied by a five- or seven-point scale assessing subject agreement or disagreement, approval or disapproval.* An example of a simple Likert item would be:

Communication Research Methods is my favorite class.
☐ Strongly Agree (1,7)
☐ Moderately Agree (2,6)
☐ Slightly Agree (3,5)
☐ Unsure (4)
☐ Slightly Disagree (5,3)
☐ Moderately Disagree (6,2)
☐ Strongly Disagree (7,1)

After reading the declarative statement, the person completing the Likert Scale selects the level of agreement/disagreement from the options provided. Each of the five or seven options provided can be translated, or mapped, to the numbers one through seven as shown in the parentheses following the options. If, in this example, the subject selected the second line from the top, moderately agree, that could be mapped as number two or number six, depending on the need and rules established by the researcher. If we wanted to assign the highest score to positive feelings about the Communication Research Methods class, we would assign a one to the strongest level of disagreement with the statement and a seven to the strongest level of agreement. In this case, a six would be assigned to our sample response.

When the Likert Scale is applied in actual research, however, each measured construct usually is mapped using several scale items. If I were measuring students' pleasure with the course, I might include such declarative statements as:

Communication Research Methods is an enjoyable experience. (+)
I find Communication Research Methods to be dull and boring. (–)
I would recommend Communication Research Methods to my friends. (+)
I see no practical advantage to taking Communication Research Methods. (–)

Notice that some of the opinion statements are positively worded, while others are more negative, as specified by the positive and negative signs following the statements. It should be obvious that each of these would require a different mapping strategy. If we are looking for a high overall score to be associated to stronger favor with the course, negative items would receive the highest number assignments, or sevens, for the most disagreement. In other words, they would be mapped as opposite to the other statements.

Once all of the responses to the variety of items have been mapped, it is possible to add the scores together to obtain an overall score for the measured construct. Because of the addition of individual item scores into a summated rating, it is assumed with this scale that included items are **unidimensional;** that is, they *measure a single quality or attribute of the construct under investigation,* in our case the quality of "liking" Communication Research Methods. This scale is assumed to be at the interval level, with the belief that each of the options is equidistant from the other options provided. However, many researchers have questioned this assumption, suggesting that, in practice, the highest levels of agreement and disagreement are seldom selected, with most subjects selecting the more central options. To eliminate some of these concerns, some researchers have begun to map seven-point scales with only the numbers one through five, and to create nine-point scales to map the numbers one through seven. These researchers simply collapse the two most extreme options at either end of the scale into a single mapped number. For example:

I find this to be a enjoyable class.
☐ Strongly agree (5)
☐ Moderately agree (5)
☐ Slightly agree (4)
☐ Unsure (3)
☐ Slightly disagree (2)
☐ Moderately disagree (1)
☐ Strongly disagree (1)

In the example, selection of strongly or moderately agree would be mapped as a five, and strongly or moderately disagree would be mapped as a one. The argument is that, because people generally don't select the extreme positions, this adapted mapping assures a more interval-based scale.

The Semantic Differential Scale. Osgood, Suci, and Tannenbaum (1957) developed the other commonly used interval scale. In assessing the meaning associated with different words, they proposed that each word had three dimensions to its meaning. The three dimensions were degree of liking, an *evaluative* dimension, degree of strength, a *potency* dimension, and degree of activity, an *activity* dimension (E–P–A). They developed a **multidimensional** scale for assessing these three dimensions *by providing subjects with a construct followed by a series of seven-point scales bounded by bipolar adjectives, selected to represent each of the separate dimensions.* For example:

pos   *neg*

Your Professor:
1. Aggressive __ __ __ __ __ __ __ Submissive
2. Weak __ __ __ __ __ __ __ Strong
3. Logical __ __ __ __ __ __ __ Illogical
4. Withdrawn __ __ __ __ __ __ __ Outgoing
5. Sturdy __ __ __ __ __ __ __ Fragile
6. Insensitive __ __ __ __ __ __ __ Sensitive
7. Bold __ __ __ __ __ __ __ Timid
8. Dependent __ __ __ __ __ __ __ Self-reliant
9. Realistic __ __ __ __ __ __ __ Unrealistic
10. Good __ __ __ __ __ __ __ Bad
11. Delicate __ __ __ __ __ __ __ Rugged
12. Active __ __ __ __ __ __ __ Passive

potency

evaluative

activity

Subjects completing the semantic differential scale are instructed to select the point between each set of adjectives that best fits their impression of the presented construct. In this sample scale, items numbered 3, 6, 9, and 10 are intended to measure an evaluative dimension, while numbers 2, 5, 8, and 11 are intended to measure the potency dimension. Finally, numbers 1, 4, 7, and 12 are supposed to measure the activity dimension. Notice that the positive and negative adjectives vary from the left to right side of the scale. This is intended to reduce the likelihood that subjects will *respond without thinking about the intended construct, or with reduced sensitivity due to an apparent pattern in the responses,* a tendency called **response set.**

Once the scale is completed by a subject, numbers are mapped on the responses much as they are for the Likert Scale. Generally, the strongest attribute is assigned the highest number, or a seven, with the weaker attribute assigned the lowest, or a one. If, for example, a subject selected the second space from the left on item number two, an item measuring the potency dimension, that choice would be mapped as a two, because *strong,* the more powerful representation of potency, is at the right of the scale. On the other hand, the choice of the second option from the left on item number five would be assigned a six, because the strongest representation of potency of those bipolar adjectives is *sturdy.* Mapped scores are generally either summated for each of the separate dimensions, or an average is calculated for each dimension.

The most significant advantage of the semantic differential scale as a multidimensional scaling technique is that any set of dimensions can replace the E–P–A dimensions used by Osgood, et al. It would be possible to measure a person's perceived credibility across the dimensions of competence, integrity, attractiveness, and power. Using the semantic differential, overall credibility can be assessed across each of these four dimensions with bipolar adjectives selected to represent each component. The competence dimension might use such adjective pairs as *experienced/inexperienced, unintelligent/intelligent,* and *knowledgeable/unknowledgeable.* Attractiveness might be measured with such pairs as *friendly/unfriendly, nice/cruel,* and *pleasant/unpleasant.* As with the previous example, mapping would assign the highest number to the most positive adjective representing the construct, with the lowest assignment to the least positive adjective.

Ratio. The final level of Stevens's hierarchy is ratio measurement. This level *retains all of the characteristics of the previous three levels, but includes for the first time a true zero point.* At this level, we not only rank-order observations with equal intervals between categories, but also include a zero point that represents the absence of an attribute. No longer is the researcher responsible for the creation of a zero point; it is, instead, an actual value representing the absence of the construct. Many physiological constructs have true zero points. For example, if you are zero inches tall, it suggests you have no height. If you have a zero pulse rate, it suggests the absence of a heartbeat. If you have zero income, you are earning nothing. And, if you are traveling at zero miles per hour, it suggests you are standing still.

Incidentally, in our discussion of interval scales, we suggested that most temperature scales used by meteorologists use an arbitrary zero point. There is, however, one temperature scale that has a true zero point, and is, therefore, a ratio scale. The Kelvin Scale has as its zero point the absence of molecular motion, or a point at which all activity stops. It is a point that cannot be negatively exceeded, as it is impossible to move below this absolute zero.

Mapping Techniques

The mapping scheme that develops as a result of the measured operational definition may use any of three general techniques for assigning numerals to observations. These three techniques common to each of the various methodologies used by communication researchers are the **interview,** the **questionnaire,** and **observation.** Both the interview and the questionnaire are known as **self-report** techniques, in that they are *intended to evoke responses directly from the individuals being studied,* usually called **respondents.** The critical difference between the interview and questionnaire is in the form of response expected. The questionnaire generally uses written questions to elicit written responses from the respondents, while the interview usually uses oral questions to elicit oral responses from the respondents. Varieties of interview and questionnaire techniques are used in experimental, interaction analysis, and qualitative research, but are most apparent in the survey methodology. In Chapter 9, Survey and Interview Designs, the various styles of questionnaires and interviews will be examined, as will general rules for the development of these specific measurement instruments.

The third general technique for mapping is observation, or *a third-party examination and evaluation of communication phenomena using a prescribed mapping technique.* Unlike questionnaires and interviews, participants are not asked for their personal contributions, but are, instead, observed by the researcher, or trained observer, who records details of behavior and maps that behavior using a measurement scheme. To clarify the difference between the self-report measurement techniques and observation techniques, imagine that we are interested in the topics commonly discussed by married couples. If we were to use a self-report technique, we might ask couples on a questionnaire, or in an interview, to describe the topics they most frequently discuss. Using an observational technique, on the other hand, we might observe several conversations between married couples, and, as researchers, determine the topics that are evident, perhaps using a mapping scheme, or list of common topics, that we previously generated. There will be further discussion of the specifics regarding observational techniques in Chapter 8, Experimental Designs, Chapter 10, Content and Interaction Analysis, and Chapter 11, Qualitative Methods.

Assessing Measurement Validity

Once the rules for mapping observations have been developed, consideration needs to be given to ensuring that the measurements are **valid,** or *yield accurate results.* Measurement validity is a significant component of an investigation's **internal validity,** *the accuracy of an investigation's results as influenced by the planning, design, and conduct of the investigation.* In other words, it is the influence that a variety of factors from within an investigation, internal to the study, have on the accuracy of the results. Measurement reliability and validity are among several factors that influence internal validity. Other factors will be discussed in future chapters. There are a variety of considerations that influence the validity of a measurement scheme: reliability, content validity, concurrent validity, predictive validity, and construct validity.

Reliability

One of the most easily established factors influencing the validity of a measurement scheme is measurement reliability, *the consistency with which a measurement yields consistent results.* If we were to construct a length measure out of an elastic material, we would discover very quickly that measurements would vary dramatically from time to time due to the elasticity of the material. On the other hand, a length measurement constructed from a metal alloy would yield more consistent results. One goal of an investigator is to develop a measurement scheme that has a high degree of consistency, or reliability. Several common techniques are used to establish that a measurement instrument is reliable: test–retest, parallel forms, split half, and intercoder reliability.

Test–Retest Approach. The simplest technique for assessing reliability *requires that a measurement instrument be administered two or more times to the same group of respondents. The results of the multiple administrations are then compared or assessed for similarity.* If the measurement instrument has a high degree of reliability, the results of the multiple administrations will be very similar. In practice, the results of the test–retest are usually analyzed using a correlation technique that yields a coefficient between zero, meaning no relationship between responses, and one, meaning a perfect relationship between administrations. Generally, a correlation of .80 or higher is accepted as suggestive of an acceptable degree of reliability.

There are, however, some significant concerns regarding the use of the test–retest method. If the multiple test administrations take place in too short a period of time, it is possible that the respondents will simply remember their earlier response, a form of subject **sensitization,** and, by responding identically, perhaps inflate the reliability measure of a potentially flawed instrument. The clear solution to this problem is to wait some time between administrations, long enough that the initial responses are forgotten. However, if the investigator waits too long, it is possible that *the respondents will have changed in some real way between administrations,* known as subject **maturation,** and the reliability coefficient may be depressed, suggesting that a perfectly reliable instrument is somehow flawed. As a result, investigators using the test–retest approach must walk a fine line in determining administration times, usually allowing at least one day between administrations, but no more than one month. Careful selection and justification of administration schedule is expected and required of researchers using this technique.

Parallel Forms Technique. Because of the sensitization and maturation concerns regarding the test–retest method, many investigators assess reliability using a set of parallel forms. In this technique, *two separate, but parallel, measures are administered to a set of respondents.* Parallel measures are instruments that attempt to map exactly the same constructs, but using different items. If we were attempting to assess the reliability of a questionnaire consisting of a set of Likert scales, we would construct a second questionnaire containing a different set of Likert items intended to measure the same constructs as the first. The parallel instruments are then administered to a group of respondents without regard for the time interval between administrations. This is acceptable because the items on the parallel forms are different, and sensitization is less of an issue. As with the test–retest method, the results are compared for similarity, usually using a correlation coefficient. Again, a correlation of .80 or greater is deemed to be indicative of a reliable measurement. The greatest liability of the parallel forms technique rests in the need to create two parallel measurements. Developing two measurements using different items, yet measuring the same constructs, is often an arduous task.

Split Half Technique.   Closely related to the parallel forms technique is the split half technique. In this technique, *a single measurement instrument is created using two or more parallel items for each construct to be mapped.* In other words, if we were creating a questionnaire we would include two or more parallel items to assess each construct of interest. The result would be very much the same as the development of parallel forms in the previous technique, except that all items would be included in the same questionnaire. Following administration to a set of respondents, the parallel items would be assessed for similarity, and correlations of .80 or greater would be accepted as indicating reliability. The primary advantage to this technique is its single administration, which makes it possible to assess measurement reliability at the same time that data are being collected for an investigation.

Intercoder Reliability.   All of the previous techniques prove most useful in assessing the reliability of self-report measurement schemes, like questionnaires or interviews. However, when observational measurement schemes are anticipated, an often-used reliability assessment involves the use of multiple observers, known as *coders.* With this technique, *two or more observers are trained in the use of the measurement scheme and assigned to observe and map the same events. Their recorded observations are then compared for consistency;* a high correlation is expected if the measurement scheme is reliable.

While the above techniques are the most frequently used in determining the degree of reliability, the list is by no means exhaustive. Many statistical packages, for example, calculate Cronbach's Alpha Coefficient, a sophisticated reliability measure that randomly selects pairs of items from a measurement instrument, compares them, and generates an overall index of reliability. However, the complexity of the calculations involved render this, and other statistical indexes, beyond the scope of this text.

While reliability is a necessary component of a measurement's overall validity, and is generally easily assessed, its presence alone is not sufficient to guarantee accuracy. To completely evaluate a measurement scheme's validity, four varieties of validity need to be considered.

Content Validity

Often called **face validity,** content validity *asks whether a measurement scheme accurately reflects the characteristics of the construct being investigated.* Does it look like it measures what it is designed to measure? To evaluate the content validity of a measurement, researchers often use the **panel approach:** *A group of individuals with expertise regarding the constructs of interest are assembled and asked to examine the measurement scheme and determine its ability to measure what is intended.* If, for example, we were to develop a questionnaire measuring a student's public speaking anxiety, we might assemble a group of professors who specialize in public speaking, and ask them to judge the instrument's ability to assess a speaker's anxiety level. Recommendations of the panel members would be used to develop a scheme with greater face validity.

Concurrent Validity

Concurrent validity *asks how a measurement scheme compares to a previously validated instrument.* Given the concept of convergence, if two schemes are purported to measure the same constructs, the results they produce should be similar. Therefore, concurrent validity is generally assessed using the **convergence technique:** *The measurement being evaluated, and one or more already validated measurements of the same construct, are administered to a group of individuals.* If the evaluated instrument has high concurrent validity, the results of the two or more measurements should be similar. For example, if we created a measure of student public speaking anxiety, we might compare it to an instrument previously generated and validated by Professor James McCroskey, a recognized leader in the area of speech anxiety. If our instrument accurately measures the same constructs as McCroskey's, we would expect both to produce similar results.

Predictive Validity

A third consideration of the researcher is *the measurement's ability to accurately predict expected contingencies.* While not all measurement schemes require this assessment, because not all purport to predict later events, some certainly do. For example, the SAT is marketed as an effective predictor of a student's likelihood for success in higher education. An evaluation of predictive validity would examine the relationship between the measurement and the later outcome, between the SAT score and college or university success. To determine the relationship, the most difficult consideration is often the definition of the predicted outcome. For example, college success might be measured as (1) the generation of a high grade-point average, (2) a well-developed integration into the college or university social situation, or (3) the successful integration into the career market following college or university graduation. It is likely that the predictive validity of the SAT would vary widely, depending on which of these definitions was employed.

Construct Validity

Establishing construct validity assures that *the measurement scheme is consistent with the theoretical framework that it evolved from or is being used with.* Because it is based on the theoretical grounding of the measurement, generally the more theory that exists regarding the measured constructs, the greater the chance of having high construct validity. It is one of the greatest challenges to the researcher. In practice, construct validity is often assessed using the **known groups method.** This method involves three steps: (1) *existing theory is used to develop two groups, one with a high level of a construct and the other a low level;* (2) *the measurement instrument being evaluated is administered to each of the groups;* and (3) *the results are compared, and, if the measurement clearly differentiates between the groups, high construct validity can be assumed.* For example, if we were to create our measurement of public speaking anxiety, we might assess its construct validity by using McCroskey's theoretical foundation to create a group with high levels of anxiety and one with minimal levels. Each of the groups would then be tested with our instrument, and the results compared. If we have high construct validity, we would expect that the two groups would receive clearly distinctive scores.

Careful consideration to each of the above validity factors should result in the development of a measurement scheme that has a great deal of consistency as well as accuracy.

5

Sampling Theory

Chapter Outline

Chapter 4 explained one important consideration of all communication investigators: the development of valid measurement schemes. Once such schemes have been constructed and verified, the next important step is deciding what observations from the real world will be evaluated with those measurements.

Terminology

The selection of the things or people to study in an investigation plays a major role in determining a study's **external validity.** *External validity* is *the accuracy with which the results of an investigation may be generalized to a different group from the one studied.* In order to understand the selection of the elements to be studied, it is important to first understand some of the basic terminology.

Population

When an investigator is interested in studying *a group of people with particular characteristics of interest,* that group is known as a **population.** For example, a researcher interested in the conversational topics of newly married couples might identify as the population all couples who have been married for less than two years. The definition provided suggests the **parameters** of the population, or the *specific characteristics that must be present* for an individual to fit that group.

Universe

If the researcher is, instead, interested in studying a *group of nonhuman elements with particular characteristics of interest,* that group is referred to as a **universe.** For example, a researcher using content analysis might choose to examine the front pages of all nationally distributed newspapers in the United States in order to determine the mix of stories present. Because the newspapers are nonhuman, though created by human communicators, the group with these parameters is referred to as a *universe.* The same term would be used to refer to a collection of drawings, journals, transcripts, or other nonhuman objects.

   The primary reason that a researcher identifies the parameters of a population or universe is to suggest the group that the intended research can be applied to or to which it can be generalized. This *group to which the results might be applied* is often called the **target population** or **target universe.**

Census

Sometimes, when the target population or universe is relatively small and finite, as is the case if we were to study the front page content from a college newspaper published during the last month, it is possible for the researcher to *collect and study all the elements in the group.* This approach is known as a **census.**

Sample

However, in the majority of communication research situations, the target population or target universe is far too large to reasonably access all of the elements. For example, if we were to study the Internet use patterns of people in the United States, it would be nearly impossible to contact and assess every individual in the population, particularly if we have a limited research schedule or budget. In these situations, we might instead select *a subset of the population or universe thought to represent the entire group,* a subset known as a **sample.**

Sampling Error

 The key to the successful development of a sample is that it be representative, or closely adhere to the parameters of the population/universe. However, anytime a sample is drawn from the population or universe there is some potential for **sampling error.** *Sampling error* is *the degree to which a sample's parameters differ from the parameters of the population/universe from which it was selected.* The likelihood of sampling error is influenced by two important factors: (1) the size of the sample created, and (2) the homogeneity of the population or universe. If all other things are equal, the general rule is that, the larger the sample, the lower the potential for sampling error. To illustrate, imagine that we wanted to discover the level of academic achievement in your class. If we were to select any single individual as the representative of your entire class, there is a significant chance that his or her academic achievement level would be well above or well below the class average. If we instead selected five members from the class, there is an improved chance that their average achievement will be nearer to the class average. If we continue to select even larger samples the error would continue to decline. However, it is important to recognize that the decline in sampling error is nonlinear: The addition of sampled elements is much more likely to reduce sampling error when the sample is small, and has less impact on sampling error as the sample increases in size. In other words, adding an additional element to a proposed sample of two will contribute significantly more to the reduction of sampling error than the addition of one element to a sample of two hundred.

The other contributor to sampling error is the homogeneity of the population or universe. If we had a population or universe in which every element was identical to every other element, or perfectly homogeneous, it would be possible to select any single element with confidence that it will represent all members of that collection. However, as the members of the population or universe become more dissimilar, or more heterogeneous, samples must increase in size to reduce the likelihood of error. In a completely heterogeneous population or universe the only approach that will completely eliminate sampling error is use of a census. In most communication research, due to the heterogeneity of elements being studied, some sampling error is acceptable. However, researchers take important precautions to limit the amount of sampling error, generally by selecting samples that are of sufficient size to allow for reasonable confidence that error is kept to a minimum, while assuring that the samples are small enough to conveniently and economically access.

Sampling Methods

Selecting a representative sample can occur in two basic ways: probability sampling and nonprobability sampling.

Probability Sampling

Probability sampling is generally most preferred by researchers. It involves *the selection of elements from a population or universe in accordance with some set of mathematical rules, thereby permitting calculation of the probability of sampling error.* There are a variety of common probability sampling techniques: simple random sampling, systematic sampling, stratified sampling, and multistage cluster sampling.

Simple Random Sampling. **Simple random sampling** is the most elementary form of probability sampling: *Each element in the population or universe is afforded an equal opportunity of being selected to the sample.* In order to guarantee each element an equal likelihood of selection, this approach requires that the researcher first have access to a complete **sampling frame,** a list of all the elements in the population or universe. Once that complete frame is available, several techniques can be used for selecting the sample: lottery, random numbers, and random digit dialing.

Lottery. With the complete sampling frame in hand, *the researcher separates the elements from one another, mixes them in a container, and selects one element at a time until the determined sample size is reached.* One approach for making the lottery selection is known as **lottery without replacement.** With this approach, *each selected element is kept out of the pool of elements, thereby reducing the entire pool by one.* The problem with this approach is that the probability of selection changes with each drawn element. For example, if 50 names were placed in a container, and one name drawn, the chance of that selection is 1:50. With that element left out of the pool, the next selection has a 1:49 chance, and the third a 1:48 chance. It is clear that not all elements have an equal likelihood of selection, making this an invalid simple random sample. Correction can be achieved by using a **lottery with replacement:** *elements are returned to the pool following their selection, thereby keeping the pool of elements equal in size throughout the selection process.*

Random Numbers. While the lottery approach is quite simple, it is often inconvenient to separate each element in the population or universe from the others. For example, we may be selecting a sample from the roster of students registered at a moderately sized college or university, numbering about 7,000. Separation and selection of elements from this rather large group using a lottery would prove to be time-consuming and inconvenient. Instead, we can number the sampling frame with each element assigned a consecutive number from 1 to 7,000. Then, a sequence of random numbers can be used to select elements from the frame. We can develop the sequence of random numbers using one of several simple computer programs or with generators accessible through the World Wide Web. Two easy to use random number generators are available at http://www.random.org and http://www.randomizer.org Each of these generators requires that you enter the number of random numbers to be generated and the range of numbers requested. For our example, we could request 100 numbers to be generated, ranging from 1 to 7,000. The random selections would then be used to select the 100 elements to be included in the sample. In the absence of a random number generator, published **tables of random numbers** are available in many statistics textbooks and handbooks. Rules for using the random numbers tables vary from table to table, so it is important for the researcher to be familiar with the variety being used.

Random Digit Dialing. While both the lottery and random number approaches require a complete sampling frame, this third option eliminates that requirement for researchers who plan to use the telephone to contact prospective elements from a population. With the **random digit dialing** (RDD) technique, a random number generator is used to create seven- or ten-digit sequences. The seven-digit sequences are then used as telephone numbers within the local area code. The ten-digit sequence is used when you want to generate the area code as well. If, on the other hand, you want to limit your contact to a single town or locality, you might generate only four-digit sequences and use those with the local calling prefix. As you might imagine, many of the numbers that are generated using a randomizer may be invalid, connected to faxes or modems, or in other ways not appropriate to your sample. Therefore, it is generally recommended that you generate at least three times the amount of telephone numbers as the anticipated size of your sample.

Systematic Sampling. This second variety of probability sampling, like simple random sampling, requires a complete sampling frame, from which *every nth element is selected following a random start.* To calculate *n* in the above definition, the researcher simply divides the number of elements in the sampling frame by the number of elements desired in the sample. If, for example, we have a sampling frame consisting of the 7,000 students on a college campus, and we want to generate a sample of 100 students, the **sampling rate,** or *n,* would be 7000/100, or 70. Once calculated, the researcher must determine a starting point on the sampling frame, most frequently through the generation of a single random number within the range of the frame size, or, in our example, from 1 to 7,000. That random element is then the first to be included in our sample. The researcher then proceeds from that point to select every *n*th element, or 70th element in our example, continuing through the frame until all required elements are selected.

There is, however, one potentially serious drawback to the use of a systematic sampling technique. *If the elements in the sampling frame are organized in a pattern, and elements are drawn from that frame systematically, it is possible that certain parameters of the universe or population may be over- or underrepresented,* a problem known as **periodicity.** To illustrate, imagine selecting a sample of television shows from the *TV Guide.* The listings in the *Guide* are ordered with broadcast channels listed first, in numeric order, followed by cable channels in alphabetic order. Selection from that ordered list may overrepresent some channels, while underrepresenting others, due to the selection of the sampling rate.

Stratified Sampling. Like the previous two techniques, **stratified sampling** requires the generation of a complete sampling frame. Its particular advantage, however, is that it permits the researcher some assurance that elements with particular characteristics are included in the sample. It does this by *organizing the elements in the sampling frame into subsets based on some characteristic of interest,* or **stratification variable,** *then using one of the previous two techniques to select a proportional representation from each subset to the sample.* To illustrate, imagine our college of 7,000 students, and a researcher interested in selecting 100 students that represent that population. In evaluating the population the researcher might recognize that 30% are freshman, 25% sophomores, 25% juniors, and 20% seniors. To assure that a representative selection of each is included in the sample, he or she would divide the sampling frame into four groups based on their class standing, the stratification variable. Then, using the **incidence,** *the proportion of the sample parameter represented within the target population,* he or she would select 30 elements from the freshman list using a simple random sampling or systematic sampling technique. Then 25 elements would be selected from the sophomore and junior lists, respectively. Finally, 20 elements would be selected from the senior subset. The result would be a sample of 100 elements that closely reflect the incidence of the stratification variable in the population.

Multistage Cluster Sampling.   **Multistage cluster sampling** is a probability sampling technique that is particularly useful when dealing with a very large target population or universe when it would be inconvenient or impossible to generate a complete sampling frame of elements. It would, for example, be an excellent option if a researcher hoped to select a probability sample of 1,000 elements from the U.S. population. In multistage cluster sampling, *the choices of elements are continuously narrowed until a complete sampling frame becomes possible, then the final elements are chosen from the sampling frame in accordance with one of the previous three sampling techniques.* Using our example, the prospective researcher might first generate a list of the 50 states in which citizens reside, and, using one of the previous approaches, select a group of representative states, perhaps five states from the complete listing. Then, for each of the five states, a listing of counties could be assembled, and a sample of five counties selected. Now the researcher has 25 counties where citizens reside. From those lists of counties, a listing of all cities, towns, boroughs, villages, and townships within the counties can be developed. From each of those listings, 5 elements can be selected, giving us 125 locations in the United States. From this, a listing of all U.S. residents can be developed and our final sample drawn from that listing using one of the previous sampling techniques. While the idea of multistage cluster sampling is quite simple, actual application may become considerably more complicated because at each stage of sampling a greater chance of sampling error is introduced. For example, in our illustration, if the five selected states all happen to be located in the Northeast, the final selection of a sample of individuals from those states is unlikely to be truly representative of all U.S. residents. Correction of these potentials for bias is possible by combining multistage cluster sampling and stratified sampling techniques, but the resulting hybrid techniques become increasingly complicated.

Nonprobability Sampling

While most researchers prefer probability sampling techniques, there are numerous occasions when nonprobability methods must be accepted, or when they combine or hybridize with probability methods. The most significant concern of the nonprobability approaches results from their nonadherence to mathematical rules, which makes it impossible to calculate the likelihood of sampling error. Therefore, the researcher's ability to generalize results to groups other than that studied become more questionable. Several common non-probability sampling techniques are found in communication research: convenience, volunteer, purposive, quota, and network sampling.

Convenience Sampling. Also called **availability sampling, convenience sampling** is the nonprobability approach in which a *researcher selects elements to study simply because they are easily accessible, and, in its pure form, without any consideration of mathematical rules.* However, this nonprobability approach is often discovered hybridizing with the probability approaches as the researcher considers his or her ability to access a sample drawn from a diverse target population or universe. If, for example, a researcher wanted to study the television viewing habits of U.S. children, he or she might discover practical limits to the geographic area his or her study can cover, perhaps finding himself or herself only able to study children in a two- or three-state area. This *limited subset of the target population or universe from which a sample is drawn* is often called the **survey population,** or **survey universe,** and is often determined on the basis of accessibility by the researcher.

Volunteer Sampling. In this nonprobability technique, sample elements are selected based on their agreement to participate in research, and, once again, in its pure form, without the use of mathematical selection rules. As with convenience sampling, this approach often is discovered blending with probability methods, at least to some degree. Ethical principles require that human subjects be informed of their participation in a study and given the option to withdraw. In its truest sense, those who continue to participate are, in fact, volunteers to whatever probability sampling technique is used. This is especially true of minors, who are required to have parental or guardian permission to participate in an investigation. The significant concern with the volunteer approach is that volunteers may not be representative of the typical population member. Evidence suggests that volunteers from a population are generally better educated, have a greater need for approval, have a clear interest in the research topic, and are more sociable and younger than the population norm (Rosenthal, 1965). This raises questions concerning the external validity of any study using volunteer sampling, even if it is combined with probability techniques.

Purposive Sampling. **Purposive sampling,** sometimes called judgment sampling, occurs when a *researcher selects an element from a population or universe to be a part of the sample as a result of the element's specific characteristics of interest to the researcher.* For example, a researcher interested in the communication hierarchy in U.S. businesses might select IBM or Microsoft to be a part of his or her sample, primarily due to the size and economic success of these businesses. Or, a researcher interested in crisis public relations might select Johnson & Johnson, due to their effective campaign following the cyanide crisis, or Exxon for its flawed campaign following the Valdez grounding. Note that mathematical rules are absent in all of the above cases. The judgment for inclusion is subjective, and made entirely by the researcher. This nonprobability technique is frequently encountered in reports of case studies.

Quota Sampling. Before the benefits of probability sampling methods, such as stratified sampling, were recognized, **quota sampling** was often used. With this approach, *elements are selected from the population or universe in proportion to the incidence of some characteristic of interest to the researcher.* For example, if an investigator wished to study the major U.S. newspapers, he or she might discover that 70% of that universe is published in the morning, with the remaining 30% published in the evening. To select a sample retaining the incidence of these characteristics, the researcher would select 70% of his or her sample from the morning papers and 30% from the evening, but with little concern for mathematical rules of selection. Quota sampling, once quite popular, lost much of its appeal when, in 1948, a quota sample of U.S. voters predicted that Thomas Dewey would be elected president. However, on election day almost 50% of the popular vote was cast for Harry S. Truman. Since that time, most researchers have shifted to the mathematical insurance of the stratified sample for such situations.

Network Sampling. A final variety of nonprobability sampling, sometimes called **snowball sampling,** is often used in qualitative research studies. **Network sampling** draws one element from a population or universe at the discretion of the researcher, much like purposive sampling. That element is then asked to provide the names of additional elements to be included in the study. Each of those elements recommends yet further elements, and the sample "snowballs" to its anticipated size. Again, mathematical rules of inclusion are absent, and the final constitution of the sample is determined by the subjective recommendations of elements.

When employing any of the above techniques for the selection of a sample, the researcher's primary concern should be the enhancement of the external validity of the study, and recognition of the role played by a representative sample. Careful consideration needs to be given to all levels of the sampling procedure, from the careful identification of a population's or universe's parameters, to the careful selection of a survey population or universe, and application of an appropriate sampling technique.

6

Research
Ethics

Defining Ethics

By this point in the research process it should be quite evident that the researcher must make a variety of decisions as the investigation develops. Many of these decisions are influenced by sets of accepted rules for proper behavior, known as **ethics.** The term *ethics* is derived from the Greek word, *ethikos,* or *ethos,* referring to character, and is defined by *American Heritage Dictionary* (1985) as "the rules or standards governing the conduct of the members of a profession." In essence, ethics provide each of us with accepted standards for our proper behavior in any specific situation. As students, you are bound to uphold a set of explicit or implicit ethical principles including vigilant striving for academic achievement and maintaining academic honesty. However, many times these ethical obligations come into conflict, and a choice has to be made. For example, if you attended today's class only to discover that there was a major examination being administered, and you had forgotten to prepare for that examination, your poor performance would come into conflict with the ethical principle of achievement. On the other hand, if you cheated on the exam to assure greater achievement, you would be violating the principle of academic honesty. In many research situations, similar conflicts are evident, and decisions have to be carefully considered.

Factors Influencing Intellectual Integrity

The primary ethical goal of a communication researcher should be *the development of honest and dependable scholarship,* or the development of **intellectual integrity.** Several factors within the research environment influence intellectual integrity:

Researcher Motivation

One factor influencing the overall integrity of scholarship is the researcher's motivation for the inquiry. Our understanding of epistemology suggests that research be motivated primarily by an interest in the topic, or by a desire to enhance the state of knowledge in a particular field. However, in the majority of situations, other, perhaps less pure, motivations are evident. One common research motivation is *professional pressure.* In some professional positions there is an expectation of research productivity, and failure to abide by those expectations can lead to serious negative consequences. A newly hired public relations practitioner, for example, might be expected to regularly survey public opinion, and failure to complete this task may result in termination. Within colleges and universities, faculty members are frequently expected to produce scholarly research, and failure to comply can result in termination, or stagnation in their professional growth. As a student, you are often required to complete a research project at risk of receiving a failing grade. As a consequence, much research is generated with the primary motivation being professional success rather than the development of knowledge.

Another motivation for research can come in the form of *peer pressure.* This pressure becomes apparent when professional contemporaries, or peers, inquire about research projects, thereby indicating the need for current development. In order to successfully integrate into the peer group, an investigator may find him- or herself, once again, investigating for reasons other than the development of knowledge.

A third source of research motivation often comes from the researcher's *personal needs and desires.* The desire to achieve some degree of fame, recognition, or notoriety has provided the driving force for much research, as has the desire for monetary gain. Personal gain rather than the pure quest for knowledge may motivate a researcher who recognizes that a professional promotion will likely accompany completed research. The same may be true for the researcher who desires to see his or her name in print or regularly attached to a particular field of expertise.

It is important to recognize that none of these several motivations are inherently bad, only that they differ from the purely epistemological foundation of science. As a part of the ethical evaluation of a proposed investigation, the researcher needs to be clear about the underlying motivation, and to personally reflect on the impact that motivation has on the primary purpose of science, which should be the development of knowledge.

Intellectual Resources

The *level of knowledge that the researcher brings to the investigation* is a second factor influencing the integrity of a scientific investigation. If the primary purpose of science is the growth of knowledge, a researcher must first recognize the current state of that knowledge base. Without that understanding, any growth would likely be haphazard. Therefore, the ethical researcher has an obligation to learn as much about the contemporary state of knowledge regarding his or her topic as possible. However, the dilemma is often one of determining how much knowledge is enough. Learning too little about the existing knowledge would ignore valuable contributions, but striving to achieve truly comprehensive knowledge may be impractical and lead to failure to ever step out into the research process.

Because of this need for adequate intellectual resources, many researchers limit their investigations to the fields within the discipline with which they are most familiar. Investigators who have traditionally studied mass communication often find themselves continuing investigation in that field, even when research problems seem to abound in other fields. The dilemma is, again, one of developing the required intellectual resources, or knowledge base, to permit epistemological growth. Similar dilemmas are faced by researchers with particular expertise in one of the research methodologies, such as the experiment, who discover an abundance of research problems to be answered using qualitative methods. Any change in discipline, field, or method demands the development of competence in the researcher's intellectual resources.

Material Resources

A third factor influencing the intellectual integrity of scholarship is the *funding available to the investigator.* All research has some economic cost associated with it, and some research is very expensive. As a consequence of these costs, researchers are often searching for sources of funding. Two sources of funding are most frequently explored. One source is the *private grant, monies provided by private organizations or institutions for the development of research.* It is probably no surprise that the organizations and institutions that provide this money have specific research agendas. They are generally interested in resolving some practical problems or developing research findings with some specific proprietary benefit to them. The dilemma is that a researcher in search of funding may feel compelled to investigate topics of interest to the grant providers rather than those in which epistemological growth might be most profound.

Government bodies are another source of research funding, in the form of *public grants.* While these monies are provided for less proprietary benefit, in most cases the researcher is compelled to demonstrate the value of the investigation to society. Also, like private grants, the application process is usually quite competitive, with numerous researchers striving for the same resources. As a result, researchers are sometimes tempted to propose more elaborate investigations than they believe practical. The dilemma is that, without funding research is impossible, but to get the material resources the researcher may feel compelled to compromise some aspect of the investigation.

Both intellectual resources and material resources can have a significant impact on the topics investigated by communication scholars. Joanne Martin (1981) has suggested that, in many situations, research problems develop as a result of the researcher's current expertise or availability of funding rather than from a desire for knowledge, a perspective she has named the **garbage can research model.**

Quality of Product

The intellectual integrity of scholarship is also influenced by the quality of the research generated. If the primary goal of science is the development of knowledge, then the concerted effort of the scientist should be the systematic enhancement of the knowledge base. The growth of knowledge should be evolutionary, with the scientist carefully searching for gaps and inconsistencies in the knowledge base and attempting to fill them. However, as a consequence of the varying motivations already discussed, some researchers find themselves falsely equating quantity with quality. An abundance of research is no guarantee that the research will integrate with and enhance the development of theory or knowledge. The ethical researcher should reflect on the investigation and its value to the epistemological cause. While this advice seems obvious, the dilemma is often compounded when faced with professional, peer, or personal pressure to produce multiple investigations, and, at times, the conflicting concern with developing a quality product.

Objectivity of Communication

You have already learned that science is community-based. In order for the community of scholars to grow and develop, clear, objective communication between its members is required. Intellectual integrity requires that researchers provide clear, concise reports of their investigations to the community, while remaining self-reflexive, alert to any errors or biases that might be present. Because it is possible that the researcher's motivation, intellectual or material resources may influence the topics studied, methods used, and, perhaps, the results obtained, it is his or her responsibility to alert the community of scholars to such biases. Likewise, if the researcher is aware of some possible flaw or error in the research procedures employed or potential bias in the methodology used, it is his or her responsibility to report it. And, by all means, researchers should not intentionally falsify research reports or generate falsified data. Finally, it is the researcher's responsibility to report all the results of an investigation, even those that appear insignificant. Growth in scholarship demands clear, accurate reporting of information, and researchers need to suggest any deviation they make from planned procedures. For example, many studies use *post hoc* statistical analysis, whereby analytic procedures are developed following the initial analysis of data, usually as a result of a possible relationship suggested by the data. The danger is that such analyses are automatically biased by the researcher's awareness of the data. Therefore, *post hoc* analyses should always be clearly indicated as such in a research report.

While the desire for complete objectivity should be evident, in practice it results in many ethical dilemmas. Researchers may find themselves unwilling to publicly reveal the potential impact of motivation, intellectual resources, or material resources on a study if they risk losing those resources or having a study rejected by a publication source. Likewise, reporting errors in research procedures may result in a loss of prestige or the nonpublication of results. Either of these contingencies can compound the ethical dilemma. Finally, many research journals, due to competition for limited space, accept for publication only studies that have significant results. This may encourage researchers with less significant findings to perform an array of *post hoc* analyses in hopes of generating some level of significance, particularly if they feel some pressure to publish results.

Community Credit

Recognizing, once again, that science is community-based, intellectual integrity demands that responsible members of the community receive appropriate credit for their intellectual work. In other words, a researcher needs to be certain that credit is given for all intellectual ideas borrowed from other members of the community. Failure to provide appropriate credit for ideas, other than one's own, constitutes plagiarism, a serious ethical breach discussed in Chapter 3.

Careful consideration of each of the above factors is critical to the development of intellectual integrity. Moreover, thoughtful resolution of the conflicts between ethical principles is required to assure the most honest and dependable scholarship.

Ethical Responsibility to Human Subjects

Because of the inherently human nature of much communication study, a great deal of research in the discipline is conducted using people as the source of data. In some cases the people are observed in their natural settings. In others they are questioned, measured, or manipulated. Regardless, researchers must remain aware that their subjects are humans and demand the respect and protection due all humans.

Role of the IRB-PHS

In order to assure that the rights of human subjects involved in research be protected, the federal government passed a common rule in August of 1991 requiring the establishment of Institutional Review Boards for the Protection of Human Subjects (IRB-PHS). These boards, consisting of no less than five qualified members, are required to review all research proposals involving human subjects in the data collection process. Such review is required by the federal common rule for all organizations or institutions that receive any federal monies, regardless of the amount. Because most colleges and universities do receive some federal funding by way of curricular development grants, student financial aid, or other federal funding, the presence of IRB-PHSs has become commonplace. There are three possible levels of IRB-PHS review. Proposals for research submitted to the IRB-PHS can be classified as **exempt** if there is no risk to the subjects involved, perhaps due to the use of existing data, or observation of public behavior, or use of survey or interview techniques. If the proposal poses no more than a **minimal risk** to subjects, the federal common rule permits an **expedited** review, reducing the potential time for approval. Minimal risk is defined by the common rule as "the probability and magnitude of harm or discomfort anticipated in the research are not greater in and of themselves from those encountered in the performance of routine physical or psychological examination or tests" (U.S. Department of Health and Human Services, 1991, 46.102(i)). If, however, the research proposal poses more than a minimal risk the IRB-PHS must conduct a **full** review, involving the entire membership of the board. No research within funded institutions or organizations can commence until approval has been granted by the IRB-PHS. Likewise, any changes to a research proposal following review by the IRB-PHS are subject to review by the board.

Ethical Considerations

Organizations and institutions that receive no federal funding are currently not affected by the common rule requirements. However, most in which research using human subjects is carried out, nonetheless, implement review procedures, though perhaps not using the formal IRB-PHS title or classification system. Therefore, regardless of your situation as a researcher, there will likely come a time when you will need to deal with a board similar to the IRB-PHS. Remember that the primary concern of those bodies is the protection of human rights. As these bodies review the protection of subject rights, they generally consider four basic rights: freedom of choice, freedom from harm, the right to privacy, and the right to be treated with respect.

Freedom of Choice. One right guaranteed to all human subjects is the ability to freely choose to be involved in research investigations. Participants should be aware that their participation in research is voluntary and that they have the right to withdraw at any time. The best guarantee that freedom of choice is provided to subjects is the use of **informed consent.** With informed consent, *participants are provided with a detailed explanation of their role in the research, the procedures that will be used and the risks and benefits that are possible, and are asked to provide their agreement to participate.* Several assumptions are required to understand the full impact of informed consent. First, it is assumed that full disclosure of the research is provided to subjects, including a description of the procedures, purposes, and attendant discomforts or risks. Subjects should be given the opportunity to ask questions and assured of their ability to withdraw from the research at any time. Second, it is assumed that the subjects can comprehend the explanation provided and their inherent rights. Therefore, highly complex or technical explanations must be replaced with ones expressed in simple, everyday language. Third, subjects must be competent to provide their consent. In other words, the subjects must be assumed to be responsible, mature individuals. However, because many investigations involve the use of subjects of varying degrees of incompetence, including minors and individuals with neurological or developmental deficits, alternatives to true informed consent must be considered. Among the most common alternative is the use of **in loco parentis consent:** *Informed consent is solicited from those legally responsible for the subjects,* such as parents, guardians, physicians, or family members. When used, in loco parentis consent is usually accompanied by **subject assent:** *The subject is provided with a cognitively appropriate explanation of the research and asked to agree to participate.* The fourth and final assumption of informed consent is that the agreement to participate be voluntary and given without coercion. Subjects need to recognize that there will be no negative consequences associated with choosing not to participate or with withdrawing from participation.

While freedom of choice is best assured by informed consent, situations exist in which providing detailed descriptions of procedures would contaminate the research results. This is particularly true in communication research when, for example, telling a subject you want to observe his or her topics of conversation might influence the topics that emerge in later observations. Several alternatives to informed consent have been proposed for those situations:

1. *Prior consent plus proxy consent.* When using **prior consent plus proxy consent,** general agreement for subject participation is solicited along with the name of a trusted acquaintance, or proxy, who will serve to provide informed consent. The proxy is provided with full disclosure of the research, and solicited for consent allowing the original party to participate.
2. *Dual sampling.* In **dual sampling,** one sample from the population is selected, full disclosure provided, and the agreement to participate solicited. If the majority of the sample provide their consent, a second sample is drawn from the same population; general agreement to participate is solicited and the research is conducted on the second sample. The reasoning is that, because both samples are selected representatively from the same population, consent by the one sample assures consent by the second.
3. *Debriefing.* In **debriefing,** subjects' general agreement to participate is solicited and the research is conducted. Following the research, subjects are provided with a detailed explanation regarding the goals and procedures of the study in which they participated. The obvious limitation is in the timing of the full disclosure. Baumrind (1979) has suggested that such information provided at the completion of a study may have more negative psychological consequences than would continued deception, a phenomenon he calls **inflicted insight.** It is, therefore, extremely important for a researcher using debriefing to seriously consider the impact of full disclosure on the subject's well-being.

Freedom from Harm.   A second right afforded to all human subjects is the right to avoid physical, social, or psychological harm as a consequence of research. To assure protection of this right, researchers need to complete a risk/benefit ratio assessment in which they completely evaluate all possible risks and discomfort to subjects and balance those against potential benefits to the individual and society. As a part of this analysis, researchers should carefully consider techniques for reducing any potential risks. One method for limiting the risk associated with a negative stimulus is limiting the time or extent of the exposure. Another is to study a population that is already exposed to that negative condition. For example, if we were to study the effect of high levels of Internet exposure, a potentially negative stimulus, on subjects' sociability, we might limit the time of such intense exposure to a few days or weeks. Alternatively, we might select subjects who are already heavily exposed to the Internet.

The key to successful risk/benefit ratio assessment is careful evaluation of all possible harms, being certain to consider social and psychological, as well as physical risks. Far too often communication researchers neglect to consider the potential risks that may accompany participation in research, including possible social ostracism or emerging antisocial behaviors. However, they are also likely to overlook some of the benefits, including increased social interaction and enhanced self-image that may accompany participation in a study.

Right to Privacy.   A third right to be afforded all human subjects is "freedom of the individual to pick and choose for himself the time and circumstances under which, and most importantly, the extent to which, his attitudes, beliefs, behavior, and opinions are to be shared or withheld from others" (Ruebhausen & Brim, 1966, 432). Due to the public nature of the scientific enterprise, particularly the dissemination of research findings within the community of scholars, this right is easily violated. It clearly suggests that subjects have the right to determine how, and how much, personal information is revealed to the community of scholars. Generally, subject privacy is protected using one of two methods:

1. *Anonymity.* The preferred technique for assuring subject privacy is **anonymity:** the researcher uses techniques that ensure that a subject's response cannot be connected with the subject who provided that response. This may be the case when a researcher uses a questionnaire, but does not ask the subjects to identify themselves, when completing the instrument. However, some caution is always necessary. If the questionnaire makes inquiries that are personal in nature, perhaps regarding such things as sex and income, it is possible that the researcher might, even inadvertently, be able to identify the responding subject, in which case anonymity is no longer assured. In true anonymity there should be no possible way for the researcher and, as a consequence, anyone else, to connect specific responses to specific research subjects. While anonymity is the preferred technique for assuring subject privacy, it is not always practical. If personal interviews are used instead of the questionnaires in the

previous example, it is obvious that the researcher could connect responses to individuals.

2. *Confidentiality.* Researchers generally provide assurances of **confidentiality** in those situations where anonymity is impractical or impossible. With this technique, though the researcher knows which responses were made by which subjects, he or she agrees not to reveal that publicly. Subjects are informed during the data-collection stage about the meaning and limits to confidentiality. For example, participants may be told that the data collected might be circulated among a select group of researchers within an organization or institution. However, when the results of the investigation are provided to the community of scholars, that information will be presented without subject-specific identifiers and using grouping strategies so that no one can identify individual answers.

Right to Respect. The final right to be afforded all human subjects is the right to receive the respect due all human beings. Often, researchers, inadvertently, forget that their subjects are human, and begin to think of them simply as data providers. This dehumanization can manifest itself in many ways. Sometimes as a result of pressure to collect data, subjects are viewed as automatons producing data, not unlike the rats in a psychology laboratory being run through a maze for a meager reward. In fact, many times researchers refer to the data collection process as that of "running subjects." This statement may be harmless, or it may be a subtle indicator of a general trend toward dehumanization.

At other times, dehumanization manifests itself when researchers view the subject as simply a source of data and fail to respect the time or energy being required. This can occur when subjects are asked to participate in a study, then required to wait in an endless queue for their specific opportunity. Or, it can occur when a researcher demands a great deal of the subjects without rest and, often, with little apparent gratitude.

The ethical dilemmas faced by communication researchers are profound and demand serious reflection to achieve the highest levels of intellectual integrity and to demonstrate concern for human subjects. Honest, dependable scholarship is the principal goal of the scientific enterprise, and the equitable, just treatment of human subjects is a necessary component.

7

Design Considerations

We have explored a number of important decisions as you have progressed through my discussion of the scientific process to this point. We began the process by developing a research problem of some degree of abstraction, whether it was a research question or a hypothesis. Once developed in its preliminary form, we began the process of identifying its major components and conceptually defining the included constructs. Clear conceptual definition permits access to the community of scholars and assessment of the current state of knowledge concerning the topic. From that assessment, we were able to refine the problem statement into a more specific form.

Once the problem statement was clearly developed, we could begin to operationally define the constructs contained therein, with particular concern for the methods with which we would measure the relative presence or absence of those constructs. We could also begin to consider the methods with which we choose the elements that we plan to study, the sampling methods to be employed. Finally, we began to consider the various ethical concerns and implications of our investigation.

Research Methodology

It is at this point that a decision needs to be made concerning the methodology to be used for the collection of the data required to answer a research problem. Over the course of the next four chapters, we will explore some of the most common methodologies used in communication research. In Chapter 8 we will explore the **experiment,** a *method that evaluates the influence of some input variable on some output variable while controlling for all other extraneous variables.* This is the method that most students visualize when they think of science. It is easy to picture the white-coated researcher immersed in a sterile laboratory using planned procedures to resolve complicated research problems. While it is inaccurate to believe that all experiments take place in a laboratory, the impression of planned, controlled procedures is both accurate and important. It is the planning and control of the experiment that permits it to be the only methodology to allow the generation of statements of causal inference, the conclusion that one construct causes a change in another.

In Chapter 9 we will explore an alternative methodology, the **survey/interview** method, in which *self-report techniques, including questionnaires and interviews,* discussed in Chapter 4, *are used to generate the required data to resolve the research problem.* The principle virtue of this method is its ability to obtain subjective information from participants. In other words, the involved parties provide information regarding their feelings, values, attitudes, and beliefs.

The products of human communication are the focus of content analysis or interaction analysis, the topics of Chapter 10. While it is possible to consider these approaches independently, they are addressed in the same chapter because both focus on the outputs of the communication process. **Content analysis** is *"a research technique for the objective, systematic, and quantitative description of the manifest content of communication"* (italics added; Berelson, 1952, p. 18). **Interaction analysis** is a *"systematic method of classifying verbal and non-verbal behavior"* (italics added; Poole & McPhee, 1985, p. 124). The similarities between these methods are apparent; both are systematic approaches, dependent on planned procedures that permit the evaluation and classification of existing communication. In the case of content analysis, that communication can be visual, verbal, or nonverbal, while in the case of interaction analysis it can be real or recorded verbal or nonverbal interaction.

While the above methods have a long history in the communication discipline, a more recent methodology, really a group of methodologies, has been contributed by sociology and anthropology. Collectively, these methods are known as **qualitative methods,** and are the subject of Chapter 11. The methods of the qualitative researcher are designed to permit detailed description of communication behavior, consistent with the mission of the phenomenologist. These methods include intense observation of communication participants, detailed interviews with communicants, examination of **artifacts,** *materials left behind as a result of communication,* as well as the creative combination of these techniques.

A number of factors influence selection of the appropriate methodology for solving a research problem. Within the community of scholars there exists some tradition regarding the methods best used to explore particular topics. These traditions become evident as the researcher immerses him- or herself in the literature of the community. Often, a methodology is selected primarily because previous investigations have used similar methods. This is not meant to suggest that researchers should never stray from tradition. Some of the most important and revealing contributions are, in fact, made by those researchers willing to "color outside the lines," or behave less traditionally.

A second factor influencing the choice of methods is the research problem itself. Problems that suggest an exploration of participants' beliefs, values, and attitudes are perhaps best suited to the survey/interview method. Problems for which the researcher is interested in establishing a causal link between constructs are most suited to the experiment. Problems that require evaluating the content of existing communication are perhaps best answered using content or interaction analysis.

It is important not to overlook a third group of factors influencing method selection, those of a practical nature. Researchers often have limited time or resources at their command and that may affect their choice of methods. The experiment, for example, is generally quite efficient in terms of the time required to collect data. A great deal of data can be generated in a relatively short time frame. Surveys and interviews are more efficient in terms of cost to the researcher, allowing much data collection from a large sample for fewer dollars. The descriptive detail required of the qualitative researcher, on the other hand, requires the expenditure of much time and effort. Also, the intellectual resources of the investigator have a practical impact on the choice of methods. Use of any method requires some knowledge about its demands, and limitations. Acquiring that knowledge takes considerable time and energy. Consequently, researchers often use the methods with which they are most familiar. The different methods also use different forms of data analysis. Experiments, surveys/interviews, and content analysis most frequently use statistical methods to simplify and draw inferences from data, whereas interaction analysis and qualitative methods often use grounded theory (discussed later) to simplify data. Acquiring knowledge of these analytic methods can require significant energy expenditure by researchers, so, once again, methods are often selected based on the existing knowledge of the investigator.

Design Validity

One of the most important concerns of the scientist is planning and designing a research methodology that yields accurate answers to the research problems. Generically, *the accuracy of an investigation* is known as its **validity.** Two varieties of validity are of interest to the communication researcher: internal validity and external validity.

Factors Influencing Internal Validity

Internal validity, you may recall from Chapter 4, is *the accuracy of an investigation's results as influenced by the planning, design, and conduct of the investigation.* A variety of factors influence the degree of confidence an investigator has in a study's internal validity.

Measurement Reliability and Validity. The consistency and accuracy with which a measurement scheme assigns numerals to events plays an important role in the overall accuracy of an investigation's results. Weaknesses in the reliability or validity of a measurement scheme will likely result in greater inaccuracy in the results of the investigation and, thereby, suppress internal validity. (Techniques for assessing and assuring measurement reliability and validity were discussed in Chapter 4.)

Procedures. As with measurement, the procedures followed by an investigator need to be assessed for reliability and validity. Reliability is generally guaranteed through the standardization of investigation procedures and settings. In short, the researcher develops a clear plan for each step to be followed during the investigation, often including a script of the narrative that will be presented to participants, descriptions of behaviors to be manifested, and detailed descriptions of any treatments or interventions that will be presented to participants. Treatments and interventions are planned procedures performed on participants as part of an investigation. Ideally, every piece of data collected will be gathered using a similar procedure to every other similar piece of data and in a similar setting. It is also important for the investigator to determine that any treatments or interventions presented to participants are valid, or accurate, representations of the research expectation. For example, if an experimental researcher were to expose a group of participants to a videotape review of course material, and a second group to a small group discussion of that material, some assessment of the validity of the treatments would be required. The researcher would probably consider the degree to which each treatment provided a review of similar concepts, using similar terminology, and similar examples, as well as an assessment of the accuracy with which the material from the targeted course was reviewed.

Maturation. A third factor influencing internal validity is the result of the *natural physical and psychological aging of participants to a study.* Anytime a study continues for an extended period, it can be expected that some participants may demonstrate some change, physical or psychological, simply as a result of the passage of time. If a researcher measured your knowledge of astrophysics at the beginning of the year and once again at the end of the year, it is possible he or she would discover a significant change in that level of knowledge. While it is possible that change was the result of some specific intervention, such as registration in a course in astrophysics, it is also plausible that the change was simply a result of the normal passage of time and random accumulation of knowledge. As this example demonstrates, maturation poses the greatest problem for investigations that continue over extended periods. Obviously, the greater the impact of maturation the less assurance an investigator has in the accuracy of his or her results.

Sensitization. Like maturation, sensitization occurs as a result of *participants' experience with the research procedures.* An introduction to sensitization was provided in Chapter 4 where I discussed the limitations of a test–retest method. You will recall that repeat exposure to a measurement instrument may result in enhanced reliability measures due to participant recall of the items included. Likewise, procedures or measurements repeated during an investigation may be recalled by participants and responded to accordingly. It is possible that this recall-driven behavior may be inconsistent with normal spontaneous behavior, and that may reduce the accuracy of an investigation's findings.

Closely related to sensitization is a phenomenon known as the **sequencing effect,** which *occurs when multiple treatments or interventions are provided to participants with each intervention followed by a measurement to evaluate change.* For example, a professor might require students to read this chapter, and administer a quiz at the beginning of the following period. The quiz would be followed by a lecture of the material that was previously read, and a quiz delivered at the beginning of the next period. That second quiz might be followed by a review session on the material, and a final quiz delivered at the beginning of the next session. If a dramatic increase in quiz scores was manifested on the final quiz, it might be tempting to suggest that increase was due to the review session. However, it may, instead, be the result of delayed comprehension of the reading done several days previously, or of the accumulated effect of the three treatments, none of which alone would produce such an impact. Researchers using multiple treatments in this way reduce the impact of the sequencing effect on their results by using counterbalancing. **Counterbalancing** is *the presentation of treatments to different participants in different order permutations.* In our example, one student might read, then listen, to the lecture, and then review, while a second might listen to the lecture, then read, then review, and a third might review, then read, and then listen to the lecture. Each possible ordered permutation would be presented, permitting the evaluation of individual as well as accumulated effects. For reference, the number of possible ordered permutations is equal to the number of treatments factorial, or K!, which is equal to the number of treatments times each whole number smaller than itself, through one. So, three treatments can have $3 \times 2 \times 1$ ordered permutations (6), while four treatments can be ordered in 24 different permutations ($4 \times 3 \times 2 \times 1$).

Statistical Regression. When researchers select elements for inclusion in an investigation as a result of each element's deviation from the population or universe norms, the study's results can be influenced by statistical regression, regression toward the mean. For example, if a professor wished to study the impact of personalized instruction by selecting students who scored in the bottom 5% on previous tests to be participants in his or her study, an obviously deviant subgroup of the population from which they were selected. He or she then plans to meet with each student for a designated time each week and use regular class testing of content to determine the effectiveness of the personal instruction. A significant improvement in the scores of the bottom 5% of students might tempt the researcher to suggest it was due to the personal attention. Instead, it might be due to *the natural movement toward the group mean, or average, that participants demonstrate when tested multiple times.*

Attrition.   Some *elements initially included in a study may be lost as the investigation progresses.* In the case of a human sample, some participants may withdraw when they become tired, disinterested, or ill during the course of an investigation. In the course of some investigations, participants die or contact with them is lost, perhaps due to their moving, changing their names, or changing their telephone numbers. When nonhuman elements, such as texts, diaries, or recorded conversation, are involved, access to the elements may suddenly be discontinued, or the elements may be lost, as in the case of an audio recording that is inadvertently erased. While most of these forms of attrition are beyond the control of the researcher, careful evaluation of the level of attrition is necessary to assure that the sample at the conclusion of the study remains an accurate representation of the target population or universe. Researchers generally include in the report of an investigation information about the amount of attrition, as well as descriptions of the known reasons for lost elements. This self-reflexive tactic permits other members of the community of scholars to determine the adequacy with which the sample represents the population or universe and, thereby, the accuracy of the research findings.

Data Analysis.   The choice of methods used for the analysis of the collected data also influences the accuracy of an investigation's results. As you may recall from Chapter 4, each of the four levels of measurement has associated with it specific analytic methods. Many statistical tests are, for example, applicable to interval or ratio level measurement, but cannot be used at the nominal or ordinal level. Choice of an inappropriate analysis technique is likely to result in inaccurate results and decreased internal validity. We will examine choice of analytic method further in upcoming chapters.

Researcher Presence.   When the researcher is present during the collection of data, his or her presence may influence the data collected. One way this may be manifested is through the **personal attribute effect.** This occurs when the *physical characteristics of the researcher, such as sex, attire, hair color, skin tone, attractiveness, perceived friendliness, or age, influences the data collected.* Participants interviewed about their consumer habits may respond differently to a business-suited interviewer than they would to one attired in jeans and flannel shirt. Likewise, female employees interviewed about corporate sexual equity policy may respond differently to a female interviewer than to a male. Careful consideration of the potential impact of researcher attributes and consistency in the appearance of attributes are the best protections for internal validity.

A researcher may also *influence data collected by inadvertently providing cues as to the desirability of provided data,* a phenomenon known as the **unintentional expec-**

tancy effect. This may occur when the researcher smiles or nods in approval to a particular response, or grimaces, or frowns when a less desired piece of data is provided. The impact of the unintentional expectancy effect can be minimized by the researcher's strict adherence to investigation procedures or through the use of a **single-blind procedure.** In the single-blind procedure *the researcher hires a confederate who knows nothing about the purpose or conduct of the study and trains that individual to do the required data collection.* Because the confederate is unaware of the expectations of the data, or "blind" to those expectations, he or she cannot provide unintentional cues.

Hawthorne Effect. When *participants in a study behave differently as a result of knowing they are being observed,* the results yielded may be inaccurate reflections of reality. This factor influencing internal validity is known as the Hawthorne effect, named after the Western Electric Hawthorne Plant in Cicero, Illinois. In a series of studies done in the 1920s (Roethlisberger & Dickson, 1939) researchers evaluated methods of improving employee productivity. Lighting levels within the plant were varied from bright to dim, and music was added and deleted from the plant. With each change, regardless of its direction or intensity, there came an increase in employee production. The only possible explanation for the increases was the response of the employees to the presence of the investigator. While the obvious solution to this threat to internal validity is to observe participants without their knowledge, the ethical implications to freedom of choice are significant.

History. *The regular uncontrolled events that participants experience during the course of an investigation* can significantly affect the results of a study. For example, if a class was surveyed regarding their attitudes about a particular course and instructor on the same day that they received notice that they had done poorly on the last examination, it is likely that event would influence the results of the survey. On the other hand, if the survey was distributed immediately following the announcement that all students were doing remarkably well, a different effect might be expected. While the influence of history in the above examples should be evident to the researcher, many times it is much more subtle, and may result from participant exposure to a news story, social situation, media event, or life experience, often without the awareness of the researcher. Researcher awareness of those events in the world beyond the study that might have some impact on the data collected is the best protection against the undue influence of history. It is his or her duty, as a self-reflexive scientist, to report any evidence of such influences.

Inter-Subject Diffusion. A final influence on the internal validity of a study *occurs when multiple participants come into contact with one another during the course of a study.* This contact may occur when data are collected from several participants simultaneously, as in the case of a survey distributed to a collected group, or when participants casually meet one another during the life of an investigation. This casual contact may occur when one participant, who has perhaps completed his or her role in the study, meets another person and discovers that he or she is also a participant in the study. In the course of the ensuing interaction the first subject may share seemingly harmless information concerning the study with the second party, who has perhaps not yet participated, thereby influencing the data that he or she provides. The obvious solution to this dilemma is to restrict inter-subject contact during the course of an investigation, but it is, however, often impractical and, in the case of lengthy studies, perhaps even unethical. In most situations, the researcher can only be sensitive to the potential impact of inter-subject diffusion and report any evidence of its influence.

Factors Influencing External Validity

External validity, as you may recall from Chapter 5, is *the accuracy with which the results of an investigation may be generalized to a different group than the one studied.* As with internal validity, there are a variety of factors that influence confidence in an investigation's external validity.

Sampling. The selection of elements to be included in an investigation plays a significant role in the ability to generalize results. It is critical that elements from which data are collected be representative of the groups to which we expect to apply results. Careful consideration of sampling strategy is the necessary first step to attaining higher levels of external validity.

Ecological Isomorphism. *Isomorphism* means "similar in form." You may recall an earlier reference to reality isomorphism, the condition that operational definitions be 'similar in form' to the real world they are intended to represent. **Ecological isomorphism,** similarly, refers to the similarity in form between the settings in which research is conducted and their real-world counterparts. Often the settings in which data are collected bear little resemblance to the real world. For example, participants in experiments regarding media use are often sequestered in a laboratory that is sparsely and functionally furnished, perhaps only with a chair and media device. This furniture is frequently positioned by the researcher to maximize exposure, so the chair is often directly facing the media device. It takes little analysis to recognize that this is a significant departure from the setting experienced by the majority of participants during their everyday media exposure. The goal of the researcher interested in ecological isomorphism is to provide research settings that are consistent with the everyday experience of the participants. While this goal is often impractical, or impossible, to achieve, marked differences between the research setting and that of the external world will significantly diminish the scientist's ability to generalize results.

Replication. Because science is replicable and evolutionary, the ability to generalize results is influenced by the number of times similar results have been generated by similar studies. The primary reason for the procedure-driven foundation of science is to permit other researchers to complete and verify the results of previous studies, hence increasing the accuracy of generalization. There are three different forms of replication: literal, general, and triangulation.

Literal replication is the exact duplication of an investigation using the same research problems, methodology, procedures, measurement schemes, analysis techniques, and population or universe, though with a different sample selected from the population or universe. Similar results between literal replications significantly improve external validity, in part due to the increase in overall sample size. Conversely, radically different results have powerful negative effects.

General replication is the duplication of an investigation using the same research problem and methodology, but with some alteration to the procedures, measurements, population/universe, and/or analysis techniques. Consistent results between general replications will, like literal replications, significantly improve external validity. However, inconsistent results may be a result of changes in the procedures, measurements, or other factors, and, therefore, have a tempered negative impact.

Triangulation is the duplication of an investigation using the same general research problem, but utilizing an entirely different methodology. As you may recall from Chapter 1, such an approach permits the researcher to look at a problem from numerous perspectives and, as a result, arrive at a closer approximation to truth. Consistent results between triangulated studies are powerful contributors to external validity. However, like general replication, inconsistent results may be due to variations in the method and, therefore, have a subdued negative impact.

Consideration of the various factors influencing the validity of an investigation is necessary for the planning and execution of an effective research methodology. The next four chapters will focus on the specific concerns, requirements, limitations, and implications of several major methodologies, their planning, design, and conduct.

8

Experimental Designs

Chapter Outline

Defining Experimental Methodology

Requirements of Causality
Temporal Ordering
Meaningful Covariance
Nonspuriousness

Factors Influencing Control
Manipulation of the Independent Variable
Group Equivalence
Control of Intervening Variables

Categorizing Experiments by Setting
Laboratory
Field

Categorizing Experiments by Level of Control
High Control
Pretest–Post-Test Control Group Design
Post-Test only Control Group Design
Solomon Four-Group Design
Moderate Control
Pretest–Post-Test Nonequivalent Group
Design
Interrupted Time Series Design
Multiple Interrupted Time Series Design

Low Control
Single-Group Post-Test only Design
Single-Group Pretest–Post-Test Design
Post-Test only Nonequivalent Control
Group Design

Categorizing Experiments by Number of
Independent Variables
Single-Factor Studies
Factorial Studies
Between-Subject Design
Within-Subject Design
Mixed Factorial Design

Planning the Experiment
Development of a Research Problem
Access to the Community of Scholars
Definition of Constructs
Development of a Measurement Scheme
Selection of a Representative Sample
Determination of an Appropriate
Design
Planning of Data Analysis
Collection of Data
Analysis of Results
Integration of the Findings

As you discovered in the previous chapter, an experiment is a technique for evaluating the influence of some input variable on some output variable while controlling for all other extraneous variables. The input variables are called **independent variables,** *the variables expected to influence a change in another variable.* The output variables are called **dependent variables,** *those expected to change as a result of the actions of the independent variables. All other variables that might somehow influence the relationship between the independent and dependent variables,* those extraneous to the relationship, are called **intervening variables.** The goal of the experimental researcher is to examine the influence of the independent variables on some dependent variable while controlling the influence of any intervening variables.

Defining Experimental Methodology

A natural science scenario may assist in our understanding of the various components. Imagine that you wished to evaluate the temperature at which liquid water vaporized. You could place the water in a beaker on a stand and apply heat using a Bunsen burner while measuring the heat at the water's surface with a Fahrenheit thermometer. You would then observe the temperature at which the water began to boil and record that as the vaporization point. In this example, heat is the independent variable and the vaporization point the dependent variable. Intervening variables would include such factors as the laboratory air pressure and impurities in the tested water, each of which may influence the result. At a lower air pressure the water may boil at 210°, while at sea level it would boil at 212°. Careful analysis and control of these intervening factors is necessary for the assurance of a valid result.

We can, likewise, construct a simple example of an experimental study using our sample research problems from Chapter 2. Each of those problem statements expresses an interest in how varying teaching styles influence student perceptions of the classroom climate. In this case the independent variable, the one expected to bring about some change, is the instructor's teaching style. The variable expected to change as a result, or the dependent variable, is student perception of classroom climate. An experiment could be constructed in which individuals were exposed to different teaching styles, perhaps lecture versus discussion, and, following the exposure, student perceptions of the class could be solicited, perhaps using a simple Likert Scale. To reduce the influence of intervening variables, the researcher might assure that both classrooms were decorated identically, that the content covered in the classes was identical, and that the instructors looked and behaved similarly, perhaps even following a prescribed script.

There are a variety of advantages and disadvantages to the experimental methodology. Because of the detailed procedures generally established in advance by the experimental researcher, primarily to control for intervening influences, this methodology allows for easy replication by others. Many classic experimental studies are, in fact, replicated sometimes with modifications, to assure greater external validity. Another advantage is the relative cost of the data generated. Generally, experiments can develop more data in less time and at less unit cost than most other methodologies. Finally, and most importantly, the experimental method is the only methodology that permits the development of statements of causal inference. Because the requirements for establishing causality can be assured, it is possible to suggest that a change in the independent variable causes a change in the dependent.

The experimental method does, however, have a major liability associated with it. As a result of the researcher's need to eliminate intervening influences, and the strict procedures usually developed, the experiment may lack ecological isomorphism, the degree to which the research setting corresponds to its real-world counterpart. The artificiality of the experimental setting can have a serious influence on the researcher's ability to generalize the results of the investigation.

Requirements of Causality

It has been suggested that one of the primary advantages of the experiment is its ability to develop causal inferences. Three conditions are required for establishing causality between variables: temporal ordering, meaningful covariance, and nonspuriousness.

Temporal Ordering

Temporal ordering simply means *in order of time.* For a researcher to suggest that an independent variable causes a change in the dependent, the independent must precede the dependent. If the independent condition comes after the dependent, it is impossible to suggest that it caused the noted change.

Meaningful Covariance

Meaningful covariance requires that *the values of the independent and dependent variables shift in a systematic way* and that there is a reason for the relationship. In other words, as one increases, the other should increase, decrease, or show some systematic curvilinear relationship, and, moreover, the relationship must be meaningful, or have some sensible reason for its existence. In short, there must be a theoretical foundation for the covariance.

Many students have a "lucky" pen, shirt, cap, or other piece of apparel that they believe is linked to their academic success. At some point, use of that object may have resulted in an unexpected success, so it has been linked to success ever since. While this linkage does have temporal ordering and covariance, the covariance lacks a theoretical base. There is no known reason for the linkage between that object and the student's success; therefore, a causal inference is impossible.

Nonspuriousness

The third requirement of a causal relationship is *the ability to dismiss, or rule out, all other factors that may explain the change in the dependent variable.* These **alternative**

causality arguments are generally dismissed through the use of experimental control. **Control** involves *the use of techniques for systematically ruling out alternative causes.* Experimental control exists along a continuum from high control to low control, with causal inference most valid at the highest levels.

In the student/lucky artifact example just discussed, it is possible, indeed probable, that the initial unexpected success could be attributed to some other alternative influence.

Absence of any one of the above conditions restricts the researcher's ability to suggest a causal relationship between variables.

Factors Influencing Control

There are three principle factors that influence the amount of control manifested in an experimental study: manipulation of the independent variable, group equivalence, and control of the intervening variables.

Manipulation of the Independent Variable

Researchers exert the highest degree of control in an experiment *when they determine the participants' degree of exposure to the independent variable.* These **active variables,** those under the researcher's direct control, provide some assurance that changes in the dependent variable are the result of the induced influence of the independent variable, and not the result of some other factor. In the study of instructor teaching style and student perceptions of the classroom climate, the assignment of students to either the lecture or the discussion by the researcher would be an example of an active variable, because administration of the independent variable is controlled by the researcher. While, with all other things being equal, active variables yield higher levels of control, they are not always practical or possible. At the opposite extreme of the control continuum are **observed variables,** *those that cannot be directly manipulated by the researcher, but must instead be observed in their natural state.* If, for example, our sample study chose to use two existing classes, one taught with lecture and the other with discussion, if the students selected the class that they were taking, we would have an observed variable. The researcher in this case would not have control over which participants were exposed to which level of the independent variable. Because it could be possible that other factors influenced the participants' choice of classes, and, therefore, their perceptions of the classroom climate, control over alternative causality arguments would be diminished.

Group Equivalence

To assure that it is indeed change in the independent variable that brings about change to the dependent, researchers regularly use multiple groups. Such groups must be demonstrably equivalent. In many cases *one or more of the groups receives some level of the independent variable, or some treatment,* and is referred to as the

treatment group, while another *group receives no imposed treatment,* and is referred to as the **control group.** In our continuing example, we have two groups, *each receiving some form of treatment,* whether it be a lecture or discussion, and those groups are compared with one another, and are therefore known as **comparison groups.**

If the researcher's goal is to compare changes in the dependent variable between a treatment and control group, or among comparison groups, he or she must assume that, *prior to the imposition of the independent variable, all the groups were equivalent with regard to the dependent variable.* This assumption is referred to as **group equivalence,** and is an important component of experimental control. There are a variety of techniques for assuring that experimental groups start with equivalent dependent measures. Near the apex of the control continuum is **random assignment,** closely related to random selection, discussed in Chapter 5. In random assignment, *participants selected for an investigation are assigned to a treatment, control, or comparison group based on some randomizing technique.* The randomizing technique can be the use of a lottery, use of a set of random numbers, or a systematic sampling technique. Students selected to participate in the experiment on teaching styles might be entered into a lottery in which every other name selected would be assigned to either the lecture or discussion class. While random assignment provides no guarantee that groups will initially be equivalent, statistical analysis allows us to determine the likelihood of substantial deviation. Generally speaking, the smaller the sample used in an experiment, the greater the probability that randomization will produce nonequivalent groups, underscoring the importance of selecting an appropriately large sample.

An alternative to random assignment, producing a slightly lower degree of control, is the use of **pretesting.** In this technique, *established treatment, control, or comparison groups are evaluated on the dependent variable prior to the introduction of any treatment.* In short, the dependent measure would be administered and analyzed before treatment begins, with the expectation that groups would score similarly. In our sample study, students in the comparison groups would be evaluated regarding their perceptions of classroom climate before the lecture or discussion treatment began, and it would be expected that their perceptions at this stage would be similar. While it may appear that pretesting is at least as effective as random assignment, the degree of control exerted is, in fact, somewhat lower. This is a result of pretesting's focus on similarities only in the dependent variable, ignoring other intervening variables that may result in later variations to the final dependent measure. In our sample, the two groups may pretest similarly, though one group, composed primarily of males, may have a disposition toward the more linear lecture approach as a result of their gender, while the other group, composed of females, may be predisposed toward the intertwined nature of the discussion. In this case, an intervening variable, gender, would influence the results of the study, and yet not be discovered through pretesting. It is, however, possible to combine both random assignment and pretesting to yield an even higher degree of control than permitted by either alone.

Group equivalence can also be assured through **matching,** though again with a slightly diminished level of control. In matching, *participants in the treatment,* *control, or comparison groups are matched on characteristics thought to be important to the dependent variable.* Two forms of matching are commonly used: constancy matching and pairing. In **constancy matching,** *all participants in all groups are kept uniform with regard to significant characteristics thought to influence the dependent variable.* In our sample study, if existing research or theory suggests that males and females respond differently to different presentation styles, the significant characteristic, gender, might be held constant across comparison groups, perhaps by using all male, or all female, participants.

In **pairing,** *each participant in the treatment, control, or comparison group is matched with participants in the other groups, based on characteristics thought to influence the dependent variable.* If gender was suspected of influencing student perceptions of a class, each male in the lecture group would be paired with a male in the discussion group, and each female would be likewise paired. If class standing was also suspected of influencing the dependent variable, each freshman male in one group would be paired with a freshman male in the other group. Pairing can become increasingly complicated as more significant characteristics are introduced. As with random assignment and pretesting, matching may also be blended with pretesting to enhance the overall control of group equivalence, though it never reaches the power of random assignment. The principle problems associated with matching are the limited generalizability of results obtained using constancy matching, and the necessity of researcher knowledge of all salient characteristics influencing the dependent variable. Because it is practically impossible to be aware of all such influences, random assignment continues to prove the more powerful assurance of group equivalence.

Control of Intervening Variables

In order to assert that an independent variable causes a change in a dependent, all other potential variables must be ruled out. In an experimental study, the procedures developed to systematically limit the influence of research setting, researcher influences, participant factors, and other extraneous variables contribute to the overall control manifested. In highly controlled studies, the research setting for all groups may be held constant, the researcher may follow a prescribed script and use a single-blind technique, and consideration may be given to participant maturation, attrition, and statistical regression. All of the factors influencing internal validity, discussed in the previous chapter, contribute to the overall level of experimental control.

Each of these three factors influences the amount of experimental control manifested, and, consequently, the ability of an experiment to generate valid statements of causality. Control exists along a continuum, with increased values corresponding with increased ability to dismiss alternative causality arguments, resulting in more powerful suggestions of causal relationships. **Experimental research designs,** the *overall plans for the conduct of experimental studies,* are categorized along three dimensions: the research setting, the amount of overall control exercised, and the number of independent variables being examined.

Categorizing Experiments by Setting

Laboratory

One technique for categorizing experimental research is based on the research setting, or location, in which the study occurs. If the *research setting has been created by the investigator, who maintains complete control over all that occurs in that setting,* the study is known as a **laboratory experiment.** Because of the planned development of the setting by the investigator, the degree of experimental control is enhanced in this setting, but often at the sacrifice of some ecological isomorphism. The laboratory experiment sacrifices realism for enhanced control.

Field

The other setting is the *naturally occurring research setting, where the investigator has no opportunity to shape the setting to his or her preference,* the **field experiment.** As a result of using the natural setting, ecological isomorphism is enhanced, but now with some sacrifice to overall experimental control. Changes in the dependent variable are more likely to be the result of some alternative cause that cannot be effectively ruled out. In practice, most experiments exist somewhere between the completely created laboratory environment and the completely natural field experiment. However, the laboratory or field labels are commonly used to suggest the tendency toward one or the other.

Categorizing Experiments by Level of Control

A second technique for categorizing experimental investigations is based on the amount of control inherent in the investigation's design. While control exists along a continuum from low to high, for convenience it is possible to consider three levels of control found in experimental designs: high, moderate, and low.

High Control

High control experimental designs are characterized by the rigor with which group equivalence is assured. Each of the three most common high control designs requires that participants be randomly assigned to treatment, control, or comparison groups. Any study that cannot or does not randomly assign participants is, by its very nature, not within this category. To assist our understanding of the various designs, we can begin with a simple scenario. Imagine that the instructor in your class recognized that students were struggling with some of the complex concepts being presented. He or she decided to prepare a simple review sheet to assist in the process, but, in his or her desire to determine the usefulness of the review, planned to perform a simple experimental study. The decision was made that some students would have the benefit of the review sheet as they studied this chapter, a form of treatment, while the remainder would receive no intervention or treatment, thereby becoming a control group. If the instructor wishes to generate the most powerful causal statements, he or she would probably choose one of several high control designs.

Pretest–Post-Test Control Group Design. If the instructor chose this design, his or her first challenge would be to randomly assign students to either the treatment or control group. Randomization techniques such as a lottery, random numbers, or systematic sampling might be used, with the final result being two groups, a treatment group and a control group. While randomization is a powerful method of assuring group equivalence, it can be enhanced when coupled with pretesting. So, before beginning to explore the material in this chapter each student would be tested on their knowledge of the chapter's content, with the expectation that all would perform similarly, regardless of whether they were in the treatment or control group. Following the pretesting, the treatment group would receive the review sheet following the normal class exposure to information, while the control group would simply participate in the normal class and receive no review materials. At the end of the presentation of the chapter, both groups would once again be tested for comprehension of content. If the review material was effective, the investigator would expect to see significantly higher scores from the treatment group as opposed to the control group on the post-test. In Figure 8.1 you can see a simplified schematic of this design. In the schematic, R represents the random assignment of subjects into a treatment (T) or control (C) group, Pr represents the pretest, X the treatment or intervention, — no treatment or intervention, and Po the post-test.

FIGURE 8.1   *Pretest–Post-Test Control Group Design*

The greatest liability of the pretest–post-test control group design is the possibility that participants become sensitized to the dependent measure as a result of the pretest. In our sample scenario, the pretest may make students aware of instructor expectations, resulting in inflated post-test scores for both the treatment and control subjects. And it is possible that the pretest sensitization may interact with the review sheet, contributing to even further distortion in the post-test measurement.

Post-Test Only Control Group Design. To counter the concerns regarding pretest sensitization, some researchers choose to sacrifice a bit of group equivalence control and shift to this alternative. If the instructor in our scenario were to make this choice, he or she would once again randomly assign students to a treatment or control group. However, there would be no test of chapter content prior to the class discussion of the chapter. The treatment group would once again receive the review materials withheld from the control group, and all students would be tested on the content of the chapter following class discussion, with the expectation that treatment students would perform better if the review material were effective (see Figure 8.2).

FIGURE 8.2 *Post-Test-Only Control Group Design*

Solomon Four-Group Design. The highest level of control inherent in an experimental design is achieved by combining both the pretest–post-test control group design and the post-test only control group design into a single design that permits some further assurance of group equivalence while remaining sensitive to pretest sensitization. If our instructor were to use this design, he or she would randomly assign the students to four groups, two treatments and two controls. One treatment and one control group would be pretested. The treatment groups would each receive the review material, with that material withheld from the control groups. All four groups would then be post-tested. The advantage to this design is its ability to examine the influence of the pretest on the final results. If the pretested treatment group differed significantly from the post-test only treatment group, it may suggest some sensitization due to the pretest. Likewise, if the pretest control group differs significantly on the post-test from the post-test only control group, it may suggest some sensitization. At the same time, treatment and control groups can be compared to determine the influence of the treatment. A schematic of this design is shown in Figure 8.3.

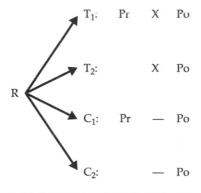

FIGURE 8.3 *Solomon Four-Group Design*

The greatest liabilities to the Solomon Four-Group design are practical in nature. Because there are twice the number of groups involved, more subjects are required. Also, it is possible that the results can be difficult to interpret. For example, what does it mean if the post-test only control group score is significantly higher than the post-test only treatment score, but the pretest–post-test treatment score is higher than the pretest–post-test control group score? The researcher might find such a result to be impossible to comprehend.

Moderate Control

While all high control designs use random assignment to assure group equivalence, such assignment is not always practical or possible. In such cases, the researcher may be forced to sacrifice some control and shift to a more moderate level design. As with the high control category, there are three commonly used moderate control designs.

Pretest–Post-Test Nonequivalent Group Design.

This design is identical to the pretest–post-test control group design, but without use of random assignment for the development of groups. It may be the design of choice if the groups to be compared are already formed, or if the researcher has no control over the formation of the groups. In our sample scenario, it is possible that the instructor may decide to compare two sections of the research methods class, one receiving a treatment and one becoming the control. If, as in most colleges and universities, the individual students decided which section in which to enroll, random assignment would be out of the question. However, some assurance of group equivalence is possible using a pretest. If the review material were effective, it would be expected that post-test results for the treatment group would be significantly higher than for the control group. However, even if such results are discovered, it is possible that they may be due to initial differences in the students in each section or to sensitization from the pretest. Therefore, the requirements for developing causal inferences are compromised by the growing inability to assure group equivalence. In Figure 8.4 a simple schematic of this design is presented. Make special note of the absence of random assignment in the schematic design, the key to its placement as a moderate control design.

$$\begin{array}{llll} \text{T:} & \text{Pr} & \text{X} & \text{Po} \\ \text{C:} & \text{Pr} & \text{—} & \text{Po} \end{array}$$

FIGURE 8.4   *Pretest–Post-Test Nonequivalent Control Group Design*

Interrupted Time Series Design.

At other times, the researcher may find him- or herself with only a single group that cannot be divided into a treatment and control, but must, instead, serve as its own control group. Our instructor may only have a single section of research methods, and find it impractical to divide the students into separate treatment and control groups. Instead, the single group is provided with a series of pretests, perhaps evaluating course understanding, over a period of time. These pretests serve to establish a baseline measure of student comprehension. After several baseline measures, the treatment, in this case the review sheet, is introduced. A series of post-tests follows to observe any changes brought about by the treatment, and to determine the lasting effect of those changes (see Figure 8.5). There are numerous advantages to this moderate control design. First, it effectively rules out pretest sensitization if all the baseline pretest scores remain similar. Second, it rules out maturation influences if there is little change from one pretest to the next. And, third, it allows the researcher to evaluate the persistence of a treatment's effect through the multiple, periodic post-tests.

$$Pr_1 \quad Pr_2 \quad Pr_3 \quad Pr_4 \quad X \quad Po_1 \quad Po_2 \quad Po_3 \quad Po_4$$

FIGURE 8.5 *Interrupted Time Series Design*

Multiple Interrupted Time Series Design. Like the Solomon Four-Group Design, the multiple interrupted time series design enhances control by combining moderate control designs. As you can see in Figure 8.6, this design requires a nonrandomly assigned treatment and control group that are pretested numerous times to establish a baseline. In our example, this could be two sections of research methods, one labeled treatment and the other control. The multiple pretests allow some enhanced assurance of group equivalence when compared to the pretest–post-test nonequivalent group design. The treatment group is provided some intervention, in our example the review sheet, and both groups are multiply post-tested. The result is a design with the highest level of inherent control found among the moderate control options.

$$T: \quad Pr_1 \quad Pr_2 \quad Pr_3 \quad X \quad Po_1 \quad Po_2 \quad Po_3$$

$$C: \quad Pr_1 \quad Pr_2 \quad Pr_3 \quad - \quad Po_1 \quad Po_2 \quad Po_3$$

FIGURE 8.6 *Multiple Interrupted Time Series Design*

Low Control

There are, however, times when group equivalence cannot be practically assured, and even greater design control must be sacrificed. In those situations, the researcher may choose a design with a low degree of inherent control. Such designs, while not allowing causal inferences, are often used for exploratory research in which the investigator is searching for some evidence of a relationship that might later be verified with a higher control design.

Single-Group Post-Test Only Design. One variation of a low control research design, the single group post-test only design permits the investigator to administer some treatment to a group and evaluate with a post-test the potential influence of the intervention (Figure 8.7). However, with only a single group involved, and no measure of the dependent variable prior to the treatment, it is difficult to determine how much influence the intervention may have had. It is entirely possible that the post-test results would have been identical even without the treatment.

$$X \qquad Po$$

FIGURE 8.7 *Single Group Post-Test Only Design*

In our classroom scenario, the instructor may determine that it is impractical to divide the class into groups or to pretest their knowledge of course content. In that situation, he or she may administer the review materials to the entire class with scores on the chapter examination used as dependent measures. If students perform well on the post-test, it is possible that the worksheet contributed to their success. However, without a control or comparison group, there is no way of ascertaining the true extent of that contribution. Likewise, in the absence of a pretest to establish a knowledge baseline, it is difficult to ascertain that any change has occurred as a result of the treatment. Post-test success may be the result of previous learning, or an inherent ability of the student, rather than an influence of the review material.

Closely related to the single-group post-test only design is the **ex post facto design,** with the only real difference being the use of an observed, rather than an active, independent variable. You will recall that an active variable is one in which the investigator has control of the degree of participant exposure, while an observed variable is one outside the control of the researcher. Ex post facto designs are often used in case study research, in which the impact of some event on a communication situation is evaluated, but the event is outside the control of the investigator. For example, an investigator may be interested in the reestablishment of mass media channels following a natural disaster such as an earthquake, hurricane, or blizzard. It is impossible for any researcher to have active control of such natural events, so they must be left to occur naturally. Once a disaster occurs, the ex post facto researcher would rush into the area and measure the reestablishment of the mass media over the next several days, weeks, or months. As with the single group post-test only design, changes observed are not necessarily due to the natural disaster—they may have occurred anyway—and, without a comparison group, we cannot determine the extent to which the disaster played a role.

Single-Group Pretest–Post-Test Design. Because of the significant limitations to the single-group post-test-only design, when provided the opportunity most exploratory researchers will elect to establish some baseline measurement prior to treatment (Figure 8.8). In this case, the instructor in our story would pretest student understanding of the chapter content, provide the entire group with the treatment review materials, and post-test their acquired knowledge of this chapter. If the review materials proved to be effective, there should be a significant increase in post-test scores when compared to the pretest. However, even with such a change, there is no assurance that it was the result of the treatment, as it could also be the result of student maturation, or sensitization created by the pretest. The only method for ruling out these alternative causality arguments would be an increase in assurance of group equivalence, either through multiple pretesting, or through the addition of a control or comparison group.

$$Pr \quad X \quad Po$$

FIGURE 8.8 *Single-Group Pretest–Post-Test Design*

Post-Test only NonEquivalent Control Group Design. A final commonly used low control design uses a treatment and control group, each created nonrandomly and not assessed with a pretest (Figure 8.9). The instructor in our scenario could divide the class into two groups, one to receive the treatment, the other having it withheld, though development of the groups would be nonrandom. The instructor might view it as impractical to pretest student knowledge of the chapter, but, instead, provide the review materials to the treatment group and withhold them from the control group. All students would be post-tested on their comprehension of the chapter content, and the post-tests would be compared. It would be expected that the treatment post-test scores would be higher than the control post-test scores if the review material was effective. However, even if that was the case, there is no assurance that the change was due to the review material. Without random assignment to groups, or the use of a pretest, it is possible that the treatment group performed better simply because it contained more talented students.

$$T: \qquad X \quad Po$$
$$C: \qquad — \quad Po$$

FIGURE 8.9 *Post-Test-Only Nonequivalent Control Group Design*

As a result of the limitations of the low control designs, development of causal inferences is seriously compromised. However, these designs do prove quite useful in exploratory settings, where researchers wish to evaluate suspicions of a relationship that can be later evaluated with greater rigor if the initial evidence seems supportive.

With each of the above designs we have concentrated on the application of a single treatment, such as the review material, and, at times, comparison with a control group receiving no treatment. However, each of the above designs can be modified to permit the use of multiple treatments. Using the pretest–post-test control group design as an example, it is possible to randomly assign students to three groups, rather than two, with two treatment groups and one control group. Following the pretesting of the groups' knowledge of chapter content, one treatment group could receive the print review materials, while the other treatment group receives the same material in a videotape format. The control group would again receive no intervention, or no review material in any form. Using this design, not only can the treatment group be compared to the control group, but the multiple treatment groups can be compared with one another, in fact serving as comparison groups.

It is also important to recognize that, while the above nine designs are among the most commonly used by researchers, they are frequently adapted to the specific needs of the investigation. As a result, many hybrids, or mixed designs, result. This may lead to some difficulty in assessing the level of inherent control. However, remember that random assignment is necessary at the highest level of the control continuum, with some assurance of group equivalence through pretesting at the moderate level, and little assurance of equivalence or the absence of multiple groups found at the lower level.

Categorizing Experiments by Number of Independent Variables

Single-Factor Studies

A third technique for categorizing experimental investigations is based on the number of independent variables being simultaneously evaluated for their influence on a dependent variable. All of the investigations that we have discussed to this point are known as **single-factor studies:** *They examine only one independent variable at a time.* In our sample scenario, the single independent variable, or single factor, being evaluated was review material.

Factorial Studies

Many times, however, researchers choose *to examine the influence of two or more independent variables, or factors, as they simultaneously influence a dependent variable.* Such investigations are known as **factorial studies.** The instructor in our story may be interested in the influence of review materials, but recognize that their usefulness might be shaped by the gender of the students using them. As a result, a two-factor study looking at review material and gender simultaneously might be proposed. When discussing this proposed investigation with his or her peers, the instructor may use a form of experimental research shorthand known as the **design statement.** This statement is *a series of numbers separated by Xs, which specify how many independent variables with how many levels are being investigated.* The instructor might say that he or she is planning a "three by two factorial investigation." In written form that would translate to 3×2, and indicates that there are two independent variables to be evaluated. This can be determined based on the number of numbers present in the statement. If the statement was a $3 \times 2 \times 2 \times 3$, it would indicate the presence of four independent variables.

The individual numbers within the statement suggest the levels of each independent variable. In our three-by-two example, the three refers to the three levels of the review material variable, one being the print review material (T_1), the second a video review (T_2), and the third a control with no review (C). The two refers to the two levels of gender being evaluated, the first being male and the second being female.

Given the shorthand design statement, it would be possible for the instructor's research peers to quickly develop a **design diagram,** *a simplified schematic or drawing of the factorial design.* A 3×2 factorial design would be represented with a two-dimensional drawing with one dimension representing the review material variable and the second the gender variable, as shown in Figure 8.10. The drawing shows all possible mixtures of those variables. Each of the separate interactions between the variables occurs within a **cell,** *a distinct block within the design diagram.* The number of cells found in a design diagram can be quickly computed by multiplying all of the levels within the design statement. For example, a 3×2 design would consist of six cells because 3 times 2 equals 6. A $3 \times 2 \times 3 \times 2$ design would consist of 36 cells, and, if diagrammed, would exist along four separate dimensions. Three common designs exist in factorial investigations.

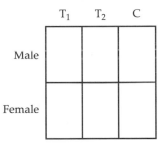

FIGURE 8.10 3×2 *Factorial Design Diagram*

Between-Subject Design. The between-subject design would most likely be used by our instructor in the sample scenario. In this design, a separate group of participants, or subjects, would be used in each of the cells so that comparison could be made between cells. A simple rule of thumb for all factorial designs is that a *minimum* of five subjects is required within each cell, though in practice most researchers average twelve to fifteen subjects per cell. Therefore, in our 3×2 design, our investigator would need a minimum of thirty subjects, with five subjects randomly assigned to each of the six cells in the design diagram. Because gender is one of the independent variables, the random assignment would need to involve a stratified sampling method to assure males and females were placed in the appropriate cells. The liability of the between-subject design is the requirement of separate sets of subjects for each cell, thereby increasing the overall number of subjects required. This becomes especially problematic as the number of factors, or number of levels, increases. If our study was a $3 \times 2 \times 2 \times 3$ design, consisting of 36 separate cells, using our general rule of thumb we would need a minimum of 180 subjects.

Within-Subject Design.   In some situations, the liability of the between-subject design can be alleviated by using the same subjects in each of the cells in the design diagram. In that case, using our rule of thumb for number of subjects per cell, only five subjects would be required for our 3×2 factorial study. Those same five subjects would be used in each of the multiple cells, though order of presentation of the cells would be counterbalanced to reduce the chance of a sequencing effect, discussed previously. As you consider the within-subject design for our sample scenario, you may notice a potential problem. If the same subjects are going to be used in each of the cells, at some point a rather radical surgical procedure is going to be required, as the male subjects are transformed to female and the female to male. So, obviously there are limitations to the within-subject design, both practical and ethical.

Mixed Factorial Design.   In those situations in which the within-subject design is impractical, but the number of subjects required for a between-subject design proves unrealistic, the researcher may combine the two approaches into a mixed factorial design. In this design, the same subjects are used across the levels of one or more independent variables, while a different set is used across the levels of the remaining independent variables. In our example, a group of five males might be exposed to each level of the review material independent variable, while a separate group of five females does likewise. In this case, the number of subjects required is reduced when compared to a between-subject design, though we can account for those variables that are not easily manipulated by introducing a between-subject component.

Planning the Experiment

As you have learned, an investigator searching for causal relationships between variables commonly chooses the experimental method. In order to plan and design an experiment, there are ten decisions the researcher needs to make.

Development of a Research Problem

As with any investigation, the first step is the development of a research question or hypothesis. Most experimental studies are based on problems involving a causal relationship between the independent and dependent variables.

Access to the Community of Scholars

Coupled with the development of the research problem is the required assessment of the knowledge base of the community of scholars. In any methodology, the result of this step is the development of a clear review of the literature, which provides the foundation for the planned investigation.

Definition of Constructs

Using the community of scholars as a reference point, the experimental researcher must develop a clear conceptual and operational definition for each of the constructs found in the problem statement. At this point, the investigator determines whether the independent variable will be an active or observed variable, and the procedures to be followed in determining its presence, or for manipulating it.

Development of a Measurement Scheme

Closely related to the definitional process, some technique needs to be established for measuring changes in the dependent variable. Care must be taken to assure that the measurement is valid and reliable.

Determination of an Appropriate Design

At this point in the planning process, the researcher needs to decide whether the investigation will occur in a laboratory or field setting, whether it will involve a single or multiple factors, and what level of control is appropriate. To assure the highest control of intervening variables, a comprehensive plan of the data collection process is generally developed, including descriptions of the procedures to be followed, the layout of the research setting, and a script of instructions to be presented by the investigator. All of the many concerns regarding internal validity are considered and resolved at this design stage.

Selection of a Representative Sample

To assure the greatest external validity, a sample of the elements in the population or universe must be made in such a way to ensure that they are representative. Generally, this is assured through the use of a probability sample.

Planning of Data Analysis

Having decided on a plan for collecting data, the investigator also needs to plan the expected approach for data analysis. Most experimental studies use *statistical analysis, which permits the application of results to groups other than those studied,* a form of analysis known as **inferential statistics.** Care is required to assure that the statistical technique planned is appropriate for the form of data collected. We will examine some of the most common inferential statistics in Chapter 12.

Collection of Data

Following the planned procedures for the conduct of the experiment, the researcher collects the required data about both the independent and dependent variables. Any deviation from procedure is clearly recorded as a part of the researcher's reflexive nature.

Analysis of Results

The inferential statistics are used to convert the raw data into **information,** *the usable results of the investigation.* Again, any deviation from the preplanned procedures is clearly recorded, particularly the use of any *post hoc* analysis, analysis conducted without a previously existing plan. The concern of the investigator is deciding on the significance of results, discussed further in Chapter 12, that suggest that independent variables have the expected influence on the dependent.

Integration of the Findings

The final step of any investigation is the integration of the new findings into the amassed knowledge of the community of scholars. Care is given to whether the results are consistent with previous investigations, the degree to which the knowledge base is expanded, the practical implications of the findings, and the growth or generation of scientific theory.

9

Survey and Interview Designs

Chapter Outline

Survey and Interview Methodology

As you recall from Chapter 7, the survey/interview method uses *self-report techniques, including questionnaires and interviews. to generate the data required to resolve research problems of interest to the researcher.* In Chapter 4 you learned that the difference between a questionnaire and an interview is that the former uses written questions to solicit written responses from participants, while the latter uses oral questions to solicit oral responses. The participants in survey/interview research are known as "respondents."

Functions of the Survey/Interview Method

Survey/interview research has proven quite popular among communication investigators, in part as a result of its ability to serve two, quite different, functions. One possible function served by this methodology is **description,** the *ability to document current conditions or attitudes, or to create a picture of conditions as they are manifested.* The U.S. Department of Labor's regular survey of unemployment exemplifies such a function. Its principal purpose is to document, or portray, the percentage of the U.S. population who are jobless during a given period of time. Likewise, surveys of consumer product preferences are, at their basic level, descriptive, providing a picture of likes and dislikes.

While the majority of surveys fulfill some degree of the descriptive function, many go beyond that and serve an analytic function as well. **Analysis** is the *ability to describe and explain why certain conditions occur or exist.* In essence, the analysis function goes beyond describing in order to begin to understand underlying causes and relationships. While the U.S. Department of Labor's unemployment survey provides a picture of current conditions, its purpose is also to develop some understanding of the conditions that may be related to fluctuations in employment. As a result, these investigations serve both the descriptive and analytic functions. The same is true of the consumer product preference surveys. Most often the interest is in determining what factors influence consumer choice so as to better predict or shape future preferences. It is often difficult to distinguish between surveys performing a descriptive function and those performing an analytic function, because the function is usually determined primarily by the intent of the principal researcher.

Advantages of the Survey Method

The survey method is popular among communication researchers as a result of its numerous advantages when compared to alternative methods. Among the most notable advantages are high ecological isomorphism, the reasonable cost of data collection, access to broadly distributed populations, and the researcher's access to subjective information.

High Ecological Isomorphism

Because the survey approach uses self-report techniques, the data are solicited from respondents who are immersed in real-world situations. As a result, the responses reflect actual, realistic situations, rather than the artificial conditions often found in the experimental method.

Reasonable Cost of Data Collection

When compared with most other methodologies, the survey is generally found to be quite economical when considering each unit of data generated. While there is quite a bit of cost variation from one survey investigation to another, generally cost is reduced due to the absence of an artificial research setting, the minimal costs associated with development of measurement instruments, and the minimal staffing requirements. In short, it is a method that can generate a great deal of data, from a large number of respondents, for relatively little capital.

Access to Broadly Distributed Populations

A third advantage to the survey method is that some approaches can solicit data from a large population that is broadly distributed geographically. Unlike the experiment, in which data collection is limited to those geographic areas directly accessible to the researcher, some survey techniques permit the collection of data from respondents far removed from the investigator. It is quite conceivable that a researcher in Washington, DC could collect data from respondents in all fifty states in the United States without ever having to leave his or her office in the nation's capital.

Access to Subjective Information

Finally, investigators can solicit information about respondents' private thoughts, feelings, or emotions due to the self-report approach used in survey research. Such subjective information is unavailable using observational techniques because they are not directly manifested.

Disadvantages of Survey Research

While the advantages to survey research are notable, it is important to recognize that the method is not perfect. Several potential disadvantages need to be considered when deciding on this methodology.

Absence of Active Variables

Because the survey method depends on the self-report of respondents, the investigator has no control of the form or extent of an independent variable, depending instead on the respondent's self-selection of that influence. As a result, much of the control associated with the experiment is sacrificed, making it increasingly difficult to rule out alternative causality arguments.

Absence of Temporal Ordering

The majority of survey designs, with one notable exception discussed below, have no procedure for assuring that one variable precedes another, or that an independent variable comes before the dependent one. You will recall that this is a primary condition of establishing causal relationships. As a result, most survey research is **correlational** in nature, suggesting *an interest in the form and extent of relationships between variables,* rather than causal relationships.

Instrumentation Bias

The wording and organization of items included in a questionnaire or interview may powerfully influence the data collected. A questionnaire that begins by inquiring about your preference in bathroom tissue is likely to shape your future responses. A later question inquiring about a most memorable television advertisement is more likely to be answered with tissue ad campaigns than might otherwise have been the case. As a result, a great deal of care needs to go into the planning and design of the survey instrument to assure the highest degree of validity and reliability.

Required Respondent Willingness

The dependence on self-report is, in itself, a potential liability because it requires that participants willingly share information. A common concern of survey researchers is the degree to which respondents purposefully provide inaccurate or incomplete data. While it is impossible to eliminate such data, careful development of survey instruments and implementation of parallel questions to assess the consistency of results can help to minimize the problem.

Required Respondent Recall

As well as being willing to share data, respondents are also expected to be able to recall the data solicited by the researcher. An apparently simple question such as, "What television programs did you watch yesterday?" may prove quite frustrating to respondents who find themselves unable to recall that detail. Besides increasing frustration to respondents, such difficulty may increase the likelihood of inaccurate responses, as participants spontaneously generate replies. Again, the careful development of the survey instrument can help minimize this problem.

Prestige Bias

Survey respondents are often selected because of the particular roles that they play within society, which leads to a potential bias in responses. For example, college professors who are interviewed regarding their media use may suggest below average consumption of television, with the majority of that use being devoted to educational programming. The reason for such response may be the professors' self-perceived role in society rather than a realistic representation of their behavior. Because they see themselves as intellectual leaders, they may avoid mention of media habits they perceive to be less than worthy of that role. Likewise, medical doctors asked about their attitudes regarding euthanasia may respond as unrealistically opposed as a result of their self-perceived role as guardians of the Hippocratic Oath and their commitment to do no harm.

Declining Participation Rate

A final disadvantage to survey research is becoming increasingly evident as the United States becomes the most surveyed nation in the world. As more people are being approached to participate in survey research, and as an increasing number of marketers attempt to disguise sales campaigns as research, the overall rate of respondent participation has declined.

Survey Designs

In the previous chapter we examined numerous designs for conducting experimental studies. Survey research, likewise, uses several different designs. Two common designs prevail in the survey methodology: cross-sectional and longitudinal. **Cross-sectional** design is the *use of self-report instruments to collect data from a single point in time in order to create a description of conditions at that moment.* A useful analogy is that of a still photograph. The cross-sectional survey, like the photograph, samples a situation at one instant and creates a concise representation of reality at that moment.

An alternative survey design is the **longitudinal** study, which uses *self-report instruments to collect data from a sample across some period of time.* The key distinction that separates this from the cross-sectional design is the multiple data collection that takes place in the longitudinal study, in essence creating a series of still pictures of reality spread out over some time frame. Analogous to a motion picture, these individual representations, viewed in a chronological progression, can show changes that occur with the passage of time. Two common longitudinal designs are commonly found in communication research. One variety is the **trend study** in which *data are collected from several different samples selected from a single population at different points in time, in an effort to evaluate changes that occur in the population.* If your instructor was interested in students' changing attitudes regarding communication research methods, he or she might create a questionnaire and distribute it to a sample of students taking research methods this semester, then again to those taking research methods in two years, and to those taking the class in four years. As you can see, a different sample from the same population is selected for each administration of the questionnaire.

The other common longitudinal design, the **panel study,** *collects data from the same sample selected from a population at several points in time, following that single sample over time, in an effort to evaluate changes that occur over time.* If your instructor was interested in how student perceptions of research methods changed as the students matured, he or she might survey your attitudes this semester, then locate the same group of students and survey attitudes near graduation, and perhaps once again in five years. The key distinction is that the same group of respondents are solicited for each of the several administrations of the survey. Because the panel study uses the same sample for each of the administrations, it tends to be more sensitive to subtle changes that occur over time. However, it is much more prone to problems with respondent attrition, as it is possible for researchers to lose contact with respondents, have them voluntarily withdraw from the investigation, or become ill, or even die.

One notable variety of the panel design, known as the **cross-lag correlational design,** is unique among survey designs in that it meets the necessary conditions to assure temporal ordering of variables, and is, therefore, able to develop causal inferences. In this design, *a presumed independent and dependent variable are measured using self-report techniques at one moment in time. Then, at a later time, the same variables are once again accessed, and the relationship between the independent and dependent variables from the earlier to later times is examined.* If the independent variable caused a change in the dependent one, there should be a strong relationship between the earlier independent and later dependent measure. However, because the independent must precede the dependent in order to cause a change, there should be little relationship between the earlier dependent measure and the later independent. A classic example of the cross-lag correlational design can be found in Lefkowitz, Eron, Walder, & Huesmann's (1972) study of the relationship between viewing of violent television programming and levels of aggression. At two times, separated by ten years, individuals were surveyed for their television viewing habits and their level of aggression. As predicted, there was a strong relationship between the earlier exposure to television violence and later increased aggression, but no relationship between earlier aggression levels and later viewing of violent television. These findings allowed Lefkowitz, et al. to conclude that evidence existed to suggest that violent television exposure might result in increased aggressiveness.

Designing the Survey Instrument

One major, and time-consuming, task facing the survey researcher is the development of a valid and reliable survey instrument, whether that is a *collection of interview questions,* an **interview schedule,** or whether it is a questionnaire. Regardless of the form of instrument, two primary considerations must be entertained in its development. First, the instrument must serve to clearly and concisely convey necessary information to respondents, so that they understand the inquiries being made. Second, the instrument must provide a clear and concise method for the respondents to provide requested information to the researcher. In short, the respondents need to understand the researcher's inquiry and be able to provide an accurate response.

Focus Group

With these considerations in mind, the survey researcher can begin instrument development. Some choose to begin the process with the assistance of a **focus group,** a *small group, usually between four and ten people, selected from the population of interest and encouraged to freely discuss the topics of interest to the researcher.* A trained moderator who has a list of general topics of interest to the researcher, and who is expected to facilitate in the discussion, oversees the group interaction. The goal of the focus group is to assess the attitudes and knowledge of the population as well as to provide some insight into possible reactions to inquiries and understanding of the population's use of language. While the information gathered from a focus group can be quite helpful to instrument design, it is not without its liabilities. To be effective, the moderator must be well trained and experienced in group facilitation, the topics must be well considered in advance, and adequate time and funding must exist to support the group activities. As a result, unfortunately, many survey instruments are designed without the benefit of the focus group.

Determining Question Type

Among the first questions that must be resolved before developing the survey instrument are those relating to the types of questions to be included and the overall kind of instrument that will result. Questions can be open-ended or closed-ended. **Closed-ended questions** are *those for which response options are provided by the researcher and the respondent is required to select from those options.* A clear example of the closed-ended question is the multiple-choice item you find on class examinations. Because of the limited response options that the respondent can select from, closed-ended questions offer the researcher easier data mapping, but also limit the amount of detail provided to the researcher.

Open-ended questions, on the other hand, *provide the respondent with no predetermined response options, and, as a result, permit the respondent to provide as much detail as he or she sees fit.* These questions are analogous to the essay items found on course examinations in which individual responses and amount of detail will vary widely from respondent to respondent. The advantage to the open-ended items is their ability to collect data that may have been previously unknown to the researcher. However, because of the potentially unlimited data and detail provided, mapping of the data proves more difficult and time-consuming.

Determining Instrument Directiveness

Based on the proportion of open-ended and closed-ended questions on a survey instrument, researchers categorize that instrument along a continuum from highly directive to highly nondirective. A **highly directive** instrument *consists primarily of closed-ended questions*, while a **highly nondirective** instrument *consists primarily of open-ended questions.*

Determining Interview Schedule Structure

While all survey instruments can be categorized based on their directiveness, interview schedules can be further categorized on the basis of their degree of structure. If an interview schedule consists of *a collection of specific questions to be asked in a specific order with no variation from one respondent to the next*, the interview is referred to as **tightly scheduled.** If, on the other hand, *the interviewer is provided with key questions, but afforded some flexibility in the ordering of the inquiry, or use of additional inquiries*, the interview is referred to as **moderately scheduled.** Finally, *if the interviewer is only provided with key topics to investigate during the interview, with wording of inquiries at his or her discretion*, the interview is regarded as **unscheduled.**

Once the survey researcher has decided on the kinds of inquiries to include, the directiveness and structure of the instrument, development of individual questions or survey items can begin. Several considerations are necessary to assure the development of effective survey inquiries.

Nine Rules for Effective Question Development

The inquiries to be included in a survey instrument demand careful development by the researcher. There are nine rules that should be followed in developing items:

1. **Make questions clear.** Care needs to be exercised to ensure that the meaning of questions is immediately evident to respondents, and that ambiguity is reduced. A researcher should be certain that the question asks for the specific variety of information required. For example, a survey of consumer satisfaction with the promotional campaign accompanying a corporate rebate program would probably want to avoid asking something so general as, "What do you think of our rebate program?" The responses to such a question are unlimited in nature and may focus on such diverse issues as satisfaction with the amount of the rebate, the speed of processing the requests, the quality of the rebate, and so forth. Such broadly phrased open-ended questions are more prone to frustrate respondents, and may lead to responses beyond the interest of the researcher.

   Questions should also use simple, easy-to-comprehend language, and avoid complex, polysyllabic words, as well as specialized terms and acronyms. As a general rule, if a question cannot be read and understood by a typical ninth-grade student, it is probably too complex in its style, though obviously that rule would need revision if the intended respondents were younger than the adult standard. Researchers should not assume that the language with which they are familiar will be understood by respondents.

When specialized terms must be included in a survey item, it is advantageous to include a clear definition of those terms.

Negative wording of questions is also prone to cause some interpretive difficulty for respondents. A question such as, "Do you not think our company should have a rebate program?" is likely to require more processing skills than the affirmatively worded version of the same question, and is, therefore, more likely to cause frustration. Items containing negation are particularly problematic for international or cross-cultural respondents, who are often unfamiliar with such stylistic idiosyncrasies.

Finally, many words in the English language have multiple meanings associated with them, which may lead to question ambiguity. For example, asking, "Do you think your instructor is hot," may be interpreted by different respondents as asking about the instructor's attractiveness, temperament, or body temperature. Careful analysis of multiple meanings associated with included words is critical to achieving question clarity.

2. **Make questions concise.** Often, in an effort to achieve greater clarity, researchers are tempted to construct long, detailed questions, explaining each term and clarifying all possible ambiguities. Respondents faced with such lengthy items may be tempted to skip sections in an attempt to get to the actual inquiry at hand, thereby limiting the usefulness of their responses. It is a difficult tightrope to walk, but the effective question must be both brief and clear.

3. **Include complete instructions.** If a survey instrument is to be effective, respondents must be aware of how to respond to included items. If the researcher expects participants to select a single, best option from a list, some indication of that needs to be included. On the other hand, if the respondent is expected to rank-order items in that list, a somewhat modified instruction would be required, including some indication of which ranking is to be assumed highest, or most preferred.

   Careful instruction is particularly important when using a specialized variety of question known as the *filter question.* In many surveys, items are included that may not be appropriate for all respondents, and it may be advantageous to include a *question that filters those respondents to a different section of the survey.* For example, a survey of media use may include a number of questions about Internet and E-mail use. However, if a respondent has no access to a computer, such questions are probably of limited use. A filter question may be introduced to redirect select respondents to other more applicable sections:

Do you have access to either E-mail or the Internet?
☐ Yes (Continue with the next question)
☐ No (Continue with question # 25)

When such questions are introduced, careful instruction regarding the respondent redirection needs to be included.

4. **Be realistic.** When formulating items for inclusion in a survey, be realistic about the expectations you have of your respondents. If you are interested in their consumer habits, it is probably unrealistic to expect them to remember all products purchased in the past year. If that data is important to your study it may be necessary to have individuals maintain a consumer log. Or, perhaps it would suffice to have them recall items purchased during their last shopping outing. Requiring unrealistic amounts of recall or analysis from respondents will likely increase frustration levels and lead to inaccurate, or perhaps even falsified, responses, or greater attrition rates.

5. **Remember the purpose of the survey.** When developing items for a survey instrument, it is important to regularly remind oneself of the purpose of the survey. Many times researchers add questions to a survey to increase its length, believing that to be an indication of its level of importance. Or, researchers begin to add questions because they think it would be interesting to know the answers, even though there may be no conceptual reason for those questions. If a question is irrelevant to the intended purpose of the survey, it is best omitted.

6. **Avoid double-barreled questions.** Double-barreled questions are those that ask for two or more responses from a single question, making the response potentially ambiguous. If a researcher was interested in media use, he or she might ask, "Do you enjoy using E-mail and the Internet?" While the question appears to be clear and concise, a respondent may have different reactions to E-mail and the Internet, liking one but despising the other. In that case, the answer to the question would be difficult for the respondent to formulate, and, if given a choice of yes or no, a valid response would be impossible. The appearance of conjunctions, particularly *and, or,* and *but,* are yellow flags, suggesting the possibility of a double-barreled item.

7. **Avoid biased words or terms.** Care needs to be exercised to ensure that words used within items do not shape the responses provided. An instructor who asks, "When you are in search of current events, do you read a newspaper, or do you just watch television," is likely to discover inflated amounts of newspaper reading as a result of the inclusion of the word *just.* Likewise, items that include specific people or ideologies are likely to introduce some bias. "Do you agree with the Republican budget proposal" will likely receive more favorable responses from Republicans than others, even if none of the respondents are aware of the specific proposal. Neutral wording is important to the development of valid survey items.

8. **Avoid leading questions.** Closely related to bias within questions are varieties of questions that suggest specific responses from participants. "Do you, like most college or university students, spend three or more hours studying for each hour you spend in class," would likely receive an overwhelmingly affirmative response, primarily because of respondents' desire to fit in. "Don't you agree that . . ." will likewise enhance an affirmative response due to the suggestion of an expected response.

   One particularly troublesome variety of leading question, known as the **double bind,** *implies an affirmative response regardless of how the participant* *replies.* An example would be, "Do you still cheat on examinations?" Even if the respondent replies in the negative, the implication is that he or she once did cheat on exams.

9. **Avoid threatening questions.** A threatening question is one that causes unease or embarrassment to respondents. While questions about a respondent's sexual behavior, criminal activities, gambling, or drug abuse are clear examples, even questions about personal issues like a respondent's age, occupation, or income can result in some tension. It is best to avoid including anxiety-causing questions in a survey whenever possible. However, many times they are important to the research question at hand. In those cases, care should be exercised to reduce the level of tension experienced by the respondent. A respondent's discomfort with revealing his or her age might be reduced by asking for his or her year of birth. While computation of age is easily accomplished, simply not having to provide the actual age may reduce anxiety. Likewise, having respondents select from a list of randomized options and providing a code corresponding to their selection may reduce potential embarrassment. For example, if asking the number of times a respondent recalls cheating on a college or university examination, a list of options, such as those below, might be provided on a separate card:

E = 5	J = 2	D = more than 10
A = 4	I = 1	H = 9
B = 3	K = 8	G = 6
L = 7	F = 10	C = 0

The respondent would select the correct option and provide the corresponding letter, thereby reducing the potential embarrassment of providing the numeric response. Also, some evidence suggests that less anxiety is experienced when personal information is solicited with open-ended questions, permitting respondents to provide as much detail in the specific form that they desire.

Common Survey Items

With the above rules in mind, the survey researcher can develop the specific items or inquiries to be included in the questionnaire or interview schedule. One method of classifying these items is based on the class of data being solicited. If the inquiry is *intended to elicit objective data from the respondents regarding their background, habits, or behavior,* the items are referred to as **factual inquiries.** One of the most common forms of factual inquiry is the **demographic item,** which *solicits information about respondents' personal characteristics such as gender, ethnicity, marital status, income, occupation,* and so forth. Inquiries that *solicit data about a respondent's beliefs, values, attitudes, opinions, or feelings* are known as **subjective inquiries.** Developing items that yield accurate data regarding subjective states is considerably more challenging than developing valid factual inquiries. Assuming that respondents are conscious of their opinions or attitudes may be erroneous. Also, opinions and attitudes are often multifaceted, meaning that a respondent with a particular attitude may respond to slightly different questions with dramatically different responses. As a result, a considerable amount of time and effort is likely to accompany the development of subjective items.

Regardless of an inquiry's factual or subjective orientation, the items included in a survey instrument are often adapted to one of several common item forms: multiple-choice, rating scales, rank order, and open-ended.

Multiple-Choice Items

A commonly used closed-ended method of obtaining factual data from respondents, the multiple-choice item *provides two or more options from which the respondent chooses the most valid.* The simplest multiple-choice item is dichotomous, providing only two choices to the respondent:

Sex:
☐ Male
☐ Female

or

Are you a communication major?
☐ Yes
☐ No

More advanced multiple-choice items may provide an array of selections to a respondent:

Your major:
☐ Philosophy
☐ English
☐ Communication
☐ Modern languages
☐ Chemistry
☐ Other (please indicate) _____

The latter example suggests an important principle of well-formulated multiple-choice items. Such items need to provide mutually exclusive, exhaustive, and equivalent options, as discussed in Chapter 4. The limited majors presented in the option array in the sample question may result in a significant number of "other" selections, a likelihood reduced if the researcher carefully considers the exhaustive nature of his or her choices. The primary advantage to the multiple-choice item is ease of construction and overall ease of data mapping.

Rating Scales

When soliciting subjective data from respondents, rating scales such as the Likert Summated Rating Scale and the Semantic Differential Scale, both discussed in Chapter 4, are quite popular. Such scales permit access to the multifaceted components of a respondent's opinions, values, attitudes, beliefs, or feelings. However, construction of valid and reliable rating scales can be quite difficult and time-consuming. As a result, researchers often use previously developed and validated scales, accessible through published collections of measurements or from previous research, at times modifying them to serve his or her specific purpose.

While the Likert Scale is most often used with literate, mature respondents, creative modifications of the scale can be used with respondents who lack the normal literacy and maturity requirements. Picture scales, such as the Yucky scale created by Zillman and Bryant (1975), can assess children's and semiliterate adults' reaction to Likert-style statements. The statements, presented orally, are responded to by selecting one of an array of simple faces suggesting emotions ranging from pleased, through neutral, to displeased. Responses are then recorded on a favorable/unfavorable scale, consistent with that of a normal Likert Scale. A similar modification was made by the University of Michigan Survey Research Center in the development of their feeling thermometer. Presenting respondents with a graphic of a thermometer divided into 10 degree increments ranging from 0 to 100, Likert-type statements are presented and respondents are instructed to select their degree of like or dislike in terms of hot or cold. Creative modifications, such as these, can expand the useful application of existing rating scales to previously inaccessible populations.

Rank Order Items

Another common survey item, the rank order question, also introduced in Chapter 4, permits the researcher to assess relative perceptions of a series of options. Respondents are instructed to rank-order items from a highest, or most favorable perception, to a least favorable. As a general rule, requiring the rank-ordering of more than twelve options is impractical as respondents may find the process tedious and the distinctions increasingly ambiguous.

Open-Ended Items

The inclusion of open-ended items on a survey instrument requires special care by the designer. The simplest open-ended item, the fill-in-the-blank item, must be clearly and concisely worded to indicate the precise form of response requested. For example, the demographic inquiry below may produce the response "yes," rather than the desired response of male or female:

Sex? _____

All open-ended items also need to be realistic in the space provided for a reasonable response. Asking participants to analyze their favorite television advertisement, and providing them with two blank lines to complete that analysis is likely to result in some respondent frustration, and the likelihood of an abbreviated analysis.

Instrument Design

Once the items for inclusion on a survey instrument have been developed, the actual design of the instrument can begin. Every questionnaire or interview schedule needs to consist of an introduction, instruction, and body sections. Each part serves a critical purpose.

Introduction

The introduction to a survey serves to encourage respondent participation by providing a brief, neutral introduction to the purpose of the investigation, as well as some demonstration of the study's legitimacy. Legitimacy can be demonstrated through the presentation of the organization sponsoring the investigation, perhaps a college or university, a corporation, or a nonprofit organization, or with a statement indicating the need for such information development.

The introduction is also important in availing respondents of their rights as human participants. All surveys should apprise respondents of the voluntary nature of their participation, permitting them the option of withdrawing at any point during the survey. Respondents should also be assured that the data provided will remain confidential, or anonymous. Finally, recognizing that respondents will need to volunteer their time and effort to complete the survey, it is generally advisable to indicate a realistic amount of time necessary for the completion of the questionnaire or interview. When the survey is to be completed by telephone, or using face-to-face techniques, the introduction is usually presented orally by the researcher, or interviewer, while computer and mail techniques usually include the introduction in written form, sometimes in the form of a cover letter.

Instructions

To ensure that respondents provide the required information, every survey instrument needs a complete and concise set of instructions. Instructions should suggest the specific form of response required of participants. Instructions for a Likert Scale might read as follows:

> Read each of the following statements and select one of the spaces between agree and disagree that best indicates your level of agreement with that statement.

When designing a questionnaire, it is generally recommended that instructions be included in a different typeface, or font, from the other sections of the instrument, in order to make them most perceptually salient.

Interview schedules pose a somewhat more difficult challenge, as instructions must be provided to the interviewer, as well as to the respondents. To ensure clarity, yet another font or typeface may be introduced for these instructions.

Body

The body of the survey instrument contains the collection of inquiry items developed for the investigation. Organization of the items becomes a key concern as the body is assembled. Most survey researchers agree that respondent participation can be enhanced if the instrument begins with several *easy-to-answer, unintrusive items,* often called **warm-up questions.** The purpose of these questions is to limit respondent anxiety and increase rapport. Many suggest using demographic questions as warm-up items. However, because some demographics are potentially sensitive, it is advisable to consider inserting those items near the end of the survey instrument. Placing them there ensures that, if respondents are overly threatened, other items will be responded to prior to a potential respondent withdrawal. Also, by including such items near the end of the instrument, there is an increased likelihood that rapport will be enhanced, increasing the likelihood of open and honest responses to sensitive inquiries.

Other items within the body of the survey instrument need to be carefully ordered so as to reduce the possibility of any response bias. One variety of response bias that is particularly troublesome is known as **response set,** which occurs *when respondents perceive a pattern to a series of item responses, and continue to respond following the pattern rather than basing their answers on the item inquiry.* If, for example, the first eight items on a multiple choice examination were answered, A,B,C,D,A,B,C,D, there is a good chance that respondents would select A for the ninth item, having perceived a pattern. Careful reduction of perceived response patterns is the best solution to this problem.

Bias can also occur as a result of item interaction and sensitization. Early survey items may shape responses to later inquiries. For example, if a survey began by inquiring about favorite media advertisements, and then inquired about the importance of media advertising in the respondent's life, there is an enhanced likelihood of a positive perception of that influence. Careful analysis of the potential for interaction is therefore necessary to limit bias.

Having exercised some care in the limitation of bias, researchers must decide on the general order of the questions within the instrument. Three commonly referred to question-order formats are the funnel, inverted funnel, and tunnel. In the **funnel format,** the researcher *begins with broadly stated questions, with successive questions becoming increasingly more focused and narrower in scope.* This format is the most commonly used, and permits acquisition of information with the least amount of a researcher-imposed frame of reference while assisting the respondent in recall of increasingly detailed information.

The **inverted funnel format** *begins with highly specific and detailed questions and successively becomes more broad and general in its inquiry.* Its primary goal is the establishment of a common, focused frame of reference for the respondents and the limitation of the broader responses to that referential frame. An inverted funnel format used in a classroom questionnaire might begin with a series of specific questions about the class, its instructor, and setting, and then proceed into increasingly broad questions concerning student perceptions of the class and their likes and dislikes. The introductory questions form the frame of reference for all future inquiries and naturally limit the responses.

The final common format is the **tunnel,** in which *all questions presented are of equal specificity and detail.* The choice of question-order format clearly shapes the responses provided, and, therefore, demands careful consideration of the survey investigator.

While structuring the items in the appropriate format, it is recommended that contextually related questions and those using similar response formats be grouped together. For example, multiple questions about a particular topic or event should be grouped together, as should open-ended items, rank order items, scale items, and multiple-choice items. Such grouping will both assist respondent recall and limit the potential frustration of confronting radically different inquiry forms.

The grouping of related items also contributes to the development of an esthetically pleasing instrument. The pleasant appearance of the instrument can be extremely important to respondents' willingness to participate. The goal for the investigator should be the development of a professional-looking instrument that reduces the likelihood of response errors. Therefore, an instrument should be free of grammatical and typographic errors, have clearly defined blocks of related questions, use an easy-to-read, yet attractive font, and include an abundance of white space. Likewise, care should be exercised that response options are explicit and realistic. For example, a multiple-choice item soliciting information about a student's class standing might be presented as:

What is your class standing?
___ Freshman   ___ Sophomore   ___ Junior   ___ Senior

This item, however, is more prone to erroneous response than if the options were presented vertically because respondents could be confused about which line accompanies which option. When the items are presented vertically, the use of response boxes can further improve response clarity by limiting potentially confusing overlapping ×s or check marks:

☐ Freshman   ___ Freshman
☐ Sophomore   instead of   ___ Sophomore
☐ Junior   ___ Junior
☐ Senior   ___ Senior

Finally, the survey designer needs to consider the overall length of the instrument. Because participation in survey research is voluntary, a long tedious instrument is almost certain to experience problems with respondent participation. There are no clear rules regarding the length of a survey instrument, but it is generally agreed that shorter is better. Completing a survey is work for a respondent, and leads to fatigue, which increases the possibility of response error and respondent attrition. Therefore, only necessary inquiries should be included in a survey, and the time required for completion should be reduced as much as possible.

Pilot Testing

Without a doubt, the best way to determine the success with which an instrument is designed is to conduct a pilot test of it. A **pilot test** is *a ministudy designed to diagnose potential problems with a survey instrument.* Generally, the researcher selects a small sample of respondents, perhaps 15 or 20, from the population of interest using either probability or nonprobability sampling. If a probability sample is selected, the pilot study can also serve as a test of instrument validity and reliability. The questionnaire or interview is then presented to these respondents and their responses solicited. Following the completion of the instrument, the researcher goes over each component of the instrument with respondents, inquiring about clarity, perceived meaning, and perceived problems with the introduction, instructions, and body. These critiques can then be used for revising the instrument, and, if the changes required are substantial, another pilot study might be required.

Administration Techniques

Once a research instrument has been developed, pretested, and appropriately revised, a technique for collecting data from the appropriate group of respondents needs to be determined. Four basic administration techniques are commonly used for data collection: mail survey, telephone survey, face-to-face interview, and computer-assisted data collection. Distinguishing between mail, telephone, and face-to-face techniques should be obvious: mail uses the postal service for data solicitation, telephone interviews require the telephone, and face-to-face interviews are the personal encounter between researcher and respondent. **Computer-assisted data collection** (CADAC) involves *the use of a computer in the design, presentation, or distribution of the survey instrument.* One variation of CADAC is **computer-assisted telephone interviewing** (CATI) in which *a computer provides the questions in their appropriate order to a telephone interviewer who inputs provided responses into the computer. A* **computerized self-administered questionnaire** (CSAQ) *permits respondents to directly input data to presented questions at a computer.* This option, when combined with Internet technology, can dramatically expand speed and access to widely distributed respondents, as long as they possess, and know how to use, the required technology. An even more simplified variety of CADAC is the distribution of a questionnaire by E-mail. The greatest overall problem with all CADAC techniques, besides the cost, availability, and maintenance of the hardware, is the difficulty of locating and learning to use survey-development software.

TABLE 9.1 *Mail Survey Technique*

Advantages

1. **Access to large geographic area:** Postal service distribution permits access to widely distributed populations, theoretically around the world.
2. **Reasonable cost:** With minimal staffing requirements, the only costs are instrument development, duplicating, postage, and data analysis.
3. **Selective sampling:** Because of the existence of commercial sampling companies, it is possible to select highly specific populations, such as "medical professionals working in U.S. university hospitals, earning over $1 million annually," and acquire mailing lists for that sample.
4. **Promise of anonymity:** If properly designed, this technique can offer true anonymity to respondents, perhaps increasing their likelihood of responding to potentially threatening inquiries.
5. **Leisurely response:** Respondents have the option of responding when they have an opportunity, even permitting their partial completion at one time and completion at a later time.
6. **Considered response:** With the leisurely response, participants also have the ability to consider their response at some length, not being forced to answer quickly, thereby, perhaps, increasing response accuracy.

Disadvantages

1. **Low response rate:** Mail surveys have a notoriously low degree of respondent participation. As few as 20% of solicited respondents may complete the instrument, and a 60% response rate is considered quite high. Several techniques for increasing mail survey response rates are indicated in Table 9.5.
2. **Slow returns:** Mail surveys may take weeks or months to return, and some may trickle in several months after their distribution. To limit this problem, researchers often set a receipt deadline, after which responses are no longer considered.
3. **Clarification impossible:** Because a researcher is not present to clarify ambiguities, mail survey items must be simple and their instructions clear.
4. **Unknown respondent:** It is difficult to determine who completed the instrument. One mailed to a medical doctor may be completed by a receptionist or other office staff member.

Each of the four administration techniques has its own set of inherent assets and liabilities, as described in Tables 9.1 through 9.4. Careful selection of the most appropriate technique to serve the researcher's specific purpose is crucial to a survey's success.

Evaluating Response Rates

Regardless of the data collection technique employed by the researcher, one important indicator of survey success is achievement of a reasonable response, or participation rate. **Response rate** is *the percentage of respondents solicited for participation in*

TABLE 9.2 *Telephone Survey Technique*

Advantages

1. **Access to large geographic area:** As with mail surveys, the telephone provides easy access to a large, widely dispersed population.

2. **RDD sampling:** Probability sampling can be accomplished with the use of random digit dialing (RDD).

3. **Speed of data collection:** Theoretically, data collection can be completed in a short period of time due to the direct contact with respondents. However, the need for callbacks due to busy respondents or numbers can slow the process considerably, though it is still generally faster than the mail surveys.

4. **Clarification possible:** Because the interviewer is in direct contact with the respondent, concerns about ambiguous questions or instructions can be dealt with, permitting somewhat more complex items to be included than would be allowed in a mail survey.

5. **Moderate response rate:** Respondent participation is generally good, often in the 40 to 60% range.

Disadvantages

1. **Staffing costs:** Telephone survey completion usually requires the assistance of a trained staff of interviewers. Training and staffing costs can be considerable.

2. **Possible researcher effects:** Direct interaction with the interviewer may result in bias from researcher attribute effect and/or unintentional expectancy effect.

3. **Marketing anxiety:** With the increase in telephone surveys as a guise for sales and marketing attempts, potential respondents are becoming increasingly suspicious.

4. **Problems with sample representation:** Telephone surveys completed during different parts of the day are likely to differentially represent the population. In the morning hours, retirees and homemakers will be most accessed. In the midafternoon, children and teens become more numerous, and by early evening, working adults are added to the mix. When samples are selected from published directories, the omission of unlisted telephone numbers may skew sample representativeness.

5. **Visual items impossible:** The use of pictures, graphics, and picture scales is obviously limited by the telephone survey's technology. All items must be capable of oral description.

a survey who complete the instrument. If, for example, 100 students were asked to participate in a face-to-face interview and 15 refused, with another 5 withdrawing their participation before completion, we would calculate the rate as 100/80 = .80, or 80%. The 20 who refused or did not complete the interview are eliminated from the active participant list, leaving only 80 active respondents.

Computation of response rate is, however, not always so straightforward. If a telephone interview was designed to solicit data from university students in their place of residence, random digit dialing might be used to generate a list of 1,000 potential telephone numbers. If only 85 students completed the interview, it would be tempting to report the extremely low response rate of 8.5%. However, on closer inspection it might be revealed that, of the 1,000 numbers dialed, 500 were to residences where no university student resided, 200 were to disconnected or invalid

TABLE 9.3   *Face-to-Face Interview Technique*

Advantages

1. **Access to observational data:** Because of the researcher's direct interaction with the respondent, data can be recorded based on observation rather than inquiry. For example, a face-to-face interviewer could probably determine respondent gender without the need for inquiry.

2. **Item variety:** The physical proximity of the researcher and respondent permit this to be the most adaptable technique, allowing the greatest variety of survey items.

3. **Rapport development:** The presence of the interviewer permits the development of a possible relationship between him or her and the respondent, thereby increasing the likelihood of response to sensitive inquiries.

4. **Clarification possible:** Because the interviewer is in direct contact with the respondent, concerns about ambiguous questions or instructions can be dealt with, permitting even more complex items to be included than would be allowed in a telephone survey.

5. **High response rate:** Respondent participation is usually the highest of all techniques, usually in the 60 to 85% range.

Disadvantages

1. **Staffing costs:** Face-to-face interviews usually require the assistance of a trained staff of interviewers. Training, staffing, and transportation costs can be considerable.

2. **Possible researcher effects:** Direct physical interaction with the interviewer may results in bias from researcher attribute effect, and/or unintentional expectancy effect, to an even greater degree than with the telephone survey.

3. **Marketing anxiety:** With the increase in interviews as a guise for sales and marketing attempts, potential respondents are becoming increasingly suspicious.

4. **Liability:** The safety of interviewers, respondents, and respondent property is leading to increased need for liability insurance on the part of the researcher, an increasingly expensive proposition.

numbers, 150 to business or corporate numbers, and 150 were perpetually busy or had no answer. Because, in these cases, respondents were not solicited for participation, they could be eliminated from the potential total, reducing the number from 1,000 to 100. Of those actively solicited, 10 refused to participate and 5 withdrew before completing the interview, leaving a total of 85 active respondents. The response rate calculated using the collection of solicited respondents would now be 100/85 = .85, or 85%, obviously a significant improvement. Of those eliminated from the 1,000 potential respondent numbers called, the most controversial is the elimination of busy/no answer numbers, because it is conceivable that these numbers could yield active respondents. However, it is equally arguable that such numbers are connected to computer or fax equipment, business lines, automatic alarm systems, and so on. The key to the decision to eliminate them from the potential pool is usually based on multiple attempts to reach the number at various times, with no change in the number's status: It remains perpetually busy or unanswered. The key to determining the pool of solicited participants is the careful analysis of

TABLE 9.4 *Computer-Assisted Data Collection Techniques*

Computer-assisted data collection includes such diverse techniques as computer-assisted telephone interviewing (CATI), computerized self-administered questionnaires (CSAQ), touchtone data entry (TDE), a touchtone telephone is used to respond to recorded questions, and disk by mail (DBM), a computer disk containing a questionnaire is sent to respondents, completed on a personal computer, and sent back to the researcher.

Advantages

1. **Easy data mapping:** Because data is being directly input into a computer, software can conveniently and instantaneously map the provided data.
2. **Appeal:** The novelty of computer-assisted data collection makes it appealing to some respondents, particularly those with technological interests.
3. **Automatic branching and skipping:** Software design can permit the automatic movement to appropriate parts of the questionnaire or interview schedule, known as *branching*, as well as the automatic avoidance of inappropriate items, known as *skipping*.

Disadvantages

1. **Technology costs:** The purchase of computer hardware is expensive, and its cost can contribute sizably to a research budget. Also, the expectation of ownership by respondents can skew sample representation, as more affluent individuals are more likely to have made the required purchase.
2. **Technological competence:** Learning to use the computer for data collection requires substantial time and effort. Respondents asked to directly input dat into the computer may become anxious about their perceived competence, increasing their likelihood of withdrawal. Researchers, otherwise quite comfortable with questionnaire or interview schedule design, may find themselves perplexed by some of the complicated data collection software.
3. **Technological compatibility:** Multiple operating systems, disc sizes, processor speeds, and displays on computers make the selection of an appropriate distribution package difficult. A CATI survey designed for use with a Macintosh operating system will likely be useless with a Windows-based computer. A DBM questionnaire will prove useless to a respondent with access to a IMac computer with no disc drive, and a colorful Internet questionnaire will appear rather drab on a monochrome monitor.

those not participating and determining their likelihood of containing elements of the population of interest. Those ruled outside of the population may be eliminated from the pool of solicited respondents. Regardless of the researcher's decision, an accurate report containing details of who was included and excluded should accompany the calculation of response rate.

But, what is an acceptable rate of response? Obviously, the higher the response rate the better, but the choice of data collection technique will influence the rate significantly. Face-to-face interviews regularly report response rates of between 60 and 85%, while mail interviews generally report only 40 to 60% participation. Response rates are best used as an index when compared to other similar investigations, suggesting how the investigation in question compares in level of participation from similar respondents, using similar techniques.

TABLE 9.5 *Techniques for Increasing Mail Survey Responses*

---

1. **Personalized cover letter:** A well-written cover letter introducing the survey and its sponsoring organization significantly increases participation. The personalization of the letter with the respondent's name and researcher signature is likely to enhance the rate yet further.

2. **Return postage paid:** Paid postage for the return of the questionnaire is critical to improved response. While business reply envelopes can reduce the cost of the return postage, they generally also reduce response rates when compared to the use of first-class stamped envelopes (Armstrong & Lusk, 1987). Some evidence even suggests that response rate increases when commemorative stamps are used in place of standard postage.

3. **Inducements:** Rewards for the completion of a questionnaire can potentially increase rate of response. A nominal sum of money may be included for the time and effort demanded of the respondent. Some potential participants may, however, be offended by the limited worth attached to their time, and refuse to respond as a result. Other nominal rewards such as coupons, gift certificates, or inexpensive merchandise may be used in place of money.

4. **Follow-up procedures:** Brief letters or postcards sent to remind respondents to complete and mail the questionnaire are important contributors to increased response. As with the cover letter, the more personal the appeal, the greater the contribution. It is important to be aware, however, that anonymous surveys will require follow-up to all potential respondents, even those that may have responded.

Regardless of the response rate computed, researchers should take a careful look at the overall response patterns. Is there any evidence of bias in the kinds of respondents included? Are males more likely to have responded than females? Are younger people more likely than older? Are Caucasians more likely than Hispanics? The goal is to evaluate to what degree sampling bias may have been introduced to the investigation, and to what degree that might influence the final results.

Planning the Survey

As you have learned, the survey method is commonly chosen by an investigator wishing to use self-report techniques to search for potential relationships between variables. In order to plan and design a survey, eight decisions need to be made:

1. **Development of a research problem.** As with any investigation, the first step is the development of a research question (hypothesis). Most survey studies are based on problems involving a correlational, rather than causal, relationship between variables.

2. **Access to the community of scholars.** As with the experimental method, the result of this step is the development of a clear foundation for the planned investigation.

3. **Definition of constructs.** Using the community of scholars as a reference point, the survey researcher must develop a clear conceptual and operational definition for each of the constructs found in the problem statement.

4. **Development of a survey instrument.** Considering the conceptual and operational definitions, the researcher must decide on a cross-sectional or longitudinal design, and develop the questionnaire or interview schedule to be used for the collection of data. Pilot testing and revision assure that the instrument is valid and reliable.

5. **Selection of a representative sample.** To assure the greatest external validity, a sample of the population must be made in such a way to ensure that they are representative. Generally, this is accomplished through the selection of a probability sample.

6. **Collection of data.** Explicitly following the planned procedures for the conduct of the questionnaire or interview, the researcher, or trained cohorts, collect the required data. Computation and analysis of response rates are used to suggest the degree to which the achieved sample represents the population.

7. **Analysis of results.** Results of the data collection must be mapped, or assigned numerals, according to rules (review Chapter 4), by the researcher. These numerals can then be analyzed for possible relationships, often using descriptive or correlational statistics to convert the raw data into information. Both of these approaches will be discussed further in Chapter 12.

8. **Integration of the findings.** As with any investigation, the final step is the integration of the new findings into the amassed knowledge of the community of scholars. Care is given to whether the results are consistent with previous investigations, the degree to which the knowledge base is expanded, the practical implications of the findings, and the growth or generation of scientific theory.

10

Content and Interaction Analysis

Chapter Outline

While survey and experimental methods systematically generate data for analysis, content and interaction analysis are rather unique in their use of *existing* communication content. As a result, these techniques are generally considered to be **nonreactive** methods because *the potential for data bias is reduced by limiting the influence of the researcher on the development of data.* The data investigated by content or interaction analysis are collections of the encoded symbols, or messages, used in communication. For content analysis, these may include verbally encoded messages, such as books, scripts, newspaper or magazine articles or editorials, journals, or manuscripts; visually encoded messages, such as photographs, film, media images, facial expressions, or art; or nonverbal messages, including vocal cues or music. For interaction analysis, the message is generally in the form of natural or controlled dyadic or small-group interaction. While many of the concerns of these two forms of message analysis are similar, to clarify differences we will investigate each independently.

Content Analysis

The roots of content analysis reach back to eighteenth-century Sweden, where 90 songs in a collection known as the *Songs of Zion* were analyzed by a group of religious scholars and clergy to determine their agreement with accepted orthodoxy. One notable group of scholars counted the use of religious symbols in the published collection and compared those with the established church-approved songbook and found no significant difference (Krippendorff, 1980).

The first large-scale application of content analysis emerged during World War II when the Foreign Broadcast Intelligence Service of the American Federal Communications Commission collected and analyzed Nazi broadcasts. The goal of the analysis was to attempt to understand and predict events in Nazi Germany based on the messages, including music, being broadcast. The success of these content analyses remained obscure until after the war due to the overwhelming amount of data being collected and analyzed. However, postwar analysis proved that the method had successfully predicted the development and deployment of new weaponry, including the German V-weapon to be deployed against the British, as well as successfully predicting several major military and political campaigns (Krippendorff, 1980).

After the war, content analysis began to spread into numerous academic disciplines. In 1952, Bernard Berelson published *Content Analysis in Communication Research*, the first integrated description of the approach, and confirmation that the method had gained scholarly acceptance. Berelson defined content analysis as "a research technique for the objective, systematic, and quantitative description of the manifest content of communication" (p. 18). The four key words in this definition are *objective, systematic, quantitative,* and *manifest. Objective* suggests that bias introduced by the researcher is minimized, and, if objectivity is achieved, like results should be obtained regardless of a researcher's personal idiosyncrasies, attitudes, or values. To accomplish objectivity, content analysis is systematic, following explicit rules for the identification of message content and treating all messages in the same manner.

Following the established rules, each message unit is assigned to a category, and the frequency of incidence is recorded, translating the message into numeric form, which makes the method quantitative. For example, a content analysis of a writer's self-reference in an essay may analyze each word, noting the appearance of self-references such as *I, me,* or the author's name. The results would be quantitative in that they would record the incidence of self-reference in the collection of words used in the essay.

Finally, Berelson suggests that studied content must be manifest, directly observable, in the message being analyzed. This characteristic of content analysis, more than any other, has been hotly debated. The argument is made that simply counting elements that are directly observed may significantly distort reality. There is, after all, a latent aspect of communication. Some information about communication is unobtainable with direct observation and must be inferred from the manifest content. Such latent analysis is not beyond the realm of the content analyst, as long as the inferences drawn are based on systematic and objective criteria. In fact, Holsti (1969), in an important work describing the functions of content analysis, suggests that it can be used for three purposes: (1) to describe the characteristics of communication messages, (2) to make inferences regarding antecedents to those messages, and (3) to make inferences about the messages' consequences. Each of the latter two functions are latent, only to be inferred from the logical extension of the data.

In summary, content analysis follows established rules and procedures to create categories into which observable units of content within a message are identified and counted. But, what are the advantages to this analytic approach?

Advantages of Content Analysis

Krippendorff (1980) suggested four advantages to content analysis when compared with other methodologies. First, "content analysis is an unobtrusive technique" in that it uses existing messages rather than ones produced solely for the investigation (p. 29). Second, "content analysis accepts unstructured material" (p. 30). Unlike surveys, interviews, and experiments, the data for content analysis are not being produced to the researcher's specification, but are, instead, produced and then provided some structure as the content analyst assigns message units to categories. Third, "content analysis is context sensitive and thereby able to process symbolic forms" (p. 30). Because content analysis uses material that is produced in some context, it can retain the association between the data and its symbolic meaning. Finally, "content analysis can cope with large volumes of data" (p. 31). Due to the systematic, objective, and quantitative nature of this technique, massive quantities of data can be categorized, especially with the use of computer assistance. In one particularly notable study, 15,000 characters appearing in 1000 hours of prime-time television fiction were analyzed (Gerbner, Gross, Signorielli, Morgan, and Jackson-Beeck, 1979); in another, 8,039 newspaper editorials were studied (Foster, 1938).

Content Analytic Procedures

Content analysis involves seven discrete steps, some quite similar to those of our previous methods, but each with its own unique set of challenges.

Developing a Research Problem. Research problems appropriate for content analysis focus on the analysis and quantification of message content. For example, this method of analysis could be used to investigate the following research problems:

> RQ$_1$: What is the incidence of aggressive acts portrayed in prime-time television programming?

RQ$_2$: How do metropolitan daily newspapers compare with regional newspapers in the extent of coverage of international, national, state, and local stories?

RQ$_3$: How has the representation of racial groups portrayed on network television changed in the past decade?

While each of these research questions is unique, and presents individual challenges, each focuses on the quantification of message content. In the first, it is the quantification of aggressive acts, while in the second and third it is the quantification of story types and racial representations, respectively.

Because content analysis is concerned with objectively and systematically quantifying message content, it is incapable of resolving questions of message impact or antecedents. The following research questions would, therefore, be inappropriate for content analytic methods:

RQ$_4$: How does exposure to aggressive television content influence violent behavior in U.S. youth?

RQ$_5$: What causes seasonal fluctuations in the amount of consumer advertising targeted at children?

While neither of these questions can be resolved using content analysis alone, it is possible that content analysis might play some role in the research design. For example, as the author of RQ$_4$, I might conduct a content analysis of aggressive portrayals in television programming, coupled with a measurement, perhaps using a survey instrument, of a sample of viewers' violent behavior. Similarly, the author of RQ$_5$ might first analyze seasonal advertising content and couple that method with data regarding advertisement planning, perhaps obtained by survey or interview methods. One famous example of the coupling of content analytic methods with another methodology are the cultivation analysis studies done by George Gerbner and colleagues (see Gerbner, Gross, Signorielli, Morgan, & Jackson-Beeck, 1979). In a series of investigations, Gerber et al. content-analyzed the dominant themes in media portrayals and compared those with the results of a survey investigating media use and perceptions about the world. They concluded that those who were exposed to the highest doses of crime and violence in the media were also more afraid of the world around them. Such integration of methods is becoming increasingly common to content analysis.

Sampling the Universe. Once the research problem has been formulated, each salient construct needs to be conceptually defined, just as with any other methodology. However, of special concern to the content analyst is deciding on the specific message content to be investigated. In RQ$_1$, it is evident that the universe of messages will consist of prime-time television portrayals. However, the universe would probably need to be delimited to some degree. Is the researcher really interested in all prime time television, or only those of the four or five major broadcast networks? What is to be the working definition of *prime time*? In RQ$_2$, a more comparative form of analysis, how will the universe of metropolitan and regional newspapers be determined? And, in RQ3, what will be the universe of network television programming? Will it consider all programming or only prime-time, morning, or situation comedy programming?

RQ3 also poses a unique challenge to the researcher. If the goal is to compare differences over time, as is the case with this problem, then the study needs to be longitudinal rather than cross-sectional. Definition of the universe must take into consideration all potential time periods to be included in the investigation.

Once the universe of messages has been determined, either a census or representative sample of the content needs to be obtained. Because a census is often impractical, methods need to be used to establish the most representative sample, a goal most frequently accomplished with probability sampling methods. The special challenge to the content analyst is assuring that elements selected are truly representative of the message universe. For example, the selection of one week of prime-time television may or may not adequately represent the universe. If the week chosen was a "sweeps" week, when television stations compete for the largest share of the audience, message content is likely to be quite different from that found during a nonsweeps week. The selection of one metropolitan daily newspaper may or may not represent that universe, and the selection of prime-time network television may not accurately reflect the racial mix of all network fare. As a result, care in the selection of sampling methods is critical and often involves some use of stratification sampling or multistage cluster sampling. As with all sampling, the general rule is, "The larger the sample size (within reason) the greater the likelihood of representativeness."

Unitizing.   Having decided on the universe and sample that will be investigated, the researcher needs to determine the specific units of analysis that will be assigned to categories, a process called *unitizing*. In some investigations, the units to be assigned to categories, or quantified, are words. For example, if we are interested in the incidence of a particular individual's appearance in a newspaper, we may count the number of times that person is mentioned. The unit of analysis can also be themes, such as might be the case if the investigator was interested in the number of local versus national stories on a newspaper's front page. This might also be the unit of analysis if comparing the liberal versus conservative themes presented in that same newspaper. Other units of analysis proposed by Berelson (1952) include characters, time/space, and items. If the analyst was concerned with how many television characters belong to various races, each character might be categorized on the basis of race, as well as, perhaps, occupation and gender. Along with this analysis, some concern might be given to the number of minutes during which each race appears in the television lineup, so time would be a factor. Or the unit of analysis would be space if the researcher wants to know the number of column inches devoted to different categories of news in the newspaper. Finally, entire items can be assigned to categories, as might be the case if one were studying the number of advertisements that appear in a newspaper. Berelson's recommendations for units of analysis are just that. The unitizing process differs slightly with every investigation. However, a well-planned content analysis needs to clearly and concisely operationally define the units of the message that will be examined and quantified.

Developing the Measurement Scheme. To carry out content analysis, each unit of analysis must be quantified with a measurement scheme, placed in a defined category. If you are interested in how many television characters belong to different races, the category scheme may include Caucasian, African American, Asian, Native American, Latino, and Other. If, instead, the concern was the amount of aggression shown to television viewers, the categories might be Violent or Nonviolent. If the problem was the relative quality of liberal or conservative themes in newspaper stories, the measurement scheme might include a rating scale, such as the semantic differential. You will notice that themes of liberal or conservative trends are more latent than is the categorizing characters by race. However, regardless of how manifest or latent the units of analysis are, careful definition of the categories or levels of the measurement scheme are required to assure objectivity. If objectivity has been achieved, any investigator using the provided definitions should be able to categorize units consistently. If you were to categorize media content as Violent or Nonviolent, a clear operational definition of both the categories needs to be developed, providing clear guidelines for content inclusion. Like all measurement, the category scheme for content analysis needs to be mutually exclusive, exhaustive, and equivalent.

Training Coders. In order to assess the reliability of the measurement scheme, content analysis generally uses two or more *individuals trained to evaluate and categorize each unit of analysis.* These individuals are known as **coders.** Most scholars agree that the selection of coders with similar backgrounds and academic training is advantageous. Once coders have been selected, they are introduced to the measurement scheme and the definitions on which the categories are based. The goal of training coders is to develop a common frame of reference so that they perceive and categorize content consistently. The training process is often quite time-consuming, and includes a number of pilot tests of the measurement scheme. Each pilot test is generally followed by a discussion of coding consistency and inconsistency, as well as concerns about definitional ambiguity. Careful consideration of the pilot sessions will enable the researcher to clarify coding problems and, as a result, improve coder reliability during actual data coding.

This measurement of the degree of consistency with which coders categorize observations, introduced in Chapter 4 as *intercoder reliability,* is an important consideration, both during training and throughout the study. Measurement of intercoder reliability during training provides a standard for potential improvement. Reliability measurement during the data-coding stage of the investigation is standard procedure and reliability coefficients are usually included in the final report of content analytic research. While there are several techniques for assessing intercoder reliability, including Scott's Pi and Craig's Kappa, perhaps the simplest approach is

Holsti's (1969) formula. Holsti's formula provides an easy to compute index of the percentage of agreement between two coders. The formula is:

Reliability = $2M/N_1 + N_2$

where M = the total number of times the coders were in agreement, N_1 = the number of coding decisions made by the first coder, and N_2 = the number of coding decisions made by the second coder.

For example, imagine that on a coding task of 100 units of analysis, coders categorized 80 units into like categories. The reliability coefficient would be 2(80)/100 + 100, or 160/200, or .80. As you may recall from Chapter 4, this would be considered a quite acceptable degree of reliability. Suppressed reliability may result from any of three factors: (1) the relative ability of coders, (2) the clarity of category definitions, or (3) random error. Due to background, experiences, and personal differences, some coders, regardless of training, are better at quantifying units than others. Generally, those who are significantly different in their coding from the majority of trained coders, and retraining has not improved their ability, are removed from the roster of coders. Reliability may also be suppressed by ambiguity in the definitions of measurement categories, though, with clarification during the pilot testing, this can often be corrected. Finally, some error is due to random circumstances, including working conditions and fatigue, among other things. As you learned previously, much random error is beyond the control of the investigator.

Coding the Content.   Once trained in the use of the coding scheme, coders assign each unit of analysis in the sample of messages to appropriate categories. To facilitate coding, investigators usually provide easy-to-use coding sheets on which coders simply check selections or provide hash marks for counts of events. When electronic media are being analyzed, recordings of the media are used whenever available to permit the coders to stop and proceed at their own pace.

When units of analysis are manifest, and category definitions are simple and unambiguous, coding can be accomplished with incredible speed using a computer. For example, if we wished to count the appearance of a particular word in a newspaper, the computer could be programmed to rapidly evaluate text, counting or isolating all stories that contain that word. Human coders could potentially follow up and provide more intricate coding to those stories that had been isolated. And, with most print media now being composed in digital form, as well as the growing accessibility of digital scanners, it is relatively easy for a researcher to develop digital copy for the computer to evaluate.

Analyzing Data and Developing Inferences.   Because most data collected during content analysis is at the nominal level, descriptive statistics, such as percentages, modes, and frequency distributions, are most frequently used (see Chapter 12). When a hypothesis is to be tested, one inferential statistic that is commonly employed is Chi-square, also discussed in Chapter 12. Chi-square is rather unique among inferential statistics in its ability to work with nominal level data.

If the data are at the interval or ratio level, as may be the case when dealing with the number of minutes of character appearance, column inches in a newspaper, or rating scales, other inferential statistics may be more accurate. Among those commonly used (see Chapter 12), are the t-test and correlation, though other more sophisticated analyses, such as ANOVA and discriminate analysis, are sometimes used.

When inferential statistics are used, researchers can test for significant population differences or relationships, providing more depth and interest to the investigation. Results of the analyses are then included in the report, and, at times, the rules of logic are used to make inferences about antecedent influences or effects.

Interaction Analysis

Like content analysis, interaction analysis is used to systematically describe communication messages. However, the messages included in this analysis are generally limited to the products of dyadic and small-group interaction. In 1985, Poole and McPhee defined interaction analysis as "a systematic method of classifying verbal and non-verbal behavior" (p. 124). Notable in this definition is the absence of the terms *objective* and *quantitative* found in the definition of content analysis. With this adaptation, interaction analysis becomes more flexible and capable of using qualitative, or descriptive, analytic procedures as well as quantitative approaches. However, the method remains systematic, following specified rules and procedures for the analysis.

Among the earliest techniques introduced for interaction analysis was a procedure by Bales (1950), Interaction Process Analysis (IPA), which can be used to study the interactions of small decision-making groups. In his technique, each person's communication acts are categorized into one of twelve categories. Six of the categories relate to task-based messages, while the other six relate to person-related, or socioemotional, messages. As is evident, the categorization of units of analysis, the communication act, is not particularly different from that of content analysis. More recent applications of interaction analysis have introduced greater flexibility to the analytic process, and, as a result, have increased the distinction between the two methods.

Functions of Interaction Analysis

Interaction analysis is most commonly used to provide answers to one of four varieties of research problems. One possible application of interaction analysis is the investigation of interactive content, the topics raised during interaction. For example, a researcher may be interested in understanding the topics discussed by married couples, or by college or university students. It is also possible that an investigator might be interested in how the selection of topic influences the interaction. The interaction about course content between a professor and student will likely proceed differently than one about a recent sporting event.

Interaction analysis can also be used to understand the functions served by interaction: How individuals use messages to accomplish some goal. To study the functions of interaction, analysts examine **strategies,** *messages designed to accomplish a personal or relational goal.* The study of inquiries used in a student–faculty interaction might indicate that questions could be used to solicit responses, to elicit further interaction, or to demand compliance. A student asking "Why did I get this grade?" could be attempting to gain further understanding, enhance his or her interaction with the faculty member, or subtly demand a change.

As well as investigating the content and functions of interaction, interaction analysis also permits the study of interactive structure: How messages are assembled into a coherent conversation. In coherent conversation, the turns taken by participants, and the sequencing of topics discussed, is regulated by a socially agreed-on prescription. This prescription is the focus of analysts interested in structure, and is known as a conversational rule. The general structure of a conversational rule (Smith, 1988) is, "If X (goal) in situation Y (context), then behavior Z (action)" (p. 238). In other words, if a participant in a particular interactive situation (context) wanted to accomplish a particular goal, a specific behavior would be mandated. Failure to follow the accepted rules of conversation can result in misunderstanding or alienation from the interaction. Among some of the most common conversational rules taught to us as children are, "Speak only when spoken to," "Respect your elders," and "Don't change the topic." As we mature, we become aware of the contextual and functional nature of these rules.

A final potential function of interaction analysis is the understanding of the effects of interaction: How the interaction relates to important outcomes. For example, an investigator might examine student–faculty interactions in an attempt to discover how alliances are formed or how alienation occurs. The researcher's interest might be the relationship between content, function, and/or structure, and the influence of the interaction.

Interaction Analysis Procedures

Interaction analysis involves six discrete steps, many quite similar to those of content analysis, though each has its unique challenges.

Developing a Research Problem.   As with all investigations, interaction analysis begins with the formulation of a research problem appropriate to the study of communication interaction. As noted above, problems may focus on the content, structure, function, and/or impact of interactions.

Assembling a Database of Interactions.   Having determined the problem in need of resolution, the interaction analyst needs to choose a strategy for collecting the interactions to be analyzed. Grimshaw (1974) suggests five sources of interaction: (1) literary material, (2) contrived material, (3) elicited interaction, (4) laboratory interaction, and (5) natural interaction. Literary material is interactive discourse selected from novels or dramatic works, and, while useful in the study of literary interaction, it is generally regarded as having low ecological isomorphism. Con-

contrived

trived material, interaction created by the researcher, is potentially more realistic. However, because it is made up by the researcher, contrived material is significantly more susceptible to researcher bias. Its use is best reserved for providing examples to theoretical concepts developed by the study of actual conversation.

elicited

In elicited interaction, the data to be analyzed are obtained by asking participants to recall, or recreate, previous interactions. An investigator interested in the conversations of married couples might ask them to describe or recreate a recent conversation, perhaps about a consumer purchase. Significantly more realistic than contrived interaction, the principal weakness with this technique is that participant recall is usually far from accurate. And, when recreating interaction, many of the nonverbal and vocal cues of natural conversation are lost.

laboratory

To retain some of the spontaneity of natural interaction, conversation can be developed in a laboratory setting. Researchers may simply record interaction that occurs spontaneously in a setting where participants are assembled, or participants can be provided with a hypothetical topic or task to talk about. In either case, recording of the conversation can be completed rather unobtrusively with concealed cameras and microphones. However, as suggested in the ethics chapter, participants should be alerted to their role in the study and that they are being recorded.

natural

The greatest ecological isomorphism is found in interaction that is obtained in a natural setting, such as participants' homes or offices. While probably the most desirable form of interaction, it is often difficult to collect. Because of the intrusiveness of recording natural conversation, volunteer sampling, rather than a probability method, is most frequently used. This method has an obvious impact on external validity. The unnatural appearance of a recording device within the home of participants is also prone to alter their subsequent interaction, a form of reactivity effect. While it is argued that much of that influence can be reduced by leaving the recording devices in place until participants become accustomed to them, there is little agreement about how long that may take.

Once a decision has been made about the source of interaction to be studied, a sample of that interaction needs to be collected. Depending on the source of the interaction, probability sampling can be used if the goal is to generalize results; otherwise convenience, volunteer, or purposive sampling can be used.

Transcribing the Database.　In one of the most time-consuming steps of interaction analysis, the recorded sample of interactions is then converted to transcripts. **Transcripts** are *verbatim textual records of the interaction, containing detail appropriate to the purpose of the investigation.* If an analyst were interested only in the topics discussed during faculty–student interactions, only a transcript of topics would be required. If, on the other hand, the interest were in the conversational rules used during such interactions, a complete record of all verbal, vocal, and nonverbal elements would likely be required.

Developing an Analytic Strategy.　As a result of the flexible nature of interaction analysis, a number of analytic strategies, like the IPA, have been developed. While each specific strategy is unique, they can generally be characterized as either deductive or inductive. In deductive analytic strategies, categories are developed based on previously conducted research or theory, much as they are in content analysis. The goal is to create a category scheme that is mutually exclusive, exhaustive, and equivalent into which units of analysis can be coded. Once developed, each category must be explicitly defined, and coders must be trained to assure maximum reliability. If the deductive analytic method is used to study the topics of conversation between students and faculty, the researcher might develop, based on previous theory, a list of potential topics into which each interactive unit could be coded.

Inductive analysis, a much more recent approach, begins with the impartial examination of messages in the interaction database. Attempting to evaluate the messages without preconceptions, the researcher develops a list of categories suggested by the data, with supporting examples provided as evidence of their validity. If one were studying the content of faculty–student interactions, the researcher would begin by examining the collected interactions and from that examination, develop a list of topics that were observed. One specific inductive analysis strategy that receives a great deal of attention from communication scholars is Glaser and Strauss's (1967) grounded theory method, discussed in greater detail in Chapter 11.

Coding Interactive Units. Before using the selected analytic scheme, the researcher must decide on the units of analysis, just as one must do with content analysis. Common units of analysis for interaction study are words, utterances, and topics. While words and topics are relatively self-explanatory, utterances deserve further clarification. An utterance is defined by Smith (1988) as "a verbal assertion," including "any comment with a stated or implied subject and predicate" (p. 240).

Application of the decided-on analytic scheme can commence once the interactive content has been unitized. Regardless of whether the chosen method is deductive or inductive, two or more coders are generally employed to examine and code each unit in order to assess the reliability of the coding scheme. Intercoder reliability coefficients, such as the Holsti formula, are generally calculated and included in the final research report.

Reporting and Integrating Results. Once the analysis has been completed, the results of the investigation must be reported to the community of scholars. The report of a deductive analysis may contain descriptive or inferential statistics, which are also found in the reports of content analysis. Inductive analysis reports, on the other hand, provide detailed description of the inductive logic used to develop a categorization scheme, as well as supportive examples. Regardless of the approach, the results are also compared with previous research and existing theory to suggest consistencies, inconsistencies, and unresolved problems worthy of future analysis.

Content analysis and interaction analysis are nonreactive methodologies for examining and describing the characteristics of communication messages. While the former is traditionally more objective and quantitative in its approach, both methods continue to develop analytic flexibility.

11

Qualitative Methods

Chapter Outline

Defining Qualitative Methods

You may recall that in Chapter 1 you encountered positivists, communication scholars whose goal is to find generalizable rules regarding human behavior. Because of their interest in generalizability, these practitioners typically adopt methodologies that generate large amounts of observational data from substantial numbers of participants or elements, quantitative methods such as those described in the previous three chapters. However, as phenomenologists have established themselves in the discipline, they have begun to introduce methodologies that generate more detailed, or "thick," descriptions of communication behavior. These descriptive techniques have earned respect within the discipline and are now used by both positivists and phenomenologists.

Such descriptive methodologies were first established in the nineteenth century when Frederick LePlay conducted an observational study of European families and communities (Bruyn, 1966). However, the methodology remained relatively unknown outside of the discipline of anthropology until the 1920s when a *group of sociologists at the University of Chicago adopted and popularized the descriptive technique.* This group of scholars, known as the **Chicago School,** spread these novel methods into a variety of disciplines during the period from 1920 through 1940. However, a resurgence in positivism during the 1940s and 1950s contributed to a decline in the use of descriptive approaches, and it was only during the 1960s that these methods again became accepted. Most scholars today recognize them as equal partners with the traditional positivistic methods in the development of an understanding of communication behavior.

The methods used to generate the thick description desired by phenomenologists are commonly known as **qualitative methods.** Bogdan and Taylor (1975) define these methods as "research procedures that produce descriptive data" (p. 4). To better understand these procedures, it is helpful to recognize their common characteristics. First, these methods require inductive reasoning to generate theories. Qualitative investigators *begin by collecting detailed descriptions of behavior, and then examine those descriptions for patterns or trends that might explain communication.* For example, a researcher might record detailed observations of student classroom behavior from which she could infer regular patterns of behavior. To assist in the ability to draw these inferences, Anderson (1987) suggests that qualitative methods be **presuppositionless;** that is, the investigator must set aside any preconceptions or hypotheses while collecting descriptive data.

Second, qualitative methods are used to examine **naturalistic human behavior.** In short, the researcher wants to observe individuals behaving as they ordinarily do in their natural settings.

Third, qualitative methods are varied and flexible. Unlike the more procedure-driven methods of positivistic methods, the qualitative researcher often uses a blend of methods to acquire the degree of detail required. It is also not uncommon for a qualitative researcher to begin with one data-collection technique, for example naturalistic observation, and later add or switch to another, such as interviewing, and even later add a third, perhaps the collection of artifacts. It is often the creative adaptation or blending of qualitative techniques that yields the most complete description of communicative behavior.

While what follows is not an exhaustive discussion, three data-collection techniques are commonly used by qualitative researchers in communication: naturalistic observation, interviewing, and collection of artifacts. A more exhaustive presentation of the variety of methods available to the qualitative researcher can be found in a number of textbooks that focus exclusively on qualitative approaches (i.e., Bogdan & Taylor, 1975).

Naturalistic observation involves *the overt or covert observation and recording of individuals' behaviors as they engage in everyday activities. **Interviewing** attempts to elicit detailed descriptions of behavior and understanding from the participants. **Collecting***

artifacts, *materials left behind as a result of communication,* provides a third, and most nonreactive source of data to the qualitative researcher. While application of these methods is flexible and adaptable, a clearer understanding of each technique can be attained by examining the procedures common to each method.

Naturalistic Observation Procedures

In observing and recording the behavior of people "in the field," or in their common milieu, the qualitative researcher generally needs to follow six somewhat intertwined steps: framing the research problem, gaining access to the observation site, selecting an observer role, reducing reactivity effect, developing observational notes, and analyzing and reporting observations.

Framing a Research Problem

As a result of the inductive nature of qualitative research, the research problems guiding these investigations are most frequently formulated as open-ended questions. For example, here are three research questions that could be investigated using naturalistic observation:

> RQ_1: How do adolescents use the Internet?
>
> RQ_2: How do patients and physicians interact during routine physical examinations?
>
> RQ_3: How do college students behave while visiting the common area of the student union?

It is also important to recognize that, as a result of the flexible and adaptable nature of qualitative methods, new, more specific, research problems can develop during the course of the investigation. For example, the researcher exploring RQ_1 might, during the course of observation, become alert to a differing use of the Internet by males and females, and, as a result, intensify his or her observation of those differences, in essence creating a new, more specific, research problem.

In choosing a research problem, the qualitative researcher must also resolve numerous pragmatic issues, particularly those relating to the who, when, and where of the observation. While RQ_1 suggests that the target of the observation will be adolescents, the investigator must decide whether to observe a single adolescent extensively or several different adolescents, though perhaps less extensively. In RQ_2, it is apparent that physician–patient interaction is the primary target of observation, but a decision needs to be made regarding whether to observe a single physician–patient pairing or a series, each with a single physician or perhaps with multiple physicians. Finally, in RQ_3, will the researcher follow a single student as he or she uses the student union or observe all students who use the public areas?

As well as determining who will be observed, the investigator also needs to decide where the observation will take place. In RQ_1, for example, Internet use probably occurs at some combination of home, school, and other locales, such as the public library. If the investigator is interested in observing a single individual, it is possible that he or she could explore Internet use in each of these settings. However, if the plan is to observe several adolescents, it is likely that a particular setting, either the home or school, will be selected as the setting of interest. Similarly, in RQ_3, a researcher observing a single individual may follow him or her through all the public areas in the student union, whereas an investigator examining students as a group would probably select specific areas for the focus of his or her observation.

Finally, some decision needs to be made about when the observation is to occur. Selection of a specific time of day during which all observation takes place may result in a less than accurate description of individuals' behaviors. For example, observing interaction in the student union during morning hours will likely result in significant differences from observation that occurs during the afternoon or evening hours. The differences would be even more dramatic if observation took place during a college recess, as compared to behavior during the active term. Each of the above decisions will quite likely influence the results of naturalistic observation, and, therefore, must be made on the basis of the investigator's research goal.

Gaining Access to the Observation Site

Once a problem has been formulated, the qualitative investigator must gain access to the locales where observation will occur. At times such access is quite simple, as in the case of a public area. Observing the interaction of individuals as they meet others on a street corner, for example, affords easy access to the investigator, who only needs to be at the site and begin observing. In other situations, however, more extensive bargaining is necessary to gain admission to an observation site. The researcher exploring RQ_2, for example, would probably face some difficult negotiation in gaining admission to a physician's physical examinations. In cases where permission must be granted for admission, *the individual who controls access to the observation site* is known as the **gatekeeper.** In some situations, access through a gatekeeper can be as simple as a request in the form of a letter or telephone call. In other situations, negotiation with gatekeepers can be significantly more complicated, sometimes requiring bargaining about when observation will take place, where the observation will occur, whom will be observed, and, perhaps, gatekeeper review of observation notes prior to their release. In such bargaining situations, it is important that the investigator remain aware of the goals of his or her study and the potential impact of agreements on the observation. There are also situations in which a hierarchy of gatekeepers needs to provide approval for a researcher's access. A number of years ago I proposed a naturalistic observation of mentally handicapped individuals residing in a group home facility. In negotiation with the first tier of gatekeepers, the people in charge of the group homes, I encountered little opposition. However, because the group homes were organized under state funding, approval was required at the state level, and was denied on the basis of the constitution of the organization, which forbade researcher access.

Selecting an Observer Role

As well as gaining access to the observation site, the naturalistic observer needs to determine how the observation will be conducted. Will the observation be overt or covert, and how actively will the researcher participate in the environment being observed? Based on these decisions, Raymond Gold (1958) identified four potential roles that might be adopted by the naturalistic observer: (1) the complete observer, (2) the observer as participant, (2) the participant as observer, and (4) the complete participant.

The **complete observer** records *behavior without any interaction between the researcher and participants, and without participants being aware that they are being investigated.* The principal advantage to this approach is that it affords the greatest degree of researcher objectivity, because he or she maintains some distance from those being observed. However, the absence of participant–researcher interaction reduces awareness of participants' subjective states and insights that are only available through direct interaction. Also, the presence of an individual unique to the setting, who appears to be observing, is likely to cause some unease for participants, and may influence their behavior, a form of reactivity effect. Finally, the role of complete observer raises the ethical dilemma of observing participant behavior without participant consent.

The **observer as participant** records *behavior with minimal interaction between the researcher and participants, and with participants who are aware that they are being investigated.* As well as reducing the ethical dilemma by providing for participant consent, this approach also permits greater awareness of participants' subjective insights because there is the potential for some interaction. However, researcher–participant interaction is kept to a minimum to retain the highest possible degree of objectivity.

The **participant as observer** records *behavior and is even more actively involved in the environment, but with the participants' awareness that they are being investigated.* This is the most commonly used observer role. Bogdan and Taylor (1975) define it as, "research characterized by a period of intense social interaction between the researcher and the subjects, in the milieu of the latter" (p. 5). As a result of the intense interaction, observers become intimately aware of the attitudes, beliefs, and values of the participants, and learn much about participant behavior through firsthand experience. However, by becoming intimately involved, the researcher may begin to sacrifice some objectivity, and risk "going native." **Going native** is *the tendency on the part of a researcher to become so involved in the situation being observed that, in adopting observed behaviors, he or she loses awareness or objectivity regarding those behaviors.* This tendency was initially identified by anthropologists who, during observations of indigenous populations, began to behave like the group being studied and began "going native."

The final role, that of **complete participant,** involves *the observation of behavior with the researcher being completely immersed in the environment being observed, and without participants being aware they are being investigated.* The complete immersion of the researcher in the setting provides access to the most firsthand knowledge, and risks the least reactivity effect because participants are unaware of their being studied. However, the successful integration of a researcher into a novel setting is likely to be quite difficult and time-consuming. Once integrated, the danger of going native is also enhanced. There is also, as with the complete observer role, the ethical dilemma of covert observation.

Reducing Reactivity Effect

Regardless of the role adopted by the researcher, the mere presence of a novel individual in a research setting may influence participant behavior. Reduction of such reactivity effects can most obviously be achieved by reducing the awareness of a researcher's presence. Covert and unobtrusive observation, such as that achieved using a one-way mirror or hidden camera, limits awareness, but raises serious ethical concerns. More frequently, awareness is reduced by the researcher adapting to the norms of the observation site, dressing like those being observed, and remaining as inconspicuous as possible. Even then, participants are likely to demonstrate some adapted behavior due to the researcher's presence. To reduce this influence even further, most naturalistic observers make a case for **sustained observation,** *observation undertaken for a long enough period of time that participants become acclimated to the presence of the researcher, and once again behave naturally.* There is, however, no agreement about how long such acclimation takes.

Developing Observational Notes

During the course of observation, the researcher develops an extensive set of notes regarding important observations. Two kinds of entries are generally recorded in the observer's notes: field notes and the observer's comments. **Field notes** are *detailed records of who did what, when, and where during the course of an observation session.* The **observer comments,** kept distinct from the field notes, are *records of the behavior of the researcher during the setting, his or her feelings during that session that might have influenced the observations, and awareness of any emerging patterns in the observation that might assist with data analysis.*

Early in an observational investigation, the notes recorded will often be quite impressionistic, detailing the layout and appearance of the research setting, describing the participants involved, and so on. As the investigation progresses, the notes generally become increasingly focused on the emerging interests of the researcher. In example of Internet use by adolescents (R_1), the initial notes might focus on the kind of computer used, the layout of the room, the form of Internet access, the presence of other individuals, participant attire, and so forth. However, as the researcher's awareness of different use patterns by males and females became apparent, his or her notes would focus more narrowly on those distinctions.

The amount of time collecting observational notes is determined primarily by the goals of the investigation. Researchers must determine at what point they have acquired a fair representation of observed behaviors while being assured that observation was sustained long enough to reduce any reactivity effect. It is not uncommon for individual observation sessions to last several hours, or for observational investigations to continue for several months before the researcher feels comfortable with the completeness of his or her observations. Many times, however, pragmatic limits, such as a publication deadline, or gatekeeper agreement, may force the researcher out of the field prior to a feeling of completeness, which creates a difficult dilemma for the investigator.

Analyzing and Reporting Observation

While the analysis of data for positivistic methodologies is generally postponed until data collection is complete, the inductive analysis of naturalistic observation begins at the same time as data collection. In naturalistic observation, the analysis is often a lengthy process involving the creation of multiple copies of the observational notes that are then cut apart into individual observations. The individual observations are then categorized according to emerging themes or patterns observed in the data. Many of these patterns emerge during the course of the observation and are suggested by the observer's comments. The individual observations are then used as evidence for the validity of the developing patterns, with the result that the analysis becomes the creation of a set of generalizations relating to the observed phenomena.

Among the best known inductive analysis techniques is Glaser & Strauss's (1967) **grounded theory method.** Using inductive reasoning *propositions are generated that are believable, comprehensive, applicable, and grounded.* In other words, the patterns suggested by the analysis should be plausible, should account for most of the observational data, should be capable of future evaluation using similar or alternate methods, and should be clearly based on the data.

Reports of the results of naturalistic observation usually consist of the series of propositions or hypotheses generated, followed by verbatim examples of observational data that support their existence. Often, frequencies of support for particular propositions are also included. For example, a researcher may note that 85 observations, or 10% of the total observations, were suggestive of the proposed pattern.

Interviewing Procedures

If the goal of the qualitative researcher is to elicit detailed description and understanding of communication behavior directly from participants through an interview, five different, though somewhat intertwined, steps need to be followed.

Framing a Research Problem

As with naturalistic observation, the problems guiding qualitative interviewing are generally worded as open-ended questions. Three examples of appropriate problem statements for the interview method suggest the possible research goals:

RQ$_4$: What is the perception of college students regarding their overall media use?

RQ$_5$: What is the perception of a long-time faculty member regarding student quality?

RQ$_6$: How do corporate employees perceive changes in the corporate structure?

As with the initial problems posed by the observational researcher, focus and refinement of interview problem statements may continue throughout the investigation, as suggested by the interview data.

Once again, the initial formulation of the problem statement requires clarification about who will be the target of the investigation and where the interviewing will occur. In RQ$_4$, a decision needs to be made regarding the number of students to be interviewed and the method for selecting those students. Due to the exploratory nature of qualitative interviewing, most frequently samples are selected using a nonprobability method, such as volunteer, purposive, convenience, or network sampling. The obvious problem with interviewing large numbers of participants is the limited amount of time and, therefore, limited detail that is available from each. RQ$_5$'s suggestion of a single source of information simplifies some of this initial decision making, though careful selection of a participant appropriate to the resolution of the research problem is still important. And, in the case of RQ$_6$, not only does the researcher need to determine how many participants to interview, but also the levels of the corporation they will come from. In hierarchical settings, such as a corporation, selection of participants from differing levels, such as upper versus middle management versus the rank and file, is likely to produce quite different interview data.

Beyond the decision of whom to interview, the researcher must decide where the interviewing is to take place. One option is to conduct the interview in the natural setting of the participant, such as a classroom or dormitory room for RQ$_4$, the faculty office or home in RQ$_5$, or the workplace in RQ$_6$. The advantage of such a site selection is that it affords some initial comfort to the participant, in that he or she is in a setting quite natural and familiar. It is also possible that some information will be shared more spontaneously in such a setting as that information is triggered by environmental cues. However, other information may be withheld if the respondent believes it is too sensitive to share in that setting. For example, a disgruntled employee would probably be less likely to display his displeasure with corporate policy if interviewed at the corporate headquarters instead of a more neutral site.

A neutral interview site, such as an office away from the participants' natural setting, or a library, restaurant, or other site, offers the advantage of neutrality, and may permit sharing of otherwise sensitive information. However, the greatest liability of such a site is that it generally requires greater time for the development of a comfortable interaction between the researcher and participant.

Deciding the Interview Format

While making decisions about whom will be interviewed and where the interview will occur, the investigator needs to also consider whether individuals or small groups be interviewed. Each approach offers some advantage. In a small-group setting, participants are often more likely to feel comfortable during the early stages of the interview, and information shared by one participant will often trigger further sharing of related information by others. However, individual interviews provide a greater sense of confidentiality to participants and, therefore, encourage the sharing of more private information.

The qualitative interview generally follows an *unscheduled funnel format* in which topics of discussion are based on the goals of the interview, but with the specific wording and ordering of questions left to the interviewer's discretion. Early questions in the interview are intended to provide some orientation to participants, with increasingly focused questions added as the interview progresses. For example, students interviewed on media use might initially be asked to relate the forms and amount of media that they use; later questions might focus on particular media and the students' specific preferences. Because inquiries are continually being refined, this approach to unstructured interviewing is often called a **focused interview.**

Also to be decided is the technique for recording interview data. While written notes are an option, recording the appropriate degree of detail while remaining alert to responses proves quite difficult for most investigators. Therefore, most qualitative interviewers choose to record sessions on audio- or videotape. The advantage of video recording is its ability to capture nonverbal nuances that might otherwise escape the researcher's attention. The somewhat more obtrusive nature of video recording equipment is likely, however, to inhibit free and open conversation between the researcher and participant, at least initially. Audio recording offers the ability to capture an accurate record of language and vocal cues without as significant a reactivity effect. Regardless of the technique adopted, it is important that the participants be alerted to the recording technique, and that they provide consent for the record to be made.

Collecting Interview Data

Once decisions have been made regarding the who, where, and how of the interview, data collection sessions can begin. Often, interview sessions will focus initially on the collection of background information from the participant and his or her perceptions of the research topic. The goals of these sessions are to develop general knowledge of the participant as well as to begin the development of rapport between the interviewer and interviewee. As rapport develops, and participants become familiar with and at ease with the interviewer, the questions can become more specific as topics of interest to the researcher emerge.

As rapport develops, and more detailed inquiries are posed, there will likely be times when the interviewer is interested in more detail than what is voluntarily provided by the participants. In such situations, *techniques to elicit increased detail from interviewees on a topic of discussion,* **probing strategies,** might be used. One commonly used strategy is the **mirror question:** *the response of the interviewee is summarized and presented as an inquiry to elicit further detail.* If, for example, an interviewee responded to the question "What do you like to do to relax?" with "Read," the researcher might mirror that response and say, "So, you like to read?" Another approach often used following an interruption in the interview is a brief review of the interview prior to the recess, which serves to refresh the participant's memory and to encourage clarification, when necessary.

Deciding when the individual interview session and the entire investigation is complete is, as with naturalistic observation, complicated. Individual sessions should be long enough to assure that rapport is developed and maintained, and that the research goals are being met, but not so long as to result in fatigue or discomfort to the participants. With some experience, researchers learn to recognize cues from the interviewees that suggest the need for a recess. The decision about when the entire data collection process is complete should also be based on the achievement of research goals, though, once again, pragmatic issues such as deadlines and interviewee commitment often play a role.

Bogdan and Taylor (1975) astutely noted that "research is craft" (p. 101), and, as such, requires practice by the researcher. Qualitative interview techniques are not easy to master and require the committed effort of an investigator to perfect. Rapport development, probing, and recognition of participant cues are skills that can only be learned in the field.

Transcribing Interview Data

As the interview data are generated they must be converted into a **transcript,** a *verbatim written record,* for analysis. Depending on the goals of the investigator, this record may contain only the words said by the researcher and participant, or it may contain nonverbal cues as well. Also included in the transcripts are interviewer comments, suggesting the behavior of the interviewer during the session, feelings of the interviewer that might have influenced the session, emerging patterns in the interview, and questions for future sessions. Regardless of the detail required, accuracy is important. Therefore, careful supervision of the transcription process is necessary, as is the need to complete transcripts as soon after a session as possible to assure the most accurate reflection of data.

Analyzing and Reporting Results

Analyzing the results of the qualitative interview, like naturalistic observation, begins with the initiation of data collection. Transcripts, as they are produced, are often copied, cut apart into individual response units, and categorized according to emerging themes or patterns. The individual responses are then used as evidence of the validity of the developing category scheme and propositions are posited. As discussed previously, the grounded theory method is a popular choice for qualitative analysis.

The report of naturalistic interview results typically presents the propositions with verbatim interview responses that support their existence as well as, perhaps, some frequency of response occurrence. To protect participant confidentiality, pseudonyms or fictitious names are commonly used to identify interviewees as they might have been in the reports of naturalistic observation.

Artifact Procedures

To reduce the influence of the investigator on the data collected, qualitative investigators may collect and analyze artifacts left behind as a result of communication. Once again, the steps required by the researcher are similar to the previous techniques and similarly intertwined.

Framing a Research Problem

Problems appropriate for resolution by artifact analysis are, like those of the first two techniques, most often worded as open-ended research questions, though their level of focus is sometimes more narrow than the initial questions posed for naturalistic observation or qualitative interview studies. Appropriate for resolution by analysis of artifacts are questions such as:

RQ$_7$: How are children's perceptions of family reflected in drawings that they produce?

RQ$_8$: How do students differ in their use of textbooks?

RQ$_9$: How are consumer patterns reflected in the refuse people produce?

RQ$_{10}$: How are students' attitudes reflected in their diary entries?

RQ$_{11}$: How are attitudes of Civil War soldiers reflected in letters they wrote to family and friends?

It is evident in each case that the research problem will be resolved by the analysis of materials left behind as a result of the communication process, whether those are drawings, letters, diary entries, or refuse.

Deciding Artifact Variety

As part of the development of a research problem, the investigator needs to decide on the variety of artifact to be examined. Qualitative analysts commonly discuss two general varieties: measures of accretion and measures of erosion. **Measures of accretion** are *artifacts that accumulate over time*. Included among the measures of accretion are such things as refuse, as well as various cases of soiling, or accumulations of dirt, coffee stains, fingerprints, or smudges. An investigator interested in RQ$_9$ would look at the categories of items and item packaging discarded by a consumer. The researcher examining RQ$_8$ might look at the accumulation of soil on the various pages of a textbook as an indicator of use. All measures of accretion may be referred to as natural or controlled. **Natural accretion** is *the buildup of artifacts that occurs without the assistance of the researcher;* **controlled accretion** occurs when *the researcher uses specific materials to control the amount or speed of accretion.* In the investigation of student use of textbooks, a researcher might use a soft ink to print pages that would easily smudge when handled by a student, thereby controlling the degree of accretion.

Also included as measures of accretion are textual and pictorial artifacts. Textual artifacts include such written materials as letters, diaries, essays, articles, logs, speeches, and scripts. Drawings, artistic renderings, and photographs are the most common pictorial artifacts. Textual and pictorial artifacts are general categorized as solicited or unsolicited, and public or private. **Solicited artifacts** are those *created at the request of the researcher,* whereas **unsolicited artifacts** are those *created without the solicitation of the investigator.* The researcher interested in children's drawings might use either variety. In one situation he or she might request that a group of students draw pictures of their families, while in another he or she might collect pictures drawn for other purposes.

Textual and pictorial artifacts also range from **public materials,** *generated for mass distribution,* to **private materials,** *generated for the exclusive use of the author or creator.* Most diary entries are private documents, intended only for use by their author or creator, whereas speeches are usually public materials, intended for an audience. Many artifacts are, in fact, a blend of public and private and are intended for use by a limited and somewhat restricted audience.

Measures of erosion are *artifacts that wear down over the course of time.* Some examples include the wearing down of painted, printed, upholstered, carpeted, or tiled surfaces as a result of use. For example, common traffic patterns in a room can be determined by examining wear patterns on carpeting or linoleum. Use of textbooks can be explored by evaluation of wear on pages or the spine. Evaluation of keyboard use can be determined by how much the letters on the keyboard have worn down. As with measures of accretion, these can be natural or controlled. A researcher interested in favored seats in a classroom might use an easily eroded paint so that seats receiving the most use will lose their paint at a controlled rate, rather than waiting for natural erosion to occur, which will take longer to become apparent.

Accessing the Artifacts

Once a decision has been made about the variety of artifacts to be analyzed, access to those artifacts is the next obstacle. If the artifacts are a part of the public record, as is the case with many public speeches, dramatic scripts, and literary works, access can be quite simple. However, if the materials are rare, or to some degree private, the process can be more difficult. Private materials are generally accessible only through negotiation with gatekeepers, those who control access, or by covert means, which will lead to serious ethical issues regarding subject privacy. When dealing with gatekeepers, care must be exercised to assure that the goals of the investigation are not compromised. Also of some concern is the potential for the selective deposit and accuracy of some artifacts. In some situations, not all the artifacts produced are retained or made available to the researcher. In the case of the investigator evaluating letters written by Civil War soldiers, only a few of the many letters written during that period have been saved or deposited. Of those artifacts that were maintained, many are incomplete or damaged, which raises questions about their accuracy.

Analyzing and Reporting Results

While analysis of artifacts can be deductive, using techniques similar to that of content analysis, the focus of analyzing artifacts as a qualitative method is on inductive analytic methods. As with the previous two qualitative techniques, artifact elements are separated and categorized based on emerging patterns observed by the researcher, with individual elements used as evidence for the validity of the category scheme. Results are reported as a series of propositions, each with supporting examples and frequencies of occurrence.

Regardless of whether naturalistic observation, interviewing, artifact analysis, or some combination of these or other qualitative methods is used, the goal of the qualitative investigator is the development of inductively based propositions regarding natural communicative behavior, with detailed, descriptive evidence of their validity.

Over the course of the past four chapters, you have examined a number of methodologies common to the study of communication. While each alone can provide some answers to problems generated by scholars of communication, the best resolution to those problems is the triangulation of methods, *the use of multiple methodologies to examine a single problem in order to develop the closest approximation to truth.* Positivists and phenomenologists, quantitative and qualitative researchers, must work together if the knowledge central to our discipline is to continue to deepen, grow, and prosper.

12

Statistical Analysis

Defining Statistics

For many introductory communication research students, few topics are as intimidating as the mention of statistics. However, an understanding of basic statistical approaches is necessary if one is to comprehend the published reports of much research. Statistics are the primary **data analysis tools,** *methods for inferring meaning from collected data,* used by quantitative researchers. They allow the transformation of **data,** *the raw material collected by the researcher,* into **information,** *the usable results of the investigation.* The transformation of quantitative data into information occurs through the use of mathematical manipulation. It is, therefore, possible to define **statistics** as *the mathematical manipulation of numerals for purposes of description or generalization of data.*

It is important to recognize that there is nothing magical about statistics. As tools of the researcher, they are only as useful and as accurate as the data that they are used to manipulate. As a result, if a researcher uses faulty research methods and generates erroneous data, the statistics generated will be inaccurate descriptions or generalizations. Likewise, if inaccurate manipulation is conducted on valid data, inaccurate results will be produced.

It is also important to recognize that not all scientific data are analyzed using statistical methods. You discovered in the previous chapter that much of the analysis done by qualitative researchers uses an inductive approach. Even those investigations, however, often employ some statistical techniques to simplify descriptions of the reported results. A qualitative interviewer might, for example, report the percentage of overall responses that were consistent with a developed category, an elementary form of statistical analysis. As a consequence, some comprehension of statistics is necessary, regardless of your methodological orientation. This chapter is not intended to make you a statistician, as that would require several intensive semesters of study, but to expose you to elementary statistical manipulations commonly used by communication researchers and show you how you can interpret the results of their investigations.

Statistical analysis can be divided into two basic forms: descriptive and inferential statistics. **Descriptive statistics** are *mathematical manipulations intended to simplify and summarize data in a convenient form, providing a synthesis of the data.* **Inferential statistics** are *mathematical manipulations intended to generalize from a sample to a population or universe, or to examine possible relationships between two or more sets of data.* The level of data being manipulated dictates the application of specific statistical methods. You will recall from Chapter 4 that data can be nominal, ordinal, interval, or ratio. The valid choice of statistical method depends on awareness of the level of data being described or generalized.

Descriptive Statistics

Graphic Summaries

When researchers have collected vast quantities of data, descriptive statistical techniques are often used to summarize that data for ease of reporting. One of the simplest of the descriptive strategies is the development of a *frequency distribution table,* sometimes called an *f*-table. Such a table *lists each measurement level that exists along with the frequency of observations that correspond to that level.* For nominal or ordinal data, frequency distributions are often quite simple. If presenting the males versus females in a research methods class, and there are eleven males and fourteen females in attendance, the distribution could be presented as M = 11, F = 14. If presenting the ordinal distribution of letter grades received on a recent examination the distribution might be A = 4, B = 8, C = 8, D = 3, F = 2.

Often, when presenting frequency data, researchers desire a more visually stimulating display rather than the simple frequency distribution table. Frequency data at the nominal or ordinal levels can be summarized in one of three graphic forms: the bar graph, the pie chart, and the line graph. The **bar graph** *compares the frequency counts of nominal or ordinal data using a series of disconnected bars suggesting* *the categories on the x-axis and frequency on the y-axis.* An example using the frequency data of examination letter grades, presented above, is shown in Figure 12.1.

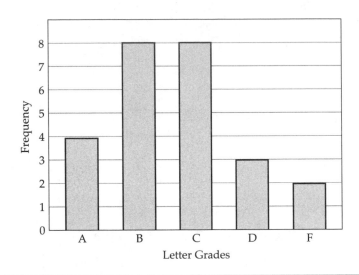

FIGURE 12.1 *Bar Graph of Examination Grade Frequencies*

The **pie chart** is used to *represent graphically the proportion of a whole represented by nominal or ordinal categories.* In order to present frequency data as a pie chart, the data must first be converted to the proportion of the whole. If the investigator is interested in the comparative frequencies of males and females in a class, as presented above, it would first be necessary to compute the proportion of the whole class that is male and the proportion that is female. Proportion is calculated by dividing the frequency in the subgroup of interest by the frequency of the entire group. In the case of male students in our example, the calculation would be 11 (the number of males)/25 (the total number of students in the class), which equals .44. The proportion of females should compute to be .56, though you can, and in practice should, check to be sure. Once the proportions are known, a pie chart can be developed by multiplying each proportion by 360 degrees, the angular measure of a circle. The result suggests the angle needed to divide that proportion of the pie. In our example, males would be represented in (.44)(360), or 158.4 degrees of the circle, and females in (.56)(360), or 201.6 degrees of the circle. Dividing out those sections of the circle will yield a pie chart such as that presented in Figure 12.2.

The third graphic method of presenting nominal or ordinal frequency data is the **line graph,** which is usually *used to suggest changes in frequencies that occur over a period of time.* If, for example the frequency of As awarded on a series of examinations was presented, the x-axis would represent the individual examinations and the y-axis the frequency of the awarded grade, as shown in Figure 12.3.

The *f*-table for interval or ratio data is quite similar to the nominal/ordinal presentation. Scores received on a 10-point quiz with their accompanying frequen-

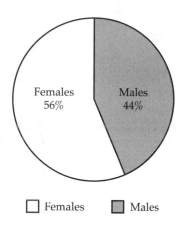

FIGURE 12.2 *Pie chart of Gender Distribution*

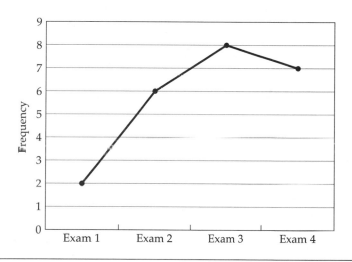

FIGURE 12.3 *Line Graph of Frequency of A's Awarded*

cies might be presented as: 10 = 1, 9 = 3, 8 = 8, 7 = 8, 6 = 3, 5 = 0, 4 = 1, 3 = 0, 2 = 1, 1 = 0. This would indicate that one person scored a ten, three scored a nine, eight scored eights, and so on. The greatest change occurs when the frequency data are presented graphically. The three common graphic representations of interval or ratio data are the histogram, the frequency polygon, and the frequency curve.

The **histogram** looks *much like a bar graph, with the key distinction being the adjoining nature of the bars.* Individual interval or ratio levels are presented along the x-axis, with the y-axis representing the frequency of observation. A histogram for the scores achieved on the 10-point quiz, referred to above, is presented in Figure 12.4.

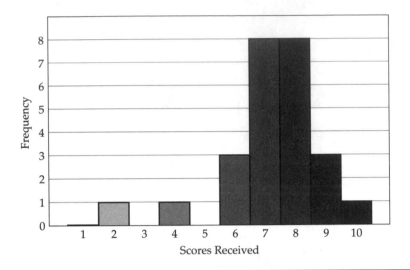

FIGURE 12.4 *Histogram of Scores Received on a 10-Point Quiz*

The **frequency polygon** *resembles a line graph, though it presents the interval/ratio levels on the x-axis, and the frequencies of observation on the y-axis.* Essentially, the frequency polygon can be developed by connecting the midpoints at the top of each bar on the histogram. Figure 12.5 shows the frequency polygon for the quiz data.

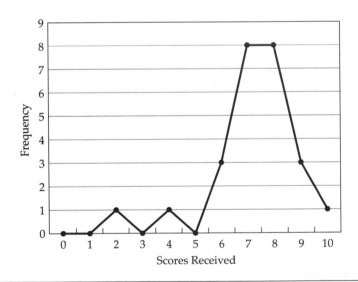

FIGURE 12.5 *Frequency Polygon of Scores Received on a 10-Point Quiz*

Finally, *if the straight, broken lines of the frequency polygon are smoothed and rounded to a best fitting curve,* we would have a **frequency curve,** such as shown in Figure

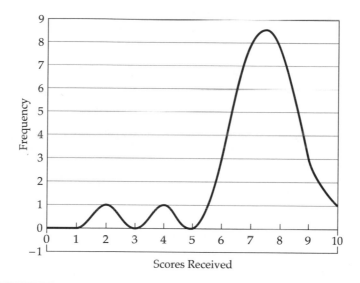

FIGURE 12.6 *Frequency Curve of Scores Received on a 10-Point Quiz*

12.6. The advantage to the frequency curve is its ability to be described by researchers based on its kurtosis, and skewness. **Kurtosis** *refers to the curves peakedness or flatness.* If the curve is *quite peaked,* as demonstrated in Figure 12.7, it is referred to as **leptokurtic.** If, on the other hand, the peak is *somewhat flattened,* as shown in Figure 12.8, it is referred to as **platykurtic.**

FIGURE 12.7 *Leptokurtic Frequency Curve*

FIGURE 12.8 *Platykurtic Frequency Curve*

FIGURE 12.9   *Negatively Skewed Frequency Curve*

Skewness *refers to whether the peak of the curve falls to the left or right of center.* If, as in Figure 12.9, it is *right of center,* it is said to be **negatively skewed.** If to the *left of center,* it is **positively skewed,** as shown in Figure 12.10. *When the frequency curve is symmetrical and bell-shaped, neither leptokurtic nor platykurtic,* it is generally called a **normal curve,** or a bell curve, shown in Figure 12.11.

FIGURE 12.10   *Positively Skewed Frequency Curve*

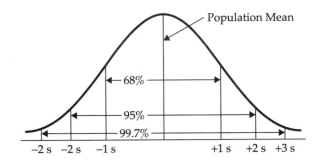

FIGURE 12.11   *The Normal Curve*

Summary Statistics

While frequency distribution tables and graphics are often used, many times researchers are interested in simplifying data without the space consumption required of tables or graphs. In such situations, summary statistics, or single numbers representative of the data, might be calculated. The two most common summary statistics are the measures of central tendency and measures of dispersion.

Measures of Central Tendency.   *Indexes of the typical score within a set of data* are the **measures of central tendency.** The three most commonly used measures are the mode, median, and mean.

Mode.   The mode, generally abbreviated as Mo, is *the level of a measurement scale that occurs with greatest frequency, or the most frequently occurring score.* It is the only measure of central tendency appropriate for all levels of data from nominal to ratio. It is determined by selecting the level of measurement, or score, that occurs most often in a set of data. For example, the mode for the gender composition of a research methods class, mentioned earlier, would be female, as that is the level with the greatest frequency of observed cases. In the array of letter grades received on an examination, presented in the same section, the modes would be B and C. In that case, two levels are tied for highest frequency of observation, both having eight cases, and the distribution would, as a result be called a **bimodal distribution,** *one with two modes.* If *three or more modes are present in a distribution,* researchers refer to it as **multimodal,** and each of the individual modes is reported. In one final example, if a group of seven students were tested and received the following scores, 55, 65, 72, 80, 90, 95, 95. the mode, or most frequently occurring score, would be 95. As is evident, particularly from this last example, the mode is insensitive to the variety of scores presented and is instead concerned only with frequency of occurrence.

Median.   A somewhat more sensitive measure of central tendency, appropriate for all data at the ordinal, interval, or ratio level, is the **median,** the *middle point in an ordered distribution of the data.* This is the point at which 50% of the scores are greater and 50% are less. In order to calculate the median, commonly abbreviated as Mdn, the researcher must first order the distribution of scores from a high to a low. If, for example, 11 students completed a quiz and letter grades were distributed as follows, 2 As, 5 Bs, 3 Cs, and 1 D, the ordered array would appear as follows:

A, A, B, B, B, <u>B</u>, B, C, C, C, D

Once ordered, the median is determined by finding the midpoint in the array. In this case, with an odd number of scores, the midpoint is at the sixth score, the under-scored B, because at that point there are an equal number of greater and lesser scores in the distribution. Using the same technique, it is possible to determine that the median of the seven test scores mentioned in the previous section would be 80. At that point, three scores are higher in the distribution, and three are lower.

When there are an even number of scores in the ordered distribution, the two middle scores are added together and divided by two in order to calculate the median. So, for example, the median of the following set of scores received on an examination, 100, 98, 94, 90, 32, 10, would be equal to 94 + 90/2, or 92. Again, this is the point at which half of the scores are greater and half lesser than the computed value. However, as is again suggested by this latest example, the median continues to be relatively insensitive to some scores in the distribution, particularly those that are most extreme.

Mean. The most sensitive measure of central tendency is the **mean,** commonly abbreviated as $\overline{X}$, and defined as the *arithmetic average of a set of scores.* The mean is appropriate only for data at the interval or ratio levels, and is computed by adding the individual scores and dividing the sum by the number of scores in the distribution. The formula for calculating the mean is:

$$\overline{X} = \Sigma X / N$$

where ΣX = the sum of scores in a distribution and N = the number of scores in the distribution.

To illustrate the calculation of the mean, imagine that we have a set of seven test scores, 55, 60, 75, 85, 90, 95, and 100. To compute the mean we would add together each of the scores, arriving at a sum of 560, and then divide that by the number of scores in the distribution, in this case seven. The mean would therefore be 560/7, or 80. The mean is the only measure of central tendency that takes into consideration all of the scores in a distribution, and it is, therefore, the most commonly used when data levels permit its computation.

Measures of Dispersion. While the measures of central tendency provide a typical score of a distribution, they provide no information about how much the scores are dispersed about them. The mean of the following seven examination scores, 80, 80, 80, 80, 80, 80, 80, is identical to the mean for the seven scores provided in the previous section, though it is clear that there is considerably more variation in the previously mentioned data. **Measures of dispersion** provide *an index of the spread or variability of scores in a data set.* The most frequently used measures of dispersion are the range, variance, and standard deviation.

Range. The simplest index of dispersion, appropriate for data at the ordinal, interval, or ratio levels, is the **range** (R). It is computed as the highest score in an ordered distribution minus the lowest score in the distribution, or

$$R = X_{hi} - X_{lo}$$

In our example of seven exam scores, all being 80, the range would be $80 - 80$, or 0, suggesting no dispersion of scores whatsoever. If we were to calculate the range for the set of scores, 55, 60, 75, 85, 90, 95, and 100, it would be $100 - 55$, or a range of 45. While the two sets have identical means, the range calculation clearly indicates greater dispersion in the latter set of scores.

Variance. The greatest limitation with range as an index of dispersion is its reliance on only the most extreme scores to determine variability. To correct for this weakness, interval and ratio data can be analyzed using **variance** (s^2), which is defined as *the average squared deviations of the scores from the mean.* While the definition may seem complicated, computation of the variance is relatively simple. The formula for its computation is

$$s^2 = \Sigma(X - \overline{X})^2/N$$

where X = each individual score, $\overline{X}$ = the mean of the distribution of scores, and N = the number of scores in the distribution.

To illustrate, take the seven examination scores from the previous section, 55, 60, 75, 85, 90, 95, and 100. To compute variance, we would first need to calculate the mean, which we have already determined to be 80. We would then subtract the mean from each individual score, with the following results:

$$55 - 80 = -25$$
$$60 - 80 = -20$$
$$75 - 80 = -5$$
$$85 - 80 = 5$$
$$90 - 80 = 10$$
$$95 - 80 = 15$$
$$100 - 80 = 20$$

Each of these deviation scores that we computed would then be squared:

$$(-25)^2 = 625$$
$$(-20)^2 = 400$$
$$(-5)^2 = 25$$
$$(5)^2 = 25$$
$$(10)^2 = 100$$
$$(15)^2 = 225$$
$$(20)^2 = 400$$

These squared deviation scores would then be added together, resulting in a sum of 1,800. That sum of squared deviation scores would then be divided by the number of scores in the distribution, in this case seven, resulting in a variance of 1800/7, or 257.14.

The general rule for interpreting variance is that the larger the score, the more variation among scores in the distribution. The greatest liability of the use of variance as a measure of dispersion is that, because it is the average *squared deviation units,* it is difficult to relate to the original data that have not been squared.

Standard Deviation. To alleviate the interpretation problem with variance, it is possible to compute *the square root of the average squared deviations of the scores from the means,* or the **standard deviation** (s). While the definition may sound quite complex, computation is as simple as taking the square root of the variance. In the case of our previous example, that would be $\sqrt{257.14}$, or 16.04. This procedure changes the index of variation back into the original data units, making interpretation more straightforward. Even more importantly, standard deviation provides a technique for estimating the probability of certain scores occurring within a sample, an important aspect of inferential statistics.

Inferential Statistics

While descriptive statistics serve to describe and summarize data sets, many times researchers wish to compare sets of data in an effort to discover significant differences or relationships between or among them. In those situations, inferential statistics come into play. These mathematical manipulations are generally divided into two varieties: analyses of differences and analyses of relationship.

Analyses of Differences

When researchers are interested in detecting potential differences between or among two or more sets of data, they may use one of several indexes of differences, some of the most common of which are the t-test, Chi-square, ANOVA, and discriminate analysis. Each of these statistical tests attempts to compare sample data set characteristics to a theoretical distribution of data, known as the normal curve, in an effort to determine whether the data sets are likely to have come from the same population. As the goal of analyses of differences is to search for statistically significant differences between the data sets, discovery of the data being from the same population distribution would support the null hypothesis, the argument that the samples are not significantly different. However, if it is possible to limit the likelihood of the data having come from a single population, it is possible to reject the null hypothesis in favor of a research hypothesis, and argue that the groups are significantly different.

The **normal curve,** presented in Figure 12.11, is *a symmetrical population distribution that is bell-shaped, with the mean of the population occurring with the greatest frequency.* The probability of selecting samples with means deviating from the population mean occur with diminishing frequency as we move away from the population mean in a positive or negative direction. Analysis of the normal curve suggests that a sample selected from a population with a deviation in the mean of within plus or minus one standard deviation unit from the population mean will likely occur in 68% of the samples drawn. A deviation of within plus or minus two standard deviations from the population mean would occur in 95% of the samples selected, and a deviation of within plus or minus three standard deviations from the population mean would account for 99.7% of the samples selected. Therefore, selection of a sample with a mean that is in excess of three standard deviation units different from the population mean is likely to occur in less than .3% of samples, or with a probability of .003 times out of one hundred samples.

Evaluation of the acceptance or rejection of a null hypothesis begins by the establishment of a **region of rejection** on the normal curve, or *a point at which data sets exceeding it would suggest that the sets came from a different population.* As is evident from our previous discussion, the further we move from the mean in the direction of the tails, the lower the chances that a sample from that population would be to demonstrate those characteristics. In establishing the region that will result in the rejection of the null hypothesis, most social scientists, including communication researchers, have, by convention, set a standard of 5%. The region of rejection is commonly referred to as the p-value, with most social scientists setting a $p < .05$ as the standard for rejecting the null hypothesis in favor of a significant difference. This means that the probability of the samples coming from the same population will occur less than five times out of one hundred if we are to reject the null hypothesis. Coincidentally, the p-value generally established by the natural sciences and medicine is $p < .01$, a somewhat more restrictive value, assuring even greater certainty that the groups come from different populations if the null hypothesis is rejected.

Once the region of rejection has been established, the researcher needs to decide if the difference test is one-tailed or two-tailed. If the research hypothesis suggests that the difference should occur in a particular direction, such as the hypothesis that females will outperform males on tests of advertising compre-hension, then any difference suggesting that the two perform similarly, or that the males outperform females, can be ignored. In that case the 5% region of rejec-tion can be located in the one tail of the normal curve, as shown in Figure 12.12. If, on the other hand, the research hypothesis is interested in any significant differ-ences, such as one suggesting that males and females perform differently on tests of advertising comprehension, the 5% p-value would be evenly divided into each tail, with the region of rejection in each tail being 2.5%, as shown in Figure 12.13.

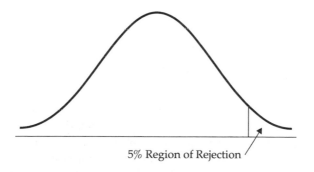

5% Region of Rejection

FIGURE 12.12 *One-Tailed Region of Rejection at p = .05*

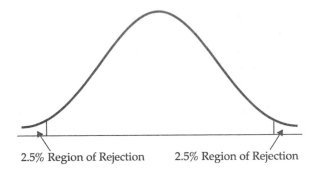

2.5% Region of Rejection   2.5% Region of Rejection

FIGURE 12.13   *Two-Tailed Region of Rejection at p = .05*

As a result, comprehension of any of the analyses of difference is the result of comparing a computed index to the normal curve in an effort to determine the probability that the sample data exceeds the region of rejection. If, in the interpretation of the computed index, the p-value is determined to be less than .05, the researcher could report that it was possible to reject the null hypothesis, that the observed differences were found significant. Even without further knowledge of analyses of difference, therefore, it is possible to begin interpreting published research based solely on the reported p-values.

Two of the simplest and most commonly used indexes of difference are the **t-test** and **Chi-square,** the computation and interpretation of which we will now examine. Students interested in the computation and interpretation of the somewhat more sophisticated ANOVA and discriminate analysis procedures are encouraged to refer to an introductory statistics textbook or to consider a course in statistical methods.

t-test.   The t-test is a simple index for computing differences between two independent groups with dependent measures that are at the interval or ratio level. The formula for computing the t-value is:

$$t = \overline{X}_1 - \overline{X}_2 / \sqrt{[(\Sigma d_1^2 + \Sigma d_2^2)/(n_1 + n_2 - 2)]\,[(n_1 + n_2)/(n_1 n_2)]}$$

where $\overline{X}_1$ and $\overline{X}_2$ are the means for each set of scores, Σd_1^2 and Σd_2^2 are the summed squared differences of each score from the group mean, n_1 is the number of scores in the first group, and n_2 is the number of scores in the second group.

Imagine that we have two groups that have been tested on a communication research examination, an interval or ratio scale, where one group is male, and the other female. Notice that the independent variable is nominal, but the important dependent variable is interval or ratio. Data at less than the interval level cannot be analyzed using a t-test. We are interested in discovering if the two groups perform significantly differently from one another. Because we are not predicting the direction of the difference, our test would be two-tailed. As communication researchers, we would most likely set our region of rejection, or our significance level, at .05, so that a $p < .05$ would be used to suggest a significant difference between groups. If, on the test, the five males scored 97, 96, 95, 94, and 93, and the females scored 95, 94, 93, 92, and 91, we could, using our understanding of descriptive statistics, compute the means: for the male group, 95 and the female group, 93.

To compute the squared difference scores for the males, we would need to subtract the mean from each individual score and square the difference:

$$97 - 95 = 2 \qquad 2^2 = 4$$
$$96 - 95 = 1 \qquad 1^2 = 1$$
$$95 - 95 = 0 \qquad 0^2 = 0$$
$$94 - 95 = -1 \qquad -1^2 = 1$$
$$93 - 95 = -2 \qquad -2^2 = 4$$

The squared differences are added together to get the value of 10 for Σd_1^2. The same procedure would be employed to determine the mean difference scores for the female group, with the female mean subtracted from each score, the differences squared, and summated. The result of this procedure should also result in Σd_2^2 equal to 10.

It is then possible to substitute data in the t formula. Because we have calculated the means for each group, the numerator of the formula will consist of 95 − 93. The first portion of the denominator consists of the summated squared difference scores of group one and group two, or, in our example, 10 + 10, divided by the sum of scores in the two groups reduced by two, or 5 + 5 − 2. The result of that computation is then multiplied by the sum of scores in the two groups, or 5 + 5, divided by the product of the number of scores in each group, or 5 × 5. The square root of the product of the two parts is then computed and divided into the numerator, the differences of the two means. Once substitution has been completed, the formula for t will look as follows:

$$t = 95 - 93 / \sqrt{[(10 + 10)/(5 + 5 - 2)]\,[(5 + 5)/(5 \times 5)]}$$

$$= 2/\sqrt{[20/8]\,[10/25]} = 2/\sqrt{(2.5)\,(.4)}$$

$$= 2/\sqrt{1} = 2/1 = 2$$

So the value of t is computed to be equal to two.

In order to interpret the results of the t-value, researchers refer to a table of percentage points for the t-distribution, available in most statistics textbooks and a number of statistical reference works. To use these tables, they must first establish whether they are interested in a one-tailed or two-tailed test. In our case, we have indicated an interest in a two-tailed test of significance. Also established must be the degrees of freedom for the computation, usually referred to as d.f. For the independent t-test, the d.f. is equal to the number of scores in group one, plus the number of scores in group two, minus two. Therefore, in our example the d.f. = 8. Using that information and reading across the table to the appropriate significance value, p = .05, we would discover that, for the groups to be found significantly different, the t-value would need to exceed 2.306. Because our t = 2, less than the required 2.306, we would be forced to accept the null hypothesis and suggest that the two groups were not significantly different.

However, by way of illustration, if we had, in our initial hypothesis, suggested that males would do better than females on the examination, and we could, therefore, use a one-tailed test, the conclusions would be different. Looking at a t-table for a one-tailed test with d.f. = 8, we would find that, to be significant at the .05 value, t must exceed 1.860. Because our t-value is equal to 2, it would be possible to reject the null hypothesis and suggest that males do, indeed, outperform females on the suggested test.

One final note of caution regarding the t-test: The formula discussed above only works when analyzing data from two independent groups. If the t-test was desired for testing two sets of data from a single group, such as, perhaps, the differences in a pretest versus post-test condition with a single group of individuals, a t-test for related groups would be required. Such adaptations of the t may be found in most introductory statistics textbooks.

Chi-square.   When the levels of measurement are at the nominal or ordinal level, and the t-test is inappropriate, the single-sample **chi-square** proves to be an easy to compute index of differences in observed frequencies between categories. The formula for computing chi-square, abbreviated as χ^2, is:

$$\chi^2 = [(O_1 - E_1)^2/E_1] + [(O_2 - E_2)^2/E_2] + \ldots + [(O_n - E_n)^2/E_n]$$

where, O_1, O_2 through O_n are the observed frequencies of each nominal category, and E_1, E_2 through E_n are the expected frequencies for each category.

Imagine that the instructor of a research methods course was interested in determining whether the composition of his or her course was significantly weighted toward freshmen, sophomores, juniors, or seniors. If it were assumed that there was no significant difference between the frequencies of each group within the class, the instructor would expect a class of 40 students to be composed of 10 freshmen, 10 sophomores, 10 juniors, and 10 seniors. This corresponds to the E-values in the chi-square formula, or the expectation that all groups will be evenly represented.

Having observed the actual composition of the class, the instructor knows that, of the 40 students present, 4 are freshmen, 20 are sophomores, 11 are juniors, and 5 are seniors. These observed frequencies correspond to the O-values in the formula.

The chi-square index is designed to evaluate the discrepancies between the observed frequencies and those expected if the groups are evenly represented. When the values of O and E are substituted into the formula for the single-sample chi-square, the result is:

$$\chi^2 = [(4 - 10)^2/10] + [(20 - 10)^2/10] + [(11 - 10)^2/10] + [(5 - 10)^2/10]$$

$$= [(-6)^2/10] + [(10)^2/10] + [(1)^2/10] + [(-5)^2/10]$$

$$= [36/10] + [100/10] + [1/10] + [25/10]$$

$$= 3.6 + 10 + .1 + 2.5 = 16.2$$

The instructor, being interested in a significance level of $p < .05$, could then consult a table of percentage points for the chi-square distribution found in a statistical reference work or statistics textbook. To determine the degrees of freedom, he or she would take the number of nominal categories being considered and subtract one. Therefore, the d.f. for our example would be four (the number of categories being evaluated) minus one, or three. In a table of the chi-square distribution, the intersect of d.f. = 3 and p = .05, is a chi-square value of 7.81473. Because our computed chi-square is greater than the critical value, it would be possible for the instructor to reject the null hypothesis, which suggests that the four groups are evenly distributed, in support of the research hypothesis that one or more of the class groups occurs with greater-than-expected frequency.

   With some modification, the chi-square index can be used to evaluate multiple samples and their division into categories. For example, our research methods instructor might be interested in whether males and females in the research methods course were similarly represented as freshmen, sophomores, juniors, and seniors. To conduct such an evaluation would require calculation of a multiple sample chi-square index, the formula for which can be found in any introductory statistics textbook.

Analyses of Relationship

When researchers are interested in evaluating the potential relationships between two or more sets of data they may use one of several indexes of relationship, some of the most common of which are correlation, regression, multiple regression, and factor analysis. Each of these indexes examines the pattern of variation between two or more sets of data in search of linear or curvilinear relationships, discussed in Chapter 2.

   The simplest, and most commonly used, index of relationship is the Pearson product moment correlation, commonly abbreviated as r. Students interested in other indexes, such as the Spearman rho, regression, multiple regression, or factor analysis, are once again encouraged to consult a statistics textbook or take a course in statistical methods.

Pearson r. For investigating the potential relationships between two sets of inter-val or ratio level data, the Pearson product moment correlation (r) proves quite useful. The formula for the index is:

$$r = \Sigma xy / \sqrt{(\Sigma x^2)\,(\Sigma y^2)}$$

where Σxy is the sum of the products of the differences between the X scores and the mean of the X scores, and the Y scores and the mean of the Y scores, Σx^2 is the sum of the squared differences between the X scores and the mean of the X scores, and Σy^2 is the sum of the squared differences between the Y scores and the mean of the Y scores.

Imagine that your instructor was interested in evaluating the relationship between student scores on a first exam and student scores on a final. Of the five students evaluated, scores for the two exams were as follows:

Student #	Exam 1	Exam 2
1	60	80
2	55	70
3	90	98
4	70	88
5	85	94

Our understanding of descriptive statistics allows us to compute the mean of the first exam scores, 72, and the mean of the second exam scores, 86. To determine deviations from the mean, the exam 1 mean is subtracted from each of the exam 1 scores to determine x:

X	–	Mean of X	=	x
60	–	72	=	–12
55	–	72	=	–17
90	–	72	=	18
70	–	72	=	–2
85	–	72	=	13

Then, the mean of the exam 2 scores is subtracted from each exam 2 score to find the second deviation score, y:

Y	–	Mean of Y	=	y
80	–	86	=	–6
70	–	86	=	–16
98	–	86	=	12
88	–	86	=	2
94	–	86	=	8

To begin completing the formula, each x score is multiplied by the corresponding y score, and the products are summed:

x	×	y	=	xy
−12	×	−6	=	72
−17	×	−16	=	272
18	×	12	=	216
−2	×	2	=	−4
13	×	8	=	104
		Σxy	=	660

Each x score is then squared and the sum of squared scores computed. The same is done for each of the y scores:

x^2	y^2
144	36
289	256
324	144
4	4
169	64
$\Sigma x^2 = 930$	$\Sigma y^2 = 504$

When the computed values are substituted in the formula for the correlation, the result is:

$$r = 660/\sqrt{(930)\ (504)} = 660/\sqrt{468720} = 660/684.63 = .964$$

Therefore, the Pearson product moment correlation between the two sets of exam scores is .964. Interpretation of the Pearson r requires understanding that the correlation coefficient can range from a −1.0, indicative of a perfect negative relationship, through a 0, suggesting no correlation, to a +1.0, indicative of a perfect positive relationship. The .964 coefficient for our two sets of data suggests a strong positive relationship between the exam scores, indicating that, as one score increases in value, the second score was likely to increase as well.

To evaluate the significance of the relationship, the correlation, a t-value can be computed using the following formula:

$$t = r\sqrt{(n-2)}/\sqrt{1-r^2}$$

where r equals the correlation coefficient and n equals the number of pairs of scores.

Using substitution, we can complete the calculation of t:

$$t = .964 \sqrt{(5-2)}/\sqrt{1-(.964)^2} = .964 \sqrt{3}/\sqrt{1-.9293}$$

$$= (.964)(1.732)/\sqrt{.0707} = 1.670/.2659 = 6.281$$

Significance of the correlation is then evaluated by referring to a table of the percentage points for the t distribution, with degrees of freedom equal to the number of pairs of scores minus two, or, in our example, d.f. = 3. Using a one-tailed distribution, with a significance level of .05, the critical value for t is determined to be 2.353. Because our computed value of t exceeds the critical value, we can reject the null hypothesis, that of no relationship, in favor of the research hypothesis, suggesting a significant positive relationship between scores on exam 1 and exam 2.

The Pearson product moment correlation can only be used when evaluating two sets of data, and only when those data are at the interval or ratio level. Other correlation coefficients, such as Spearman's rho, are appropriate if the data are at the ordinal level, while yet other related indexes, such as factor analysis or regression analysis, permit evaluation of multiple measurements or the prediction of one set of variables based on changes in another set. Pearson product moment correlation is also only sensitive to linear relationships between data sets. Data that are strongly related in a curvilinear manner may be incorrectly assessed as being unrelated if evaluated using the Pearson r.

Both descriptive and inferential statistics serve as powerful tools in the analysis of research data and the development of information. This chapter has provided you with a cursory overview of some of the most common statistical procedures used by communication researchers, and, perhaps, whetted your appetite to learn more.

Glossary

Abstract A print collection of periodical article locations arranged topically and followed by a brief summary of each listed article's content.

Active variable A variable to which the researcher determines the degree of participant exposure.

Alternative causality arguments Statements suggesting a cause-effect relationship between factors other than the independent variable and a dependent variable.

Alternative hypothesis A hypothesis suggesting a different form of relationship than that proposed by an original hypothesis.

Applied research Research whose goal is the resolution of a practical problem.

Analogical reasoning A logical method that begins with a specific case and applies it to another specific case based on the similarities between the two.

Analyses of differences Inferential statistics used to detect potential differences between/among two or more sets of data.

Analyses of relationships Inferential statistics used to detect potential relationships among/between two or more sets of data.

Analysis A function of the survey/interview method that permits the description and explanation of why certain conditions exist or occur.

AND A Boolean logical operator that searches for all sources that contain both/all keywords in the statement.

Annotated bibliography A collection of sources related to a researcher's topic of interest with each citation followed by a brief annotation.

Annotation A summary of the content of a source including evaluative comments regarding the source, supplied by the researcher.

Anonymity The assurance for human subjects' that the researcher is unable to connect participant responses to the individuals who provided the responses.

Applied research Research whose goal is the resolution of a practical problem.

Artifacts Materials left behind as a result of communication.

Attrition The loss of research elements over the course of an investigation.

Authority A low rigor epistemological method characterized by the acquisition and acceptance of knowledge as a result of its presentation by a respected source.

Availability sampling Convenience sampling.

Bar graph Graphic representation of nominal or ordinal frequency data using a series of disconnected bars.

Basic research Research whose goal is the development of better theory.

Between-subject design A variety of factorial study in which a different group of subjects is used in each of the cells in the design diagram.

Bimodal distribution A set of data with two modes.

Blind review policy A procedure followed by many scholarly journals whereby articles are selected for publication without knowledge of the contributing author, thereby assuring selection based on quality rather than reputation.

Boolean logical operators Logical rules, including AND, OR, and NOT, used in computer-based resource searches to complete a customized search.

Boundary conditions The components of a theory statement that suggest all other factors that must be true for the theory to remain valid.

Causal reasoning   logical method that attempts to establish a cause effect link between events.

Cell   A single, unique block within a design diagram.

Census   The collection and investigation of all elements within a population or universe.

Chicago School   The group of sociologists at the University of Chicago who adopted and popularized qualitative methods.

Chi-square   Statistical analysis of differences for two or more groups with dependent measures at the nominal or ordinal level.

Clarity   A characteristic of a valuable theory: The terms used are clearly and precisely defined and the logic is consistent.

Closed-ended question: A variety of survey/interview inquiry in which response options are provided by a researcher and respondents must select from those options.

Closed-ended research question   A research question that specifies the form or direction of the relationship between constructs, permitting the exploration of a particular variety of relationship.

Coders   Individuals trained to assess and map data.

Comparison groups   Two or more groups within an investigation receiving different levels of an independent variable.

Complete observer   A naturalistic observation role characterized by the observation of behavior without any interaction between the researcher and participant, and without participants being aware that they are being investigated.

Complete participant   A naturalistic observation role characterized by the researcher being completely immersed in the environment being observed, but without participants' awareness that they are being investigated.

Computer-assisted data collection (CADAC)   The use of a computer in the design, presentation, or distribution of a survey instrument.

Computer-assisted telephone interviewing (CATI)   A variety of computer-assisted data collection in which a computer provides the questions in their appropriate order to a telephone interviewer who inputs provided responses into the computer.

Computerized self-administered questionnaires (CSAQ)   A variety of computer-assisted data collection that permits respondents to directly input data to presented questions at a computer.

Conceptual definition   The process of reducing the ambiguity of terms used in a problem statement by relating them to other constructs.

Conceptual fit   A characteristic of a good operational definition that suggests how well the definition retains the majority of the characteristics described by the conceptual definition.

Concurrent validity   A variety of validity that explores the relationship between a measurement scheme or procedure and another, previously validated, instrument or procedure using the same constructs.

Confidentiality   The assurance for human subjects' that, while the researcher will be able to relate responses to individual participants, those relationships will not be revealed publicly.

Constancy matching   A variety of matching in which all participants in all groups are kept uniform with regard to significant characteristics thought to influence the dependent variable.

Constructs   Terms within a problem statement that represent the things in which the researcher has an interest.

Construct validity   A variety of validity that examines a measurement's or procedure's consistency with the theoretical framework from which it evolved.

Content analysis   A methodology for the objective, systematic, and quantitative description of the manifest content of communication.

Content validity   A variety of validity that indicates a measurement's or procedure's ability to accurately evaluate or manipulate that which it purports to.

Continuous   Variables or constructs that can take on any value within a range from some low to some high.

Contrived material   Interactive content created by a researcher.

Control   Techniques for systematically ruling out alternative causes within an investigation.

Control group   The group in an investigation that receives no imposed treatment.

Controlled accretion   The buildup of artifacts using materials that permit control of the amount of or speed of accretion.

Convenience sampling   A nonprobability sampling technique whereby elements are selected because they are easily accessible.

Convergence technique A technique for evaluating concurrent validity in which the measurement or procedure being evaluated, and one or more already validated instruments or procedures using the same constructs, are administered to a group of individuals and examined for similarity of results.

Conversational rule A socially agreed-on prescription governing the structure of interaction.

Correlational Concerned with the form and extent of relationships between/among variables.

Counterbalancing The presentation of treatments or measurements to different participants in different permutations.

Cross-lag correlational design A variety of panel study that meets the necessary conditions to establish causality. In this design, a presumed independent and dependent variable are measured using self-report techniques. Then, at a later time, the same variables are once again measured and the relationship between the earlier and later times is evaluated.

Cross-sectional design A research design for the collection of data from a single point in time in order to create a description of conditions at that moment.

Curvilinear relationship A variety of linkage that suggests any relationship that is less direct than a linear relationship.

Data The raw material collected by a researcher during an investigation.

Data-analysis tools Techniques for inferring meaning from collected data.

Database Electronically searchable or machine-readable indexes and abstracts.

Debriefing The assurance of a human subject's freedom of choice when asked to participate in a research study. Following the data collection, subjects are informed of the goals and procedures of the study in which they participated.

Deductive reasoning A logical method that begins with one or more general rules and applies those rules to a specific case to develop a conclusion.

Demographic item A variety of factual inquiry soliciting information about participants' personal characteristics.

Dependent variable A variable that is expected to change as a result of the actions of the independent variable.

Derived terms Terms within a problem statement that have vague or ambiguous meanings.

Description A function of the survey/interview method that permits the documentation of current conditions or attitudes, or generation of pictures of conditions as they are manifested.

Descriptive statistics Statistics used to simplify and summarize data in a convenient form, providing a synthesis of the data.

Discrete Variables or constructs that take on a limited number of values and change in distinct steps.

Design diagram The graphic representation of a design statement.

Design statement A series of numbers separated by ×s that specify how many independent variables with how many levels are being investigated in a factorial study.

Double-barreled questions Survey/interview inquiries that solicit two or more responses from a single question.

Double bind question A variety of leading question that implies an affirmative response regardless of how participants respond.

Dual sampling The assurance of a human subject's freedom of choice when a sample is drawn from the population, thoroughly informed of the research, and asked to participate. A second sample is then selected, and, following general agreement, used in the investigation.

Ecological isomorphism The degree of similarity in form between the settings in which research is conducted and their real world counterparts.

Effects Those components of a theory statement that are expected to be influenced by the generative forces.

Elicited interaction Interactive content obtained by asking participants to recall or recreate previous interaction.

Empiricism A moderately rigorous epistemological method characterized by the development of knowledge through the sensory observation of real events.

Epistemology The branch of philosophy interested in the study of how humans acquire knowledge.

Equivalent A characteristic of an effective nominal measurement whereby the same attribute of the variable being mapped is compared and evaluated.

Ethics Rules and standards for proper behavior in any given situation.

Evolutionary A characteristic of science that refers to the growth and change of scientific findings over time.

Exempted review The level of IRB-PHS review permitted when there is no risk to participating subjects.

Exhaustive The characteristic of an effective nominal measurement in which every observation has one category into which it may be mapped.

Expedited review The level of IRB-PHS review permitted when only a minimal risk is posed to research participants.

Experiment A methodology for evaluating the influence of one or more independent variables on a dependent variable, while controlling for all intervening variables.

Experimental operational definition The operational definition that defines the steps a researcher must take in order to manipulate levels of a construct.

Experimental research design The overall plans for the conduct of experimental studies.

Ex post facto design The single-group post-test only design that uses an observed, rather than an active, independent variable.

External validity The accuracy with which the results of an investigation can be generalized to a different group than the one studied.

Face-to-face survey/interview A survey/interview technique in which data are collected during a direct encounter between the research and participant.

Face validity Content validity.

Factorial studies Experimental research designs that examine the influence of two or more independent variables as they simultaneously influence a dependent variable.

Factual inquiries Questions intended to elicit objective data regarding participant's background, habits, or behaviors.

Feeling thermometer The pictorial rating scale developed by the University of Michigan Survey Research Center for use with semiliterate populations.

Field experiment An experiment conducted in a setting outside the control of the investigator.

Field notes The record of naturalistic observation containing information about who did what when and where during the course of an observation session.

Filter question A variety of survey/interview inquiry that selectively redirects respondents to different sections of a questionnaire or interview schedule.

Flexibility A characteristic of a valuable theory that indicates the theory can change as new observation dictates.

Focus group A small group of, usually, between four and ten subjects selected from a population of interest and encouraged to freely discuss topics of interest to a researcher.

Focused interview An unstructured, funnel format interview often used in qualitative research.

Freedom from harm The right of a human subject to avoid physical, social, or psychological harm as a consequence of participating in a research study.

Freedom of choice The right of a human subject to freely choose to be involved in research investigations.

Frequency curve A graphic representation of interval or ratio frequency data in which the lines of the frequency polygon are smoothed and rounded in a best-fitting curve.

Frequency distribution table (*f*-table) A descriptive statistical method that lists each measurement level that exists along the frequency of observations that correspond to that level.

Frequency polygon The graphic representation of interval or ratio frequency data.

Full review The level of IRB-PHS review required when more than a minimal risk is posed to research participants.

Funnel format The questionnaire/interview schedule organization that begins with broadly stated questions followed by questions of increasingly greater focus and narrowed scope.

Garbage can research model Joanne Martin's (1981) suggestion that research problems evolve from researcher expertise or funding availability rather than from a desire for knowledge.

Garbology Analysis of refuse as artifact.

Gatekeeper An individual who controls research access to an investigation site or to participants.

General replication The duplication of an investigation using the same research problems and methodology, but with some alteration to procedures, measurements, the population or universe, and/or analysis techniques.

Generative force The component of a theory statement that motivates a change in other components.

Going native The tendency of a researcher to become so involved in a situation being investigated that awareness and objectivity are sacrificed.

Grounded theory method The method of inductive data analysis developed by Glaser and Strauss (1967) that generates comprehensive, believable, applicable, and grounded hypotheses.

Group equivalence The assumption that, prior to the imposition of an independent variable, all groups within an investigation were equivalent with regard to the dependent variable.

Hawthorne effect An effect produced when participants in a study behave differently as a result of knowing they are being observed.

Heuristic value A theory's ability to generate new areas for future study.

Highly directive instrument A questionnaire or interview schedule that consists primarily of closed-ended questions.

Highly nondirective instrument A questionnaire or interview schedule that consists primary of open-ended questions.

Histogram The graphic representation of interval or ratio frequency data using a series of adjoining bars.

History The regular, uncontrolled events that participants experience during the course of an investigation.

Hits The results of a computer-based search for reference works.

Holsti's formula A measure of intercoder reliability.

Hypothesis A declarative statement that suggests a predicted relationship between two or more constructs.

Incidence The proportion of the sample parameter represented within the target population or universe used in the selection of a stratified sample.

Independent variable A variable expected to influence a change in another variable.

Index A print collection of periodical article locations arranged topically.

Inducements Rewards offered for participation in an investigation.

Inductive data analysis The categorization of data based on emerging themes or patterns evident in the data, using the data as evidence for the validity of hypotheses developed.

Inductive reasoning A logical method that begins with the collection of several specific cases and, from them, develops some general rule.

Inferential statistics Statistics intended to generalize from a sample to a population or universe, or to examine possible relationships between/among sets of data.

Inflicted insight Baumrind's (1979) concern that information provided in a debriefing may have more negative psychological consequences than continued deception.

Information The usable results of an investigation.

Informed consent A method of ensuring a human subject's freedom of choice by providing a detailed explanation of the research, its goals and procedures, and risks and benefits prior to soliciting agreement to participate.

In loco parentis consent Informed consent solicited from those legally responsible for the welfare of potential human subjects.

Institutional Review Boards for the Protection of Human Subjects (IRB-PHS) Government-mandated bodies in organizations or institutions receiving federal funding that serve to protect the rights of human research participants.

Intellectual integrity The ethical principle concerned with the development of honest and dependable scholarship.

Intellectual resources The level of knowledge that a researcher brings to an investigation.

Interaction analysis A methodology for the systematic classification of verbal and nonverbal behavior in dyadic and small-group interactions.

Interaction Process Analysis (IPA) An early variety of interaction analysis developed by Bales (1950) for the study of small-group decision making.

Intercept sampling A probability sampling technique in which every n^{th} person to pass a selected spot chosen by the researcher is solicited for participation in an investigation.

Intercoder reliability A technique for assessing measurement reliability in which two or more observers are trained in the use of the measurement scheme and assigned to map the same events, with the consistency of their respective observations being evaluated.

Interlibrary loan The cooperative effort of libraries to make collections available to other institutions on request.

Internal citations References within a written document that suggest the source of information as found in the reference list.

Internal validity The accuracy of an investigation's results as influenced by the planning, design, and conduct of the investigation.

Interrupted time series design An experimental research design in which a single group of subjects is multiply pretested prior to a treatment, then multiply post-tested.

Inter-subject diffusion The effect produced when multiple participants come into contact with one another during the course of an investigation.

Interval measurement The third level of the Stevens's measurement hierarchy. It consists of the rank-ordering of observations with equal distances between mapped categories and the inclusion of an arbitrary zero point.

Intervening variable A variable that might somehow influence the relationship between the independent and dependent variables.

Interview A self-report methodology in which oral questions are used to elicit oral responses from research participants in order to resolve research problems.

Interview schedule A collection of inquiries to be used in an interview.

Intuition A low rigor epistemological method characterized by the acquisition and acceptance of knowledge because it "feels right" or because it is provided by some extrasensory source.

Inverted funnel format A questionnaire/interview schedule organization that begins with highly detailed questions, but the questions become successively broader and more general as the inquiry continues.

Inverted-U relationship A curvilinear relationship that suggests as one construct changes in value, the other construct will initially increase in value to some point where it will plateau and then begin to decrease.

Judgment sampling Purposive sampling.

Keywords Significant words used in the title or description of a catalogued reference work.

Known groups method A technique for assessing the construct validity of a measurement in which groups are formed using some theoretical foundation and then evaluated using the proposed measurement scheme.

Kurtosis The relative peakedness or flatness of a frequency curve.

Laboratory experiment An experiment conducted in a research setting created and controlled by the investigator.

Laboratory interaction Interactive content obtained from a researcher-controlled setting.

Latent Variables or constructs that cannot be directly observed but must be inferred from other observable constructs.

Leading questions Survey/interview inquiries that suggest the expected responses from participants.

Leptokurtic A frequency curve with a prominent peakedness.

Levels of measurement An index to the degree of quantification inherent in a measurement scheme.

Likert Summated Rating Scale A common unidimensional interval measurement that consists of a series of positively and negatively worded declarative statements, each accompanied by a five- or seven-point scale that assesses subject agreement or disagreement, approval or disapproval.

Linear relationship A variety of linkage that suggests that, as one construct varies, the other will change in a consistent manner.

Line graph A graphic representation of the changes in nominal or ordinal frequency data over time.

Linkages Terms within the problem statement that specify the form or direction of the relationship expected between or among constructs.

Literal replication The exact duplication of an investigation using the same research problems, methodology, procedures, measurement schemes, analysis techniques, and population or universe.

Literary material Interactive content selected from novels or dramatic works.

Literature review An essay summarizing or synthesizing the current state of knowledge regarding a topic of interest.

Longitudinal design A research design in which data are collected across some period of time.

Lottery A variety of simple random sampling in which elements are separated from one another, mixed in a container, and selected one at a time until a predetermined sample size is achieved.

Lottery without replacement A lottery where each selected element is kept out of the pool of elements thereby reducing the entire pool by one.

Lottery with replacement A lottery where each selected element is returned to the pool of elements thereby maintaining the size of the pool throughout the selection process.

Mail survey A survey using the postal service for distribution and data solicitation.

Manifest Variables or constructs that can be directly observed.

Mapping scheme The goal of a measured operational definition: Procedures are developed for the assignment of numerals to observations.

Matching A technique for assuring group equivalence in which participants in treatment, control, and comparison groups are matched to one another on the basis of characteristics thought to be important to the dependent variable.

Material resources The funding, materials, and personnel required for the conduct of an investigation.

Maturation A change in participants due to the passage of time.

Mean The measure of central tendency that identifies the arithmetic average of a set of data.

Meaningful covariance A requirement of causality when it is expected that the values of the independent and dependent variables will shift in a systematic and sensible manner.

Measured operational definition An operational definition that describes the steps an investigator must take to ascertain the existence or quantity of a construct.

Measurement The assignment of numerals to observations according to some specified rules.

Measurement reliability The consistency with which a measurement yields consistent results.

Measurement validity The accuracy of a measurement scheme.

Measures of accretion Artifacts that accumulate over time.

Measures of central tendency Descriptive statistics that provide an index to typical scores within a set of data.

Measures of dispersion Descriptive statistics that provide an index to the spread of variability of scores in a data set.

Measures of erosion Artifacts that wear down over the course of time.

Median (Mdn) The measure of central tendency that identifies the middle point of an ordered distribution of data.

Minimal risk The probability and magnitude of harm or discomfort anticipated in the research is not greater in and of themselves from those encountered in the performance of routine physical or psychological examination or tests.

Mirror question A probing strategy in which the response of an interviewee is summarized and presented as an inquiry to elicit further detail.

Mixed factorial design A variety of factorial study that combines a between-subject design and a within-subject design.

Mode (Mo) The measure of central tendency that identifies the level of a measurement scale that occurs with the greatest frequency.

Moderately scheduled An interview schedule that consists of key questions to be asked of respondents, but with the researcher afforded some flexibility in the ordering of the inquiry, or in the use of additional inquiries.

Multidimensional measurement A measurement scheme that evaluates two or more qualities or attributes of a construct under investigation.

Multimodal distribution A set of data with three or more modes.

Multiple-choice items A variety of closed-ended question in which participants are instructed to select the most valid of two or more researcher-provided options.

Multiple interrupted time series design An experimental research design in which two groups of subjects are multiply presented with one group exposed to a treatment, and then both are multiply post-tested.

Multistage cluster sampling A probability sampling technique used when an investigator is faced with very large populations or universes: The choices of elements are successively narrowed until a complete sampling frame becomes possible, with the final elements chosen from that frame.

Mutually exclusive A characteristic of an effective nominal measurement in which every observation must fit into one and only one of the mapping categories.

Natural accretion The buildup of artifacts without the assistance of a researcher.

Natural interaction Interactive content obtained in participants' natural settings.

Naturalistic observation A qualitative method that involves the overt or covert observation and recording of individuals' behaviors as they engage in everyday activities.

Negative linear relationship A linear relationship that suggests that, as one construct changes in value, the other construct will change in the opposite direction.

Negatively skewed A frequency curve that peaks to the right of center.

Network sampling A nonprobability sampling technique, often found in qualitative research, in which one element is drawn from a population/universe, and that element recommends others, who likewise recommend yet others.

Nominal measurement The lowest level of the Stevens's measurement hierarchy: It consists of the assignment of a name, label, or category to a variable, but with no quantification of the numeral intended.

Nonprobability sampling The selection of elements from a population or universe without the use of mathematical selection rules.

Nonreactive methods Research methods in which the potential for data bias is reduced by limiting the influence of the researcher on the development of data.

Nonspuriousness A requirement of causality whereby it is possible to dismiss or rule out intervening factors that may explain changes in the dependent variable.

Normal curve A symmetrical population curve that is bell-shaped, with the mean of the population occurring with the greatest frequency.

NOT A Boolean logical operator that searches for all sources that contain the initial keyword, but omits those that contain the keyword following the NOT instruction.

Null hypothesis A hypothesis of no relationship.

Numbers Numerals used in the measurement process that have quantitative meaning.

Numerals Symbols used in the measurement process that have no inherent quantitative meaning.

Observation A mapping technique in which a third party examines and evaluates communication phenomena using a prescribed mapping scheme.

Observed variable A variable that cannot be directly manipulated by the researcher, but must instead, be observed in its natural state.

Observer as participant The naturalistic observation role characterized by the observation of behavior with minimal interaction between the researcher and participants, and with participants who are aware that they are being investigated.

Observer comments A record of qualitative research that indicates the behavior of a researcher during an investigation, the feelings of the researcher that might have influenced the data collection, and awareness of any emerging patterns that might assist in data analysis.

One-tailed hypothesis A hypothesis that suggests a particular form or direction to an anticipated relationship.

On-line resources Materials obtained via the Internet or by e-mail.

Open-ended questions A variety of survey/interview inquiry that provides respondents with a wide latitude of response options, permitting them to provide as much detail as they see fit.

Open-ended research question A research question that leaves the direction or form of a relationship between constructs open, and asks whether any relationship exists between/among them.

Operational definition The observable indicators of a construct's relative presence or absence, or which procedures the investigator will follow in order to measure, observe, or manipulate the construct.

OR A Boolean logical operator that searches for all sources that contain any of the keywords included in the statement.

Ordinal measurement The second level of Stevens's measurement hierarchy: It consists of the rank-ordering of numerals from some low to some high, but with no assumption of equal spacing between the levels.

Overview materials Research resources that provide a general introduction to the various fields within the communication discipline.

Pairing A variety of matching in which each participant in the treatment, control, or comparison group is matched with participants in the other groups, based on characteristics thought to influence the dependent variable.

Panel approach A technique for assessing content validity by assembling a group of experts from within the appropriate field and asking them to evaluate the measurement's or procedure's ability to measure or manipulate what is intended.

Panel study A longitudinal survey design in which data are collected from the same sample selected from a population at several points in time, and following that single sample for a specific period of time in an effort to evaluate changes that occur.

Parallel forms technique A technique for assessing measurement reliability in which two separate but parallel measures are administered to a set of respondents and examined for consistency of results.

Parameters The specific characteristics required for inclusion in a category or group.

Paraphrase A rewording of an original work using the researcher's own words and style.

Parsimony A characteristic of a valuable theory that indicates that the theory uses the simplest logical presentation.

Participant as observer A naturalistic observation role characterized by the observation of behavior with active involvement of the researcher in the environment, and with participants' awareness that they are being investigated.

Pearson product moment correlation(r) Statistical analysis of relationships that investigate relationships between two sets of interval or ratio level data.

Periodicals Print publications issued at regular, recurring intervals such as magazines, journals, or newspapers.

Periodicity A potential problem with systematic sampling that occurs when the elements in the sampling frame are organized in a pattern, resulting in the over- or underrepresentation of certain parameters.

Personal attribute effect An effect produced when the physical characteristics of a researcher impacts the data provided by research participants.

Phenomenology The school of communication inquiry interested in the understanding of human communicative behavior from the actor's perspective.

Pie chart A graphic representation of nominal or ordinal proportional data.

Pilot test A ministudy designed to diagnose potential problems with an investigation, its procedures, or instruments.

Plagiarism The unauthorized use of the language and ideas of another while representing them as one's own.

Platykurtic A flattened frequency curve.

Population A group of people who share particular characteristics of interest to the researcher.

Positive linear relationship A linear relationship that suggests that, as one construct changes in value, the other construct will change in the same direction.

Positively skewed A frequency curve that peaks to the left of center.

Positivism The school of communication inquiry interested in the discovery of the finite set of rules governing all communicative behavior.

Post-test only, control group design An experimental research design in which a treatment and control group are randomly assigned. The treatment group receives some intervention that is withheld from the control group, and both are post-tested for comparison.

Post-test only nonequivalent control group design An experimental research design in which a treatment and control group are established; one group receives a treatment withheld from the other, and both groups are compared on post-tests of the dependent variable.

Predictability A characteristic of a valuable theory that requires that the generative force regularly yield a predictable effect.

Predictive validity A variety of measurement validity that reflects the ability of the measurement to accurately predict expected contingencies.

Prestige bias The tendency of self-report participants to provide answers to inquiries based on their self-perceived role in society.

Pretesting A technique for assuring group equivalence by evaluating an established treatment, control, or comparison group's performance on a dependent variable before the introduction of any treatment.

Pretest–post-test control group design An experimental research design in which a treatment and control group are randomly assigned and pretested for greater assurance of group equivalence. The treatment group receives some intervention withheld from the control group, and both are post-tested for comparison.

Pretest–post-test nonequivalent group design An experimental research design in which a treatment and control group are created and pretested for group equivalence. The treatment group receives some intervention withheld from the control group, and both are post-tested for comparison.

Presuppositonless Anderson's (1987) suggestion that qualitative methods are interested in collecting descriptive data while setting aside any preconceptions or hypotheses held by the researcher.

Primary source A manuscript written by the person who completed the investigation.

Primitive terms Terms resulting from the conceptual definition process that the community of scholars agrees have the same meaning.

Prior consent plus proxy consent A method of ensuring a human subject's freedom of choice: The person's general agreement to participate in an investigation is sought, as well as the name of a trusted acquaintance who will be provided with full disclosure of the research and who will provide consent for the subject to participate.

Private grant Monies provided by private organizations or institutions for the development of research.

Private materials Artifacts and texts created for the exclusive use of their author or creator.

Probability sampling The selection of elements from a population or universe in accordance with some set of mathematical rules, thereby permitting calculation of the probability of sampling error.

Probing strategies Interview techniques used to elicit increased detail from interviewees on a topic of discussion.

Proceedings Collections of papers presented at meetings or conventions, published by many professional organizations.

Public grant Monies provided by government bodies for the development of research.

Public materials Artifacts and texts generated for mass distribution.

Purposive sampling A nonprobability sampling technique in which elements are selected to a sample as a result of specific characteristics of interest to the researcher.

Qualitative methods A group of methodologies used to produce descriptive data.

Questionnaire A self-report technique in which written questions are used to elicit written responses from research participants.

Quota sampling A nonprobability sampling technique, popular until 1948, in which elements are selected from the population/universe in proportion to the incidence of some characteristic of interest to the researcher.

Random assignment A technique for assuring group equivalence in which participants selected for an investigation are assigned to treatment, control, or comparison groups based on some randomizing technique.

Random digit dialing (RDD) A variety of simple random sampling used when researchers anticipate contacting elements by telephone, and telephone numbers are produced using a random number generator or a table of random numbers.

Random numbers A variety of simple random sampling in which a sampling frame is consecutively numbered and elements are chosen as a result of digits generated by a computer program or from a specialized table.

Range (R) A measure of dispersion that is the difference between the highest and lowest scores in an ordered data set.

Rank order items Survey/interview inquiries that instruct participants to order a collection of items from highest to lowest.

Ratio measurement The highest level of the Stevens's measurement hierarchy: Observations are rank-ordered with equal distances between levels, and a true zero point is included.

Rationalism A moderately rigorous epistemological method characterized by the development of knowledge through the application of the rules of logic.

Reactivity effect The influence of researcher presence on the data collected.

Reality isomorphism A characteristic of a good operational definition that indicates how consistent the definition is with the way the constructs exist in the real world.

References A roster of scholarly works that have been used by the researcher.

Reflexive A characteristic of science whereby potential errors in logic or observations made by investigators are revealed so that they can be corrected.

Region of rejection The point on the normal curve at which data sets would be ruled as emanating from a different population/universe.

Reliability The consistency of a measurement scheme's results, or the consistency of a research procedures implementation.

Replication The ability to reproduce or recreate an investigation.

Research question An interrogative statement exploring the relationship between two or more constructs.

Respondents The group of individuals who complete a self-report measurement instrument.

Response rate The percentage of respondents solicited for participation in an investigation who complete the investigation.

Response set A mental tendency that develops when participants perceive an apparent pattern to responses and begin to respond to an inquiry or scale item without thinking, or with reduced sensitivity.

Right to privacy The right of a human subject to pick and choose the time and circumstances under which, and the extent to which, attitudes, beliefs, behaviors, and opinions are shared with or withheld from others.

Right to respect The right of a human subject to receive the respect due all human beings.

Risk/benefit ratio assessment A means of ensuring a human subject's freedom from harm: All the possible risks and discomforts to participants are evaluated and balanced against potential benefits to the individual and society.

Running subjects A seemingly innocuous statement that refers to human subjects of the data collection process that may indicate an infringement on their right to respect.

Sample A subset of a population or universe selected to represent the entire population or universe.

Sampling error The degree to which a sample's parameters differ from the parameters of the population or universe from which it was selected.

Sampling frame A complete list of all the elements in a population or universe.

Sampling rate The frequency with which elements are selected in a systematic sample.

Scholarly journals Primary sources of timely periodical information that provide the most significant fuel for most scholarly efforts.

Science The most rigorous epistemological method in which knowledge is developed through a combination of rationalism and empiricism.

Scope A characteristic of a valuable theory that refers to its ability to be used in a variety of contexts.

Secondary source A manuscript that is a summary of a primary source completed by an author other than the original investigator.

Self-report techniques Mapping techniques intended to evoke responses directly from the individuals being investigated, including interviews and questionnaires.

Semantic Differential Scale The multidimensional interval measurement developed by Osgood, Suci, and Tannenbaum that provides subjects with a construct followed by a series of seven-point scales bounded by bipolar adjectives.

Sensitization Changes in research participants as a result of their experience with research procedures.

Sequencing effect The sensitization that occurs when multiple treatments are provided to participants; each intervention is followed by a measurement to evaluate change.

Simple random sampling A probability sampling technique in which each element in the population or universe is afforded an equal opportunity of being selected to the sample.

Single-blind procedure A research method in which a researcher hires a confederate who knows nothing about a study's purpose or conduct and trains that individual to do the required data collection, but does not provide details about the data expected.

Single-factor studies Experimental research designs that examine the influence of only one independent variable or the dependent variable.

Single-group pretest–post-test design An experimental research design in which a single group is pretested, exposed to some treatment, and post-tested.

Single-group post-test only design An experimental research design in which a single group is exposed to some treatment, with a subsequent measure of the dependent variable.

Skewness The left or right shift of the peak of a frequency curve.

Snowball sampling Network sampling.

Solicited artifacts Artifacts created at the request of a researcher.

Solomon four-group design An experimental research design that combines both the prestest–post-test control group design and the post-test only, control group design.

Split half technique A technique for assessing measurement reliability in which a single measurement instrument is constructed with two or more parallel items for each construct to be mapped.

Standard deviation (s) A measure of dispersion that is the square root of the average squared deviations of a set of scores from their mean.

Statistical regression When research participants are selected based on their deviation from population/universe norms, the tendency over subsequent measures to naturally migrate toward the population/universe mean.

Statistics Mathematical manipulations for the purpose of description or generalization of data.

Strategies Interactive messages designed to accomplish a personal or relational goal.

Stratification variable The characteristic of interest to the researcher used to divide the sampling frame into subsets in order to select a stratified sample.

Stratified sampling A probability sampling technique in which the elements in the sampling frame are divided into subsets based on some stratification variable, and a proportional representation of each subset is included in the sample.

Subject assent In cases where in loco parentis consent is used, human subjects are provided with a cognitively appropriate explanation of the anticipated research and asked for agreement to participate.

Subjective inquiries Questions intended to elicit data about participants' values, beliefs, attitudes, opinions, or feelings.

Survey A self-report methodology in which questionnaires are used to generate the data required to resolve research problems.

Survey population/universe A limited subset of the target population/universe from which a sample is drawn.

Sustained observation A technique for reducing reactivity effect by observing for a long enough period that participants become acclimated to the presence of the researcher and behave naturally.

Syllogism The simplest form of deductive logic.

Systematic sampling A probability sampling technique in which every n^{th} element from a sampling frame is selected for study.

Tables of random numbers A published collection of randomly generated digits used for sample selection.

Target population/universe The group of human or nonhuman elements to whom/which the results of an investigation might be applied.

Telephone interview An interview in which the telephone is used for contacting respondents and collecting data.

Temporal ordering A requirement of causality: The independent variable must precede the dependent variable.

Tenacity A low rigor epistemological method characterized by the acquisition and acceptance of knowledge as a result of its survival over time.

Testability A characteristic of a valuable theory: The theory can be examined for its validity using empirical methods.

Test-retest approach A simple technique for assessing measurement reliability: A measurement is administered two or more times to the same group of respondents and then evaluated for consistency of results.

Theory A simplified generalization about how or why something occurs.

Threatening questions Survey/interview inquiries that cause unease, discomfort, or embarrassment to respondents.

Tightly scheduled An interview schedule that consists of a collection of specific questions to be asked in a specific order with no change in presentation from one respondent to the next.

Transcript Verbatim textual records of interactive or interview content that contain detail appropriate to the purpose of an investigation.

Treatment group The group in an investigation that receives some level of the independent variable under investigation.

Trend study A longitudinal survey design in which data are collected from several different samples selected from a single population at different points in time, with the purpose of evaluating changes that occur in the population.

Triangulation The conduct of research using a variety of research methods for the investigation of any phenomenon in order to develop a closer approximation to truth.

Truncate To shorten keywords to enhance a computer search.

t-test A statistical analysis of difference for two independent data sets with dependent measures that are at the interval or ratio level of measurement.

Tunnel format A type of questionnaire/interview schedule organization in which all the questions are of equal specificity and detail.

Two-tailed hypothesis A hypothesis that does not specify the form or direction of an anticipated relationship.

Unidimensional measurement A measurement scheme that evaluates a single quality or attribute of a construct under investigation.

Unintentional expectancy effect An effect produced when a researcher provides cues regarding the desirability of provided data to research participants.

Unitizing The process within content/interaction analysis of identifying the units that will be assigned to categories.

Universe A group of nonhuman elements with particular characteristics of interest to the researcher.

Unscheduled A variety of interview schedule in which the interviewer is provided with key topics to investigate, but the exact wording of individual inquiries is not specified.

Unsolicited artifacts Artifacts created without the solicitation of a researcher.

U-relationship A curvilinear relationship that suggests that a positive or negative change in the value of one construct will result in an initial decline in the second construct, followed by an eventual increase.

Utility A characteristic of a valuable theory: The theory must contribute to understanding of communication.

Validity Accuracy.

Variable A construct capable of taking on two or more values.

Variance (s^2) A measure of dispersion that is the average squared deviations of a set of scores from their mean.

Volunteer sampling A nonprobability sampling technique in which elements are selected to a sample based on their agreement to participate in research.

Warm-up question A survey/interview question that is innocuous and easy to answer, intended to reduce respondent anxiety and increase rapport.

Within-subject design A variety of factorial study in which the same set of subjects are used in all cells in the design diagram, thereby minimizing the number of required subjects.

Yucky scale A pictorial rating scale developed by Zillman and Bryant (1975) for use with children and semiliterate adults.

References

American Heritage Dictionary (2nd College Edition). (1985). Boston: Houghton Mifflin.

American Psychological Association. (1999, June 1). *Electronic reference formats recommended by the American Psychological Association.* Retrieved July 13, 1999 from the World Wide Web: http://www.apa.org/journals/webref.html

American Psychological Association. (1994). *Publication manual of the American Psychological Association* (4th ed.). Washington, DC: Author.

Anderson, J. A. (1987). *Communication research: Issues and methods.* New York: McGraw-Hill.

Armstrong, J. S., & Lusk, E. J. (1987). Return postage in mail surveys: A meta-analysis. *Public Opinion Quarterly, 51,* 233–248.

Babbie, E. (1983). *The practice of social research* (3rd ed.). Belmont, CA: Wadsworth.

Bales, R. F. (1950). *Interaction process analysis: A method for the study of small groups.* Reading, MA: Addison-Wesley.

Bandura, A. I. (1969). *Principles of behavior modification.* New York: Holt, Rinehart, and Winston.

Barnouw, E. (1989). *International encyclopedia of communications* (4 vols.). New York: Oxford University Press.

Baumrind, D. (1979). IRBs and social science research: The costs of deception. *IRB: A Review of Human Subject Research, 1,* 1–4.

Berelson, B. (1952). *Content analysis in communication research.* New York: Free Press.

Bogdan, R., & Taylor, S. J. (1975). *Introduction to qualitative research methods: A phenomenological approach to the social sciences.* New York: John Wiley & Sons.

Bruyn, S. T. (1966). *The human perspective in sociology: The methodology of participant observation.* Englewood Cliffs, NJ: Prentice-Hall.

Communication yearbook. (1977–). Thousand Oaks, CA: Sage.

DeVito, J. A. (1986). *The communication handbook: A dictionary.* New York: Harper & Row.

Foster, C. R. (1938). *Editorial treatment of education in the American press.* Cambridge, MA: Harvard University Press.

Frankfort-Nachmias, C., & Nachmias, D. (1992). *Research methods in the social sciences* (4th ed.). New York: St. Martin's.

Frey, L. R., Botan, C. H., Friedman, P. G., & Kreps, G. L. (1991). *Investigating communication: An introduction to research methods.* Englewood Cliffs, NJ: Prentice-Hall.

Gerbner, G., Gross, L., Signorielli, N., Morgan, M., & Jackson-Beeck, M. (1979). *Violence profile no. 10: Trends in network television drama and view concepts of social reality, 1967–1978.* Philadelphia, University of Pennsylvania, Annenberg School of Communication.

Glaser, B. G., & Strauss, A. L. (1967). *The discovery of grounded theory: Strategies for qualitative research.* Hawthorne, NY: Aldine.

Gold, R. L. (1958). Roles in sociological field observation. *Social Forces, 36,* 217–223.

Grimshaw, A. D. (1974). Data and data use in an analysis of communicative events. In R. Bauman & J. Sherzer (Eds.), *Explorations in the ethnography of speaking* (pp. 419–424). London: Cambridge University Press.

Helmstadter, G. C. (1970). *Research concepts in human behavior.* New York: Appleton-Century-Crofts.

Holsti, P. R. (1969). *Content analysis for the social sciences and humanities.* Reading, MA: Addison-Wesley.

Hult, C. A. (1996). *Researching and writing in the social sciences.* Boston: Allyn & Bacon.

Kerlinger, F. N. (1979). *Behavioral research: A conceptual approach.* New York: Holt, Rinehart and Winston.

Krippendorff, K. (1980). *Content analysis: An introduction to its methodology.* Beverly Hills, CA: Sage.

Kuhn, T. S. (1962). *The structure of scientific revolutions.* Chicago: University of Chicago Press.

Lefkowitz, M. M., Eron, L. D. Walder, L. O., & Huesmann, L. R. (1972). Television violence and child aggression: A follow-up study. In G. Comstock & E. A. Rubenstein (Eds.), *Television and social behavior: Television and adolescent aggressiveness* (Volume 3, pp. 35–135). Washington, DC: Government Printing Office, U.S. Department of Health, Education, and Welfare.

Littlejohn, S. W. (1978). *Theories of human communication.* Columbus, OH: Charles E. Merrill.

Martin, J. (1981). A garbage can model of the psychological research process. *American Behavioral Scientist, 25,* 131–151.

McCroskey, J. C. (1977). Oral communication apprehension: A summary of recent theory and research. *Human Communication Research, 4,* 78–96.

Nunnally, J. C. (1978). *Psychometric theory* (2nd ed.). New York: McGraw-Hill.

Osgood, C. E., Suci, G. J., & Tannenbaum, P. H. (1957). *The measurement of meaning.* Urbana: University of Illinois Press.

Poole, M. S., & McPhee, R. D. (1985). Methodology in interpersonal communication research. In M. L. Knapp & J. R. Miller (Eds.), *Handbook of interpersonal communication* (pp. 100–170). Beverly Hills, CA: Sage.

Roethlisberger, F. J., & Dickson, W. J. (1939). *Management and the worker.* Cambridge, MA: Harvard University Press.

Rosenthal, R. (1965). The volunteer sample. *Human Relations, 18,* 403–404.

Ruebhausen, M. O., & Brim, O. G. (1966). Privacy and behavioral research. *American Psychologist, 21,* 432.

Rubin, R. B., Rubin, A. M., & Piele, L. J. (2000). *Communication research: Strategies and sources* (5th ed.). Belmont, CA: Wadsworth.

Sage annual reviews of communication research. (1972–). Thousand Oaks, CA: Sage.

Smith, M. J. (1988). *Contemporary communication research methods.* Belmont, CA: Wadsworth.

Stevens, S. S. (1946). On the theory of scales of measurement. *Science, 103,* 677–680.

Stevens, S. S. (1951). Mathematics, measurement, and psychophysics. In S. S. Stevens (Ed.), *Handbook of experimental psychology* (pp. 1–49). New York: John Wiley.

U.S. Department of Health and Human Services. (1991). *OPRR reports: Protection of human subjects.* Washington, DC: U.S. Government Printing Office.

Wallace, W. L. (1971). *The logic of science in sociology.* Hawthorne, NY: Aldine.

Wimmer, R. D., & Dominick, J. R. (1994). *Mass media research: An introduction* (4th ed.). Belmont, CA: Wadsworth.

Zillmann, D., & Bryant, J. (1975). Viewers' moral sanctions of retribution in the appreciation of dramatic presentations. *Journal of Experimental Social Psychology, 11,* 572–582.

Index